The Common Book of Witchcraft and Wicca

from the Ancestors

The initial version of "The Common Book of Witchcraft and Wicca" is copyrighted to Witch School, International, Inc. © 2014 for the layout, structure, and specific print editions thereof. The "book" itself, i.e. all of the individual content elements, is being published under a Creative Commons license (see below).

This version was designed, produced, and to some extent edited by Eschaton Books, and is being published under these ISBNs:

EBOOK - 978-1-57353-902-9

PAPERBACK - 978-1-57353-903-6

HARDCOVER - 978-1-57353-904-3

For more information on obtaining copies of the paperback print edition, please visit:

http://www.EschatonBooks.com

All the individual elements of this book are being published under a Creative Commons Attribution 4.0 International License - http://creativecommons.org/licenses/by/4.0/ - which means that it is "Approved for Free Cultural Works" by Creative Commons.

COVER IMAGE
Druid's Temple - a Mini Stonehenge
by Chris Heaton

Source: http://www.geograph.org.uk/reuse.php?id=1419678

Image Copyright Chris Heaton.
This work is licensed under the Creative Commons Attribution Share Alike 2.0 Generic License. To view a copy of this license, visit http://creativecommons.org/licenses/by-sa/2.0/

Pagans don't have a holy book, they have libraries.

- Phaedra Bonewits

TABLE OF CONTENTS

xiii	*Foreword*	Don Lewis
xvii	*Preface*	Ed Hubbard
1	*Theagenesis*	Oberon Zell
15	*The Nature of the Soul*	Don Lewis
18	*Chant: - "Elemental"*	Correllian Tradition
19	*Human Heritage and the Goddess*	Abby Willowroot
22	*Chant - "Daughter of Darkness"*	Correllian Tradition
23	*The Difference Between Modern Wicca and Oldline Witchcraft*	A.C. Fisher Aldag
31	*Biographies, Part One: Appolonious – Cabot*	Don Lewis
41	*Once, Long Ago ...*	Abby Willowroot
45	*Defining The Sea Priestess*	Rev. Stephanie Leon Neal

54	*Chant - "Stories"*	Correllian Tradition
55	*The Five Mystic Secrets*	Don Lewis
77	*5 Mystic Secrets Essay – Keller*	Colin A. Keller
79	*5 Mystic Secrets Essay – Brown*	Melissa Brown
83	*5 Mystic Secrets Essay – Seneker*	Rev. Daniel S. Seneker
92	*Art - "5 Airts"*	Don Lewis
93	*Biographies, Part Two: Clutterbuck – Fox*	Don Lewis
103	*Surviving the Holiday Season*	A.C. Fisher Aldag
111	*Growing Sacred Spaces*	Abby Willowroot
113	*What is a Coven?*	William Halstead
121	*Some Thoughts on Souls and Trees*	Don Lewis
127	*Choosing a Spiritual Path*	Abby Willowroot
130	*Chant - "Fire Chant"*	Correllian Tradition

131	*Moon Lore and Magick*	
		A.C. Fisher Aldag
135	*The Black Moon*	
		A.C. Fisher Aldag
142	*Art: - "The Buzzing of Bees"*	
		Don Lewis
143	*Magical Tools*	
		Abby Willowroot
146	*Chant - "Grandmother! Grandmother!"*	
		Correllian Tradition
147	*Biographies, Part Three: Gardner – Morrison*	
		Don Lewis
159	*Chant - "The Arousal (From She Arose)"*	
		Correllian Tradition
162	*Art: - "Creation"*	
		Don Lewis
163	*Ritual and Renewal*	
		Abby Willowroot
165	*Dual Sabbat Ritual Cycle*	
		Don Lewis
221	*Samhain Is Not Over Yet!*	
		A.C. Fisher Aldag
234	*Chant: - "Ourobouros"*	
		Correllian Tradition
235	*Flower Water*	
		Don Lewis

237	*Wassailing the Trees*	A.C. Fisher Aldag
241	*Correllian Soul Creed*	Rev. Stephanie Leon Neal
244	*Chant - "The Sun Shall Rise"*	Correllian Tradition
245	*A Commentary on "A Correllian Creed"*	Rev. Terry Power, HP
252	*Chant - "Sing a Song of Safety" (From She Arose)*	Correllian Tradition
253	*Wiccan Morality*	Don Lewis
268	*Chant - "Colors of Life"*	Correllian Tradition
269	*A Commentary on the Nine Virtues*	Rev. Terry Power, HP
280	*Chant - "Four Ladies"*	Correllian Tradition
281	*Deep At Your Core*	Abby Willowroot
283	*The Plow Play*	A.C. Fisher Aldag
285	*Biographies, Part Four: Morton – RavenWolf*	Don Lewis
299	*Crossroads Magick*	A.C. Fisher Aldag

306	*Chant - "You were the First One"*	Correllian Tradition
307	*Shadow as a Spiritual Force*	Raven Digitalis
315	*Suffering*	Don Lewis
322	*Chant - "Moment of Change"*	Correllian Tradition
323	*Kindness*	Abby Willowroot
325	*Spell Work: The Power of NOT*	A.C. Fisher Aldag
330	*Chant - "Magick's Everything"*	Correllian Tradition
331	*Welcome to the Dark, Still Waters – Chapter One*	Rev. Stephanie Leon Neal
338	*Art: - "Isis Nephthys"*	Don Lewis
339	*Welcome to the Dark, Still Waters – Chapter Two*	Rev. Stephanie Leon Neal
348	*Chant - "Rejoice and Give Thanks!"*	Correllian Tradition
349	*Dispelling*	A.C. Fisher Aldag
356	*Chant - "Moonlight and Firelight"*	Correllian Tradition

357	*Essay on Time Magic*	
		Don Lewis
367	*Surviving the Season, Part 2*	
		A.C. Fisher Aldag
375	*Biographies, Part Five: Robertson – Zell*	
		Don Lewis
383	*An Elemental Degree System Suggestion*	
		Alan Salmi
393	*Art: - "Pentagram Guy"*	
		Don Lewis
394	*Chant - "Child of Light" (from She Arose)*	
		Correllian Tradition
395	*Testament of Ed the Pagan*	
		Ed Hubbard
401	*Afterword*	
		Brendan Tripp
403	*Art: - "Hecate"*	
		Don Lewis

FOREWORD

by **Don Lewis**

*Why does the world need a
Common Book of Wicca and Witchcraft?*

The Common Book of Wicca and Witchcraft is a compendium of copyright free materials dealing with Wicca and Witchcraft. All the materials within it may be freely shared without the need for any further permission. These materials have been created for the world, and are explicitly intended to be shared. Why? Because we believe that sharing knowledge can create a better world.

But why Witchcraft? Why Wicca?

Why Witchcraft ? Witchcraft is the art of manipulating reality. Through magic the Witch uses internal powers to shape the external world. But Witchcraft is more than this — implicit in the shaping of reality is the idea of taking responsibility for your own life and doing what you need for yourself, rather than waiting for others to do it for you. To know that you can shape reality, frees you from dependence upon others. This is one reason so many people fear Witchcraft. Most people have been taught from birth to believe in being dependent upon the actions of others, whether governments, "experts", charities, churches, or Gods. Most other movements teach dependency, and fear independence above all else. Most organizations have also been taught from time immemorial to use people's dependence upon them as a means of control. Dependence is a powerful tool of social control that Witchcraft disrupts, because when you know that you can shape reality through magic, you have a means of resisting any attempt to make you dependent. The Witch need not sit and wait for the crumbs from the table of others — the Witch can make their own table. Not that magic is a simple art or easy to master, but even a little magic opens the door to freedom.

Why Wicca? Wicca is a new religion based upon a number of older religious movements. Eclectic Wicca has diverse origins, and blends many metaphysical ideas and practices of the past into a religion for the future. Why do we need a new religion for the future? Well, look around the world and that answer should be an easy one. The planet is soaked in the blood of religious warfare, as ancient enemies repeat the same religious wars over and over again. Accused "Witches" are being burned in Africa, and "Witch Children" tortured or murdered in horrifying ways. Religious minorities are being beheaded and otherwise murdered throughout the Middle East, while religious extremists battle at the election booth for the control of Western governments. It is a bad situation. Meanwhile the planet itself reels from the effects of long-term abuse and pollution, while Western religious leaders deny that there is or could be a problem, and insist that the "Jesus will take care of it," or that that any of various apocalyptic scenarios override the need to take corrective action. If the world ever needed a new religion, surely now is the time!

We live at a crucial moment in history. We stand at the crossroads, a place long sacred to the Witch. It is a crossroad between the failed policies of the past vs. the potential for a better future. It is a crossroad between destroying the planet vs. saving it. A crossroad between scorning the poor and empowering a tiny oligarchy vs. building a better society that allows social justice for all its members. It is a crossroad between eternal religious wars based on ancient hatreds mandated by supposedly holy books vs. the freedom to overcome the past make a more peaceful future. Magic gives us the freedom to shape a new reality, and Wicca gives us the intellectual freedom to envision a better reality free of the ingrained and often unconscious prejudices of the old religions. Instead of spending our time suppressing religious minorities and enforcing a bronze-age orthodoxy, Wicca frees us to take the needed actions to save our planet as well as to move forward into space.

Wicca is based in nature, and this includes the understanding that nature includes all of existence, not just our own back yard. The Witch studies and seeks to understand all things, knowing that all things are sacred. Our knowledge is based in the spiritual, but also embraces the scientific. We do not reject scientific ideas, though our views on some things may differ from those of atheistic mainstream science. The future we seek to craft is one of Magic AND Science, knowledge ancient AND modern, side-by-side.

And we know that we will see that future. We will return, for we know that death is but one side of a coin that is eternally flipping. We MUST be concerned about the future, because it is our future, not just our descendants, for we will be reborn into it. It is easy for those who think that they live but once to lay waste to the planet and destroy its resources, for they think this will not impact them and they have little care or concept for what will come after. But we who practice the incarnational sciences know that we return, and that what we leave behind us when we die is also what we inherit when we are reborn. The knowledge that the Soul is eternal and leads many lives transforms our relationship to the earth and our relationship to the future, for we know that there is no convenient exit from the consequences of our actions and no apocalypse to reset the game. The Witch knows that WE must take responsibility and build the world we wish to live in — for we will be reborn into the world we have built.

Because we know these things, we cannot stand idly at this crossroad. We must choose our future and we must build it — OR we must live this life and lives-to-come in a future built by others. We can build a future of love or we must suffer a future of fear. It is as simple as that. The choice is ours — and because we have the knowledge of magic, the ability to build the future of our choice is also ours.

Wicca and Witchcraft offer the world a future different from the apocalyptic dystopia so actively sought by so many of the old religions. A future of hope, a future of beauty, a future of promise.

> M. Rev. Donald Lewis is the Chancellor and First Priest of the Correllian Tradition (http://www.correllian.com), co-founder of Witch School (http://www.WitchSchool.com) the world's largest school of metaphysics, and Production Head for Magick TV (http://www.Youtube.com/MagickTV)
>
> Rev. Don is the author of the Witch School series of books available from Llewellyn (http://www.Llewellyn.com), as well as numerous other works including Rev. Don's Omnibus of Invocations and Incantations for All Occasions and the Tarot of Hekate available from http://www.WitchSchoolStore.com and the Video Lessons for the First Degree available from http://www.RevDonLewis.com

PREFACE

by **Ed Hubbard**

The Common Book of Witchcraft and Wicca was developed through a "crowd funding" project on the IndieGoGo.com site. This section is drawn from the introductory materials describing the book there.

Hi, I am Ed Hubbard, and my project will allow us to create a Common Book of Wicca and Witchcraft. I want this book to be shareable and available to all as an eBook, as well as a print copy. This Common Book will be considered open source, via Creative Commons, and can be widely shared. I feel that this is an important time in our history and we are at a crossroads.

In the legal world of Copyrights, Trademarks, and Digital Rights, we are facing a more restrictive future of written, audio and video based materials, and how they may be used. This bears directly on our freedom of religion, freedom of speech, and freedom of use. In order to avoid these restrictions, I see the Common Book of Wicca and Witchcraft as able to bypass most of the problems with copyright issues. This will give my fellow Wiccans, Witches, and Seekers the freedom to teach, with quality materials, the basics of our faith. My hope is that you will want this for yourself and your family as well.

Why Wicca? For me, once I accepted Wicca, it changed and saved my life. From my soul, my inner self, I felt healing and understanding that nothing else was ever able to answer, and I discovered how beautiful the natural world is. Being Wiccan as well as a Witch was life affirming and comforting in so many places in my life. It gave me the freedom to believe as I wanted, and since then, I have dedicated myself to teaching. The Common Book of Wicca and Witchcraft is the next step in what I believe can help bring comfort and understanding to so many others.

The Problem:

The current teaching manuals of any coven, circle, or temple — unless they are using their own personal home-grown Book of Shadows — have to be purchased from a publisher, who printed them for the original authors. While this is "standard procedure" for the dissemination of materials such as these in our society, it has produced an "unintended consequence" of many of our faith practices and rituals ending up subject to copyright regulations which potentially cause them to only be able to be shared under certain narrow conditions. And as nominal "ownership" of much of the teaching material slides from the original authors and to corporate entities, the "bean counter" drive to protect intellectual property could make it much more difficult to use any copyrighted material beyond the scope of reading and practice.

In a particular case in 2012, one of our most beloved chants had been being used freely and incorporated in many derivative works over a long period of time. The frequent alteration of the chant, as it was adapted group-to-group, ended up angering its original author, and she actively sought to narrow the usage, and eliminate the various "unapproved" forms of the chant. She was able to do so because the chant was copyrighted in the seventies, and was able to make a legal case.

This is why we want to have a book of common knowledge that allows covens, circles, witan shrines, temples, and groves to teach at least the basics to people who want to learn. This has always been our goal; to provide an education to anyone, anytime, anywhere.

All materials incorporated in the book will be derived from common knowledge, research, and properly annotated and referenced sources. We will have a review panel to ensure the material does not violate copyrights of any authors or publishers. If we are required to have permission to print, we will either acquire permission or we will remove the passages that violate copyright.

The Common Book of Witchcraft & Wicca

THEAGENESIS:
The Birth of the Goddess

by **Oberon Zell**

This paper represents the first published account of what has come to be known as "The Gaea Hypothesis" (the name suggested by novelist William Golding in 1972). It was the immediate result of a visionary experience that Oberon had on the night of September 6, 1970. This "revelation" was delivered in the form of a sermon to the congregation of the church of All Worlds on September 11, 1970. Subsequently, it was published as the lead article in Green Egg — the journal of the Neo-Pagan movement — Vol. V, No. 40 (July 1, 1971), republished in the first issue of The Witches Broomstick magazine (Feb. 2, 1972), excerpted in Dr. Leo Louis Martello's book, Witchcraft; The Old Religion (University Books, Inc. 1973), and delivered as a keynote lecture at the Third Annual Gnostic Aquarian Festival in Minneapolis, MN, Sept. 21, 1973. This updated and annotated edition is being prepared for the California Institute of Integral Studies' symposium on "Gaia Consciousness: The Goddess & the Living Earth," April 6-10, 1988.

Conceptualizations of Divinity vary from religion to religion, with adherents of each faith misunderstanding, often grotesquely, the nature of the Divine as understood by the members of other faiths. Thus conservatives of a given religious system often tend to feel that all other religions are "false" but their own, and that other people all worship the Devil, while liberals will go to the opposite extreme and contend that all religions essentially worship the same Deity, under different guises and customs. Both of these points of view grossly misrepresent the fundamental distinctions among the various religions, and try to adapt alien world-views to fit into their own frameworks of experience.

It may be said that all religions are "true," as indeed are all sincerely held opinions, in the sense that personal reality is necessarily subjective. In other words, what you believe to be true, is true, by definition. A Voudoun death-curse is as real to its victim, and as effective, as being "saved" is to a Christian fundamentalist, or the kosher laws are to an Orthodox Jew. A flat Earth, with the stars and planets revolving around it, was as real to the medieval mind as our present globe and solar system are to us. Hysteric paralysis and blindness are as real to the sufferer as their organic counterparts. The snakes and bugs of alcoholic and narcotic deliria are real to the addict, and so is the fearful world of the paranoiac. From the standpoint of human consciousness, there is no other reality than that which we experience, and whatever we experience is therefore reality — therefore "true." We can only distinguish the experience of the objective world from those which lie entirely within our own minds when we compare notes with other people and arrive thereby at a consensus of reality. This consensus, however, is also subjective within the entire community, and is also liable not to be synonymous with objective reality (as in the case of the Geocentric cosmos). The question then arises, "How can we know objective reality?" and the answer, of course, is that we can't; not totally. However, we can arrive at very close approximations of objective reality by careful applications of the scientific method combined with creative insight, and by refusing to fill in the gaps in our knowledge with blind "leaps of faith."

Thus religions may be considered more or less objectively true (while recognizing that they are all subjectively true) by evaluating how much they depend on blind faith and belief over scientific understanding (and recognizing that we only speak of belief in the absence of knowledge; no one would say "I believe two plus two equals four"); how much they depend on tradition and authority over intellectual curiosity and honesty; how much (or how little) they are able to accommodate new discoveries in science and how much (or how little) these discoveries substantiate their theories and world-views. These are the criteria for objective validation of religious viewpoints. No subjective validation is needed (or even possible).

Ancient tribal peoples — that is, Pagans — diversified though they were, held among them certain common viewpoints. Among these were: veneration of an Earth-Mother Goddess; animism and pantheism; identification with a sacred region; seasonal celebrations; love-respect, awe and veneration for Nature and Her mysteries; sensuality and sexuality in worship; magic and myth; and a sense of humanity being a microcosm corresponding to the macrocosm of all Nature. These insights, however, were largely intuitive, as science had not yet progressed to the point of being able to provide objective validation for what must have seemed, to outsiders, to be mere superstition. Twentieth-century Neo-Paganism, however, has applied itself and the science of its era to that validation, and has discovered astounding implications.

A single cell develops physically into a human being by a process of continuous division and subdivision into the myriads of cells eventually required to comprise an adult body; groups of cells specializing to become the various organs and tissues needed for full functioning of the organism. Now, when a cell reproduces, the mother cell does not remain intact, but actually becomes the two new daughter cells. Since the same protoplasm is present in the daughter cells as was in the mother cell, the two daughter cells still comprise but a single organism; one living being. The original cell ceases to exist in that form, but its life goes on in the continuous evolution of the growing organism. Thus, the three trillion or so cells of the adult human body continue to comprise a single living organism, even though different cells may be highly specialized, and some may even be mobile enough to travel independently around in the collective body. No matter how complex the final form of the adult organism, no matter how diversified its component cells, the same thread of life of the original cell, the same protoplasm, continues coursing through every cell in that body. Since the gametes, or sex cells, are also included in this ultimate diversification of a single original cell, the act of reproduction carries this same thread on in the offspring, combined with the equivalent threat of protoplasm from the other parent. Thus your children, while spatially distinct from you, are in fact as much a part of your growing, evolving organism as your blood cells (which can easily be removed and survive independently of your collective body) or somatic cells (which can also be extracted and grown in independent tissue cultures). Your children are still "you" — your own living protoplasm continues on in their cellularly-diversified bodies. And in your children's children for all generations to come. All the cells in all your descendants will still comprise but ONE LIVING BEING.

Tracing our evolution back nearly four billion years, through mammals, reptiles, amphibians, fish, and so on, we eventually wind up with ONE SINGLE CELL that was the ANCESTOR OF ALL LIFE ON EARTH. Even though there were undoubtedly many proto-cells formed in those ancient seas [or clays, as is now thought — OZ, 1988], the first one to develop the capacity to reproduce would have quickly consumed all the available free proteins and amino acids floating in the sea, effectively preventing the development of any competitors. Cell reproduction occurs at a fantastic geometric rate, which, unchecked, would result in all the planet being buried beneath the progeny of a single cell within months. Obviously, what checked this fantastic reproductive potential was a limited food supply, which would have included any not-yet-formed or newly-formed competitive cells. But when this original mother cell reproduced itself, and continued to do so for aeons, some of its daughter cells mutating and evolving into new forms, it still, as in the human body, continued to comprise but a SINGLE total organism. When a cell divides and subdivides, NO MATTER HOW OFTEN, the same cellular material, the same protoplasm, the same life, passes into the daughter cells, and the granddaughter cells, and the great-granddaughter cells, FOREVER. NO MATTER HOW OFTEN or for how long this subdivision goes on, the aggregate total of the new cells continues to comprise ONE SINGLE LIVING ORGANISM!

[Note: Lewis Thomas, in Lives of a Cell, 1974, observes: "The uniformity of the Earth's life, more astonishing than its diversity, is accountable by the high probability that we derived, originally, from some single cell, fertilized in a bolt of lightning as the Earth cooled. It is from the progeny of this parent cell that we take our looks; we still share genes around, and the resemblance of the enzymes of grasses to those of whales is a family resemblance."]

[Note: Science News "News of the Week," Jan. 16, 1988: "Seekers of Ancestral Cell Debate New Data: A new, computerized method of analyzing bacterial genes is stirring controversy among biologists seeking to characterize the ancestral cell from which all life evolved. The novel program predicts that all living things evolved from a single-celled organism that had a penchant for living in boiling sulfur springs. The prediction conflicts with the popular notion that life began in a tepid primordial soup..." — SN, Vol. 133, No. 3]

Every amino acid (except glycine) found in the proteins of living organisms can exist in two forms, each one the mirror image of the other. Since they have the same spatial relationship as a pair of gloves, one type is arbitrarily designated "right-handed" (D, dextro) and the other "left-handed" (L, levo). The two forms are identical in chemical composition and physical properties. Were it not for the fact that they rotate a beam of polarized light in opposite directions, they would be indistinguishable. Now, when amino acids are synthesized in the laboratory, an equal amount of D and L forms are produced. Moreover, NASA recently [1970] reported the discovery of 17 different amino acids in a meteorite, with an almost equal number of D and L forms. In any given cell, of course, only one of these two variant forms can exist; either all the cell's protein would contain D-acids, or they would all contain L-acids. And when the cell divides, whichever form was contained in the mother cell would be perpetuated in the daughter cells. If all life on Earth did not originate with a single cell, we would expect to find various creatures and plants with D-acids and others with L-acids. However, this is not the case: it is an established biochemical fact that ALL LIFE ON EARTH CONTAINS ONLY L-AMINO ACIDS! The equivalent D-acids are simply not found in any living organisms on this planet. Therefore, it is a biological fact that ALL LIFE ON EARTH COMPRISES ONE SINGLE LIVING ORGANISM! Literally, we are all "One."

The blue whale and the redwood tree are not the largest living organisms on Earth; the ENTIRE PLANETARY BIOSPHERE is.

[Note: Dr. Leslie Orgel of the Salk Institute, La Jolla, CA, commenting on origins of Life on Earth: "But the evidence that interests us most...is the uniformity of all living systems on Earth today...If life had arisen and evolved spontaneously here...it seems at least possible that many very different forms of life would be competing with each other. But in fact we know that all living things have evolved from a single cell, which inhabited Earth about three or four billion years ago—and there don't seem to be any traces of any extinct competitors which arose in different ways..." The implication was obvious. The first living cell, a single seed of protoplasm, a single microscopic organism, might have replicated itself billions and billions of times in short order. Its replicas would adjust to warmth or cold, evolving accordingly. In the course of time they would branch out along many different paths, and evolve as enzymes, genes, insulin, hemoglobin; they would organize into bone and muscles and organs and coordinate their work; they would begin the beating of hearts, the pumping of lungs, the vibrations of nerves, and ultimately, the flashes of thought. — In Search of Ancient Mysteries by Alan and Sally Landsburg, 1974, Bantam.]

Let us consider the following corollaries:

An organism is composed of many organs — more, obviously, in complex organisms than in simple ones. As an embryo develops, groups of cells specialize into each of the organs that the adult organism will require. At very early stages in cell differentiation, unspecialized cells can be moved from one part of the embryo to another, and the transplanted cells will still develop into whatever organs are needed in their new locations. Just so, the Planetary Organism (to which I will hereby give the scientific name of "Terrebia") needs various organs in order to function properly.

Note: As is customary in scientific nomenclature for living species, I based my name for the planetary organism on the Latin for "Earth life." When, in 1972, James Lovelock independently came up with the observation of the organic unity of all terrestrial life, his friend, the novelist William Golding, suggested the name of the ancient Greek Earth Goddess: "Gaia." Even though Greek is customarily used only in designating extinct species, in this case I yield primacy of the name to Golding, as I much prefer the connotations thereof. But I will use the American spelling, "Gaea," to distinguish my development of the concept from Lovelock's. Henceforth in this updated edition of my paper I will replace "Terrebia" with "Gaea."— OZ, 1988]

Continuing the analogy with the human body, each animal and plant on Earth is the equivalent of a single cell in the vast body of Gaea. Each biome, such as pine forest, coral reef, desert, prairie, marsh, etc., complete with all its plants and animals, is the equivalent of an organ in the body of our biospheric Being; sub-structures and tissues consisting of types of plants and animals, such as trees, insects, grasses, predators, grazing ungulates, etc. All the components of a biome are essential to its proper functioning, and each biome is essential to the proper functioning of Gaea. If some essential elements of a biome are removed or destroyed, it may be possible for relatively unspecialized "cells" of plants and animals to differentiate out by adaptive radiation to become all the required components. The most classic recent case of this is the radiation of marsupials in Australia, following the demise of the dinosaurs, to fill all the ecological niches occupied elsewhere by placentals with creatures virtually identical in structure and habits with their placental equivalents. Moreover, recent [as of 1970] papers and books on the genetics of evolution, including Biophilosophy, stress that modern Darwinian theory has abandoned the notion of individuals determining the direction of the evolution of a species. Rather, the entire species seems to migrate towards a fortuitous ecological niche as if it had a sense of whither it needed to go. If all the mutations in the direction of such a change are destroyed, the species will produce more.

The non-living components of the planetary structure of the Earth itself serve the developing organism if Gaea much as the non-living components of our own bodies serve us. These components are the Lithosphere, the Hydrosphere, and the Atmosphere. The Lithosphere, the rock and mineral foundation of our planet, functions in the body of Gaea much as the skeleton functions in the human body — as foundation and structural support (like the Lithosphere, our own skeleton is largely mineral). The Hydrosphere, the water of oceans, lakes and rivers that covers three fifths of the surface of the Earth, functions homologously with the plasma in the blood of the human body, which, incidentally, has a composition very like the water in those primeval seas wherein life first appeared. The ocean tides may even be viewed as our planetary pulse, driven by the heartbeat of our orbiting moon. The atmosphere serves the great organism of Gaea much as it does us, as individual "cells" — in a carbon-cycle respiratory process, involving breaking down carbon dioxide into carbon and oxygen by plants and building carbon and oxygen back up into carbon dioxide by animals.

[Note: The observations which led to Lovelock's formulation of the Gaia Hypothesis were concerned with the Atmosphere, in the same way that my own observations were of the Biosphere. Lovelock, an atmospheric biochemist, analyzed and noted a remarkable homeostasis of atmospheric composition and surface temperature over the past three billion years, and concluded that this could only be attributed to a biospheric regulatory mechanism. — OZ, 1988]

What is the ultimate source of energy for Gaea — her "food?" Sunlight, which, through photosynthesis in green plants, converts materials of the Lithosphere, Hydrosphere and Atmosphere into the materials of life: the Biosphere.

Now, it follows that if a biomic component occupies a particular ecological niche in a given biome, it does so because it belongs there and is necessary to the proper functioning of that biome, and hence of Gaea. Further, if some plant or animal is missing from a particular biome, it is probably because it doesn't belong there. Now, everybody realizes that the human body will not function properly if one removes, replaces or rearranges parts of it. You may survive if your leg is amputated, but you certainly won't walk as well as before. This same principle of coherency applies to Gaea, as we are beginning to learn only too well. We cannot kill all the bison in North America, import rabbits to Australia, clear-cut or burn off whole forests, or plow and plant the Great Plains with wheat and corn without seriously disrupting the ecosystem. Remember the dust bowl? Australia's plague of rabbits? Mississippi basin floods? Recent drought in the Southwestern US? Gaea is a SINGLE LIVING ORGANISM, and her parts are not to be removed, replaced or rearranged without consequence.

Just as in the human body the brain and nervous system is the last organ to develop, so in Gaea the last biome to develop is the Noosphere, composed of Earth's aggregate population of Homo Sapiens.

[Note: "In man," says Lovelock, Gaia has the equivalent of a central nervous system and an awareness of herself and the rest of the Universe. Through man, she has a rudimentary capacity, capable of development, to anticipate and guard against threats to her existence. For example, man can command just about enough capacity to ward off a collision with a planetoid the size of Icarus.

Can it then be that in the course of man's evolution within Gaia he has been acquiring the knowledge and skills necessary to ensure her survival?" — "The Quest for Gaia," New Scientist, Feb. 6, 1975]

What function does humanity, as the Noospheric organ, the planetary "brain," perform? It would seem at the present stage of evolution that the function of a biome of awareness would be to act as steward of the planetary ecosystem. Humanity's purpose in Gaea, our responsibility, is to see that her whole organism functions at its highest potential and that none of her vital systems become disrupted or impaired. We might judge the state of humanity's functioning in the macrocosmic realm by evaluating our performance of this organic responsibility.

[Note: Since writing the preceding paragraph back in 1970, I have radically altered my perception of humanity as a kind of planetary cerebral cortex, which function I am now firmly inclined to attribute to the Great Whales. Apropos of this attribution, I am now even more appalled than ever at humanity's near-extermination of these vastly-brained leviathans, as I cannot avoid viewing it as a kind of planetary lobotomy. I have developed this idea at some extent in another paper, entitled "Mind Beneath the Silver Sky." Regarding our own proper function, I have come to perceive us in a far different role: that of a reproductive system. For it is not true that the brain and nervous system is the last organ to develop in an organism; the ultimate objective of a living system is to reproduce itself, and the reproductive organs are the final product of physical development, be it embryological or evolutionary. Maturation essentially means achieving reproductive capability. I envision our greater purpose, capability and destiny as agents of planetary reproduction via extraterrestrial colonization and terraforming. However, I still include an ancillary and continuing function of ourselves as peripheral neurons and planetary stewards; after all, we as humans need not die in childbirth, but ideally continue to live long and productive lives beyond merely reproducing ourselves. — OZ, 1988]

When in the human body some cells start multiplying all out of control and excreting toxins into the bloodstream, we have a cancer. One of the ways cancer can be controlled is by radiation treatment At this moment, humanity as a species is multiplying wildly out of control and excreting vast quantities of deadly pollutants into the air, water and soil, If our own cancerous population growth is not halted — indeed, drastically reduced — our numbers and poisons will severely cripple or kill our planetary organism,

Gaea. Perhaps nuclear war — a global "radiation treatment" — will be needed ... But it is still to be hoped that it is not to late for us to wake up to our responsibility of stewardship.

[Note: In reading these words, 18 years later, I am appalled at how casually I invoked nuclear holocaust as an antidote for the cancer of our species. Studies on the "nuclear winter" scenario, as well as the recent discoveries concerning asteroid/comet impacts as agents of massive extinctions in the past, have severely curtailed any prospect of Gaea's ability to survive a nuclear war. She has her own devices for regulating overpopulation: plague, famine, drought, flood, etc. Or we could save ourselves a lot of grief and just decide not to have so many children ... — OZ, 1988]

Gaea is nearing maturity. All the physical ecological niches have been filled, and the recently developed Noosphere now extends over the entire globe... Projecting a bit, it would seem most reasonable that Teilhard de Chardin was correct in his vision of an emerging planetary consciousness, what he called the "Omega Point" (The Phenomenon of Man) and Carlton Berenda calls "The First Coming of God" (The New Genesis). The maturation of a Planetary Biosphere requires the evolution of total telepathic union among the "cells" of its Noosphere (its most intelligent species; humanity). When such an intelligent species ultimately develops telepathy to the extent that it eventually shares a single global consciousness, a PLANETARY MIND awakens in the "brain" (Noosphere) of the Biosphere.

[Note: "Lewis Thomas can readily see the worldwide community of humans as a kind of giant brain, exchanging thoughts so rapidly 'that the brains of mankind often appear, functionally, to be undergoing fusion.' With mankind as its 'nervous system,' the whole earth becomes, in one of Thomas's highest flights of fancy, a breathing organism of finely meshed parts, all growing together under the 'protective membrane' of the planet's own atmosphere." "The Boswell of Organelles," Newsweek, June 24, 1974]

This is our human destiny — our ultimate function in the organism of Gaea.

[Please, gentle readers; forgive this hubris. I've outgrown it. I consider that we could — and should — be participants in this awakening of planetary consciousness, but I hardly believe any longer in our exclusive claim to sentience on this planet! As I mentioned earlier, I heartily do believe that whales, for instance, are way ahead of us in this department. Actually, I think that the planetarization of consciousness would, by its very nature, include "all creatures great and small..." — OZ, 1988]

And just as the brain in the human body is capable, via the conscious mind, of controlling virtually everything that goes on in the body and a good deal that goes on outside it, so a planetary consciousness would be in complete control of virtually everything that goes on in the planet — from earthquakes to rainfall to ice ages to mountain building to hurricanes — and perhaps influence the rest of its local stellar system as well.

[Note: Dane Rudhyar writes: "... mankind is to fulfill a definite function in the total operation of this vast, yet closely integrated, system of activities which we call the planet Earth — provided we do not think of the Earth as merely a mass of matter. This function appears to be to extract consciousness out of all the activities within the Earth-field — a field which may extend at least to, and perhaps in a sense include, the Moon." — The Astrology of Self-Actualization and the New Morality, pp. 24-25]

At this point it becomes necessary to define Divinity:

Divinity is the highest level of aware consciousness accessible to each living being, manifesting itself in the self-actualization of that being. Thus we can truly say, "All that groks is God" (Heinlein; Stranger in a Strange Land). Divinity is a cat being fully feline, grass being grassy, and people being fully human. Collective Divinity emerges when a number of people (a culture or society) share enough values, beliefs and aspects of a common life-style that they conceptualize a tribal God or Goddess, which takes on the character (and the gender) of the dominant elements of that culture. Thus the masculine God of the Western Monotheists (Jews, Christians, Moslems) may be seen to have arisen out of the values, ideals and principles of a nomadic, patriarchal culture — the ancient Hebrews. Matrifocal agrarian cultures, on the other hand, personified their values of fertility, sensuality, peace and the arts in the conceptualization of Goddesses. As small tribes coalesced into states and nations, their Gods and Goddesses battled for supremacy through their respective devotees. In some circumstances, various tribal divinities were joined peaceably (often through marriage) into a polytheistic pantheon, being ranked in status as their followers' respective influences determined. In other circumstances, one particularly fanatic tribe was able to completely dominate others and eliminate their own deities, elevating its God to the status of a solitary ruler over all creation, and enforcing His worship upon the people, usually upon pain of death. However, no matter to what rank a single tribal deity may be exalted by its followers, it still could be no other than a tribal divinity, existing only as an embodiment of the values of that tribe. "Gods are only as strong as those who believe in them think they are" (Alley Oop). When the planetary consciousness of Gaea awakens, She too will be Divinity — but on an entirely new level: the emergent deity Carlton Berenda postulates in The New Genesis. Indeed, even though yet unawakened, the slumbering subconscious [and dreaming?] mind of Gaea is experienced intuitively by us all, and has been referred to instinctively by us as Mother Earth, Mother Nature — The Goddess for whom She is well named. Indeed, this intuitive conceptualization of feminine gender for our planetary Divinity is scientifically valid, for biologically unisexual organisms (such as amoeba or hydra) are always considered female; in the act of reproduction they are referred to as mothers and their offspring as daughters.

[Note: I came later to the conclusion that Gaea may have indeed achieved consciousness in more ancient times, and that she was actually "knocked unconscious" by the worldwide cataclysms and attendant destruction of Her worshippers which ended the Bronze Age and ushered in the Age of Iron around 1500 BCE. This hypothesis is more fully developed in my 1977 research paper, "Cataclysm and Consciousness — From the Golden Age to the Age of Iron." — OZ, 1988]

Thus we find that "God" is in reality Goddess, and that our ancient Pagan ancestors had an intuitive understanding of what we are now able to prove scientifically. Thus also we expose the logical absurdity of a concept of cosmic Divinity in the masculine gender. These few pages, however, have only been the briefest of introductions to the implications of a discovery so vast that its impact on the world's thinking will ultimately surpass the impact of the discovery of the Heliocentric structure of the solar system. This is the discovery that the entire Biosphere of the Earth comprises a single living Organism.

* * * * * * * * * * * * * * * * * *

Otter G'Zell is a 52-year-old Sagittarian with Aquarius rising who has accomplished many things in his long and colorful career. A modern Renaissance man, Otter is a transpersonal psychologist, metaphysician, naturalist, theologian, shaman, author, artist, lecturer, teacher, and ordained Priest of the Earth-Mother, Gaea. He holds academic degrees in sociology/anthropology, clinical psychology, and theology. Otter founded the Church of All Worlds in 1967, which became the first Neo-Pagan church to obtain full Federal recognition in the US. First to apply the term "Pagan" to the newly emerging Earth Religions of the '60s, and through his editorship of the Green Egg (1968-1975), Otter was instrumental in the coalescence of the Neo-Pagan movement, which for the last 20 years has been reclaiming the religious heritage of Celtic Europe. (Membership in the Neo-Pagan community is currently estimated at around 100,000 people.) In 1970, Otter formulated and published the thealogy of deep ecology which has become known as The Gaea Hypothesis. He met and married his soulmate, Morning Glory, at the Llewellyn-sponsored Gnostic Aquarian Festivals in 1973 and '74, where he was a keynote speaker. Otter and Morning Glory co-founded the Ecosophical Research Association in 1977, and their research into arcane lore and ancient legends resulted in the Living Unicorn project, begun in 1980. In Feb. 1985, Otter organized an ERA diving expedition to Australia and New Guinea which identified the species of the mysterious "Ri" and solved the ages-old mystery of the Mermaid, and in 1987 he conducted a research tour of ancient oracles and archaeological sites throughout Mediterranean Europe.

Otter is the author of numerous published articles on history, Gaean thealogy, magic, shamanism, mythology, anomalies, dinosaurs, archaeology, cosmology and related topics, and has been interviewed and quoted extensively in many books on New Age religious movements and the occult. With many years of theatrical experience, Otter has been an entertaining and knowledgeable public speaker and guest on a number of radio and television talk shows around the country (and in Canada and Australia), as well as being a regular featured speaker at various New Age, psychic and occult conventions. Otter is also an accomplished ritualist, creating and conducting rites of passage, seasonal celebrations, mystery plays, Earth-healings and other rituals for up to 3,000 people.

Otter's artwork has illuminated the pages of various fantasy and science-fiction magazines since the late 1960's. He has also illustrated a number of books (most recently, Wheels of Life by Anodea Judith) and short stories as well as designed posters, record album covers and T-shirts. But Otter's favorite art projects are his ongoing sculpture series of ancient Goddesses and of prehistoric and mythological creatures, many of which have been widely marketed.

For eight years prior to 1985 Otter lived in monastic retreat in the mountains of northern California, creating a homestead and a Pagan retreat center. During this period he was largely inaccessible for public appearances, though he continued to exercise a considerable influence in the Neo-Pagan community through the large festivals, vision quests, ceremonies, and ritual events held on the land. Presently working as a free-lance graphics artist and computer operator, Otter continues to reside in Mendocino County, CA with his extended family and exotic menagerie.

For further information on Otter, see Drawing Down the Moon by Margot Adler (1979; revised and expanded edition 1987); Do You Believe in Magic? by Annie Gottlieb (1987); Witchcraft, the Old Religion by Leo Louis Martello (1973); The Encyclopedia of American Religions by J. Gordon Melton (1979; 2nd ed. 1986); and Religious and Spiritual Groups in Modern America by Roger Elwood (1974).

THE NATURE OF THE SOUL

by **Don Lewis**

In the beginning was the God/dess, and S/He was alone in the darkness, for S/He was the darkness which was all that was. And in this darkness which existed before the dawn of creation and which was God/dess, were all of the things that would later take form existing in an unmanifest state. They were Her dreams, Her thoughts, Her fantasies – but they were mere shadows because they were as yet unmanifest. This was the first darkness, the first night – and S/He was the first dreamer.

And in the fullness of time the God/dess focused Her energy upon these, Her dreams, there in the primordial darkness. S/He focused Her energies and from Her deep desire came forth the first creation –the God. The God burst forth from the primordial darkness in an explosion of light and flame, shooting forth in all directions. And all that was warm, and active, and changeable in the darkness went forth with the light, which was the God. And all that was cool, receptive, and eternal in the darkness remained in the darkness which was the Goddess. This was the first dawn, the first creation, the first act of manifestation –and all subsequent creation has occurred in the same way, through the focus of energy.

The God spread forth in manicolored fiery glory, and His essence began to cool and take on form. The Goddess remained in Her darkness and watched. Both Goddess and God were transformed by this act of creation, as creation is always transformation, but primordial God/dess remained within Them both, and was Their

Soul, the ultimate center of being. This was the first day, from which all subsequent days have taken form.

The Goddess was fascinated by the God, Who was Her own dreams given form, and She desired Him exceedingly. She longed to take that which She had created back into Herself, to be One with it. But the God did not wish to unite with the Goddess, for He feared that such a uniting would end His own existence -and He loved existing. And so He fled from Her, and in fleeing created the Seven Planes of being. At last the God in His flight established the Physical Plane, and here He took the form of inert matter and pattern.

The Goddess saw the rainbow of the Seven Planes, and the emergence of matter, and She desired the God even more. As His nature was motile He continued to change and expand and diversify, and the more She watched the more the Goddess desired to reunite with Him. At last She decided that She must do something. So She looked within Herself to the deepest part of Her, which was primordial God/dess —that part which had existed from before creation, and which still contained within Itself the potential and knowledge of all things. Goddess asked God/dess how She could reunite with the God, how Spirit and Matter could be One again. And primordial God/dess answered, "To Rise, You Must Fall."

"To Rise, You Must Fall." It was not possible for Goddess to bring God back into Herself as He had been before creation. What was done could not be undone. But it was possible for Her to go to Him. It was possible for Goddess to unite with God and experience creation if She entered into creation with Him. And so the Goddess fell. She separated off parts of Herself, and sent them into matter. These parts were the Monads. Each Monad was a perfect microcosm of Goddess at the moment She separated it from Herself.

Each Monad had a different focus, different desires and issues that it brought into creation, representing the mind of Goddess at the moment of its separation from Her. The Monads entered into matter, and through their experiences became Souls –and thus was the ensouled universe created.

Each Monad became many, many Souls, and each Soul lived many, many lives, all seeking to experience the world of matter to the fullest –seeking out every experience, every lesson, every perspective they could have. So many Souls, so many lives, so many experiences that the pattern they wove is of infinite complexity. Each of us is one of these lives of one of these Souls, which is part of one of these Monads. Not only that, but new Souls, new lives, and new experiences are constantly taking shape in every moment of continued existence. This is how Goddess reunited with God by entering the world of matter.

The Goddess fell by creating the nine Monads and the millions of Souls. Her rise was in the endless billions of lives and their infinite experiences. She descended through the Seven Planes to unite with God in matter, Soul entering into matter. Then, Goddess united with the God, They rose back up through the Seven Planes through the experiences of the millions of Souls in the world of matter. The more lives, the more experiences, the more fully Goddess is expressed in the world of matter, until in the end it will be a perfect union of Spirit and Matter, Goddess and God, just as it was in the beginning except infinitely expanded in scope and character.

ELEMENTAL CHANT

I am Air! I am Air! Rising high and flying far!
I am Fire! I am Fire! Burning hot and burning long!
I am Water! I am Water! Flowing fast and flowing free!
I am Earth! I am Earth! I am stable and enduring!

>I am Air! I am Fire! I am Water! I am Earth!
>Dance with me! Dance with me! Dance with me!

I am Air! I am Air! Rising high and flying far!
I am Fire! I am Fire! Burning hot and burning long!
I am Water! I am Water! Flowing fast and flowing free!
I am Earth! I am Earth! I am stable and enduring!

>I am Air! I am Fire! I am Water! I am Earth!
>Dance with me! Dance with me! Dance with me!

I am Air! I am Air! Rising high and flying far!
I am Fire! I am Fire! Burning hot and burning long!
I am Water! I am Water! Flowing fast and flowing free!
I am Earth! I am Earth! I am stable and enduring!

>I am Air! I am Fire! I am Water! I am Earth!
>Dance with me! Dance with me! Dance with me!

HUMAN HERITAGE AND THE GODDESS

by **Abby Willowroot**

Deep in each human heart is a memory, a simple and powerful one.
It is the memory of sanity, the memory of being simply human.
We are each of us, the product of millions of years of evolution.
We carry inside of us, many ancient knowings and understandings.
We are the dream of our ancestors, proof of their survival lives in us.

The remembrance of the Goddess is held in the hearts of humanity.
She has begun to re-emerge and is again celebrated and honored.
She was the sustenance and guiding protectress of our ancestors.

The noise of the world around us often drowns out
the simple whisper of human truths.

You will hear these truths if you allow yourself to honor Nature and spend time quietly and without expectation. Sit under a tree and watch grass move in the breeze, or silently watch the ocean, or a lake, or a field of grass or grain. It will open you to the Universe and magic.

If you live in a city, or cannot get out, quietly watch a house plant as it breathes. Listen and do not judge what you hear, just simply allow it to bubble up and reach the surface of your consciousness. Relax, and soon you will be entrained and breathing in harmony together.

Memories of our shared heritage often emerge through drumming, chanting or dancing. Even though you may have forgotten, the cells of your body remember these ancient truths. When you connect mind, body and spirit, magic happens and the Universe opens to you.

Wisdom floats through the air on the powerful rhythms of a drum beat. The sound opens your being. You need not practice, or be a musician, to play a drum, you have only to pick up a drum, relax, and begin. Your body will remember . . . you are a human, it is part of you.

Honoring the Goddess in drumming, dance, chant and song should not be rehearsed, it should flow from you as an offering of your essence. It is not your skill that makes it powerful, it is your spirit. Your true self is released and celebrated when you dance.

A Remembering Chant

I sing to the Goddess
my voice is strong
I drum to the Goddess
an ancient song

I do not know the words
I simply make a sound
my hand strikes the drum
remembering an ancient sound

I dance to the Goddess
my feet upon the Earth
I sway to find the rhythm
of an ancient birth

I dance, I sing, I drum, I chant
the memories grow clear
I dance, I sing, I drum, I chant
and the Goddess is here

For remembering, it is often helpful to light a candle and gaze into the flame. Firelight is as old as human history. When the flickering light of a candle is perceived by your brain, it opens passage ways and paths to long forgotten genetic memories.

See the memories dance and shine in the timeless light of a candle. Ancient memories waiting to be discovered by you.

We are our ancestors, their experiences and memories live within us. They are in our brains, in our cells, in our marrow, they are the sacred core of our very being. Reconnecting with these ancient memories fills one with a deep and unshakeable knowing. The powerful realization at a gut level, that all humanity, all life and all energy is connected in a magical web of inter-dependence.

We are all cells in the body of the Goddess, each unique, each with a special task, and special gifts. Knowing this at your core, brings peace, harmony and unimaginable joy.

http://spiralgoddess.com/Heritage.html

DAUGHTER OF DARKNESS

Daughter of Darkness
Mother of Light
Grandmother Holy Moon
Shining bright!
-
Daughter of Darkness
Mother of Light
Grandmother Holy Moon
Shining bright!
-
Daughter of Darkness
Mother of Light
Grandmother Holy Moon
Shining bright!

THE DIFFERENCE BETWEEN MODERN WICCA AND OLDLINE WITCHCRAFT

by **A.C. Fisher Aldag**

This is my opinion and not necessarily that of other writers, contributors, or staff of Magickal Media.

Witchcraft with a capital W existed here in America long before Wicca was imported by Sybil Leek and Raymond Buckland. What many Pagan scholars do not seem to realize is that religious Witchcraft was and is very much active for decades in America, right up to the present day, but not as neo-Pagans currently practice. Wiccans frequently use the model of God and Goddess worship, invoking the four elements / directions, casting circle as a place to perform magickal acts, and other practices which incorporate a combination of ceremonial magick, international legend ("myth") and devotion. These practices derived primarily from Gerald Gardner, who was a folklorist that studied various traditions of Witchcraft, ceremonial magick, pre-Christian legend, and worldwide cultures, then combined them with Masonic and other fraternal rites to make a cohesive whole.

I believe that many of Mr. Gardner's rites were actually derived from observing the religio-magickal rituals of existing witches and Witches in Britain (and I make a case for this theory in my article series on <u>The Witches' Voice</u>, which is called "Another Pagan History"). I've drawn this conclusion because several of Mr. Gardner's

Wiccan ceremonies directly parallel the rites performed by American Witches who had no contact with Gardner or his coven descendants. These individuals, families and groups have stated that they learned their Craft from family members and neighbors who brought their practices from "the old countries", and who had syncretized their religio-magickal rites with that of Native cultures, long before Wicca was brought to America. Further, several of Mr. Gardner's rituals encompass folkloric tales, dances, legends and magio-religious ceremonies performed by working-class rural people and inner-city folks right up until the 1940s and 50s, when a combination of WWII and television caused the traditions to fizzle out (Christianity did not kill Paganism, as modern Wiccans would have us believe. It was Ed Sullivan). Many people are reviving these customs today. However, many more people practiced their magickal religions right up to present times. We'll get to how Witchcraft differs from Wicca in a moment.

Location: Many of the Witches I've encountered were from the rural Upper Peninsula of Michigan, as well as the northern parts of Appalachia, the mountains and farmsteads of Indiana / Kentucky / Ohio / West Virginia, and the farthest Northern portions of Wisconsin. My own tradition comes from Mandan, a tiny copper-mining and timbering village near Copper Harbor in the Upper Peninsula, a town that no longer exists due to the economic crash of the 80s. After my husband performed a hoodening (wearing an animal skin and antlers in a ceremonial dance and children's simulated hunt) for a local parade, several individuals from our small town came forward to state that they'd been involved in or observed a similar rite. After publishing "Another Pagan History", several people corresponded with me privately to state that when they were kids, they'd participated in religious Witchcraft, Shamanic practice, and some of the meso-Pagan customs mentioned in the article series. These folks wrote from all across America, Canada and Britain. I figure there are Witches everywhere. Ethnicity: Most of the Witches I've encountered are of Celtic descent, including Welsh, Irish, Scots, and northwestern English, mixed with the blood of the Saxon invaders of those districts. Dozens are of Cornish heritage, who'd never heard of Mr. Coltraine. Over time in America, they'd intermarried with the "Three Fires" nations (Pottawatomi, Odawa, Chippewa) as well as Lanapi, Cheroki, Menomeni, and other tribes. However I've also spoken to traditional Witches of Mexican, African, Roma and Asian descent. People who come from a heritage of Witchcraft seem to marry each other, regardless of national ancestry. Some, not all, syncretized each others' practices. I've found Cymri (Welsh) folk who had bottle trees to scare away baneful entities, Native Americans who use the tarot for divination, and "Pellars" (spell casters) of Cornish descent who used sticks and tree configurations to cast or interpret runes (no, not the Runes as taught by Mr. McNallen and Mr. Thorsson ... not the Norse alphabet. Still, they were called runes with a small r). None of these folks claimed knowledge of Wicca or neo-Paganism. Some were functionally illiterate. Others had heard of the modern Pagan movement, but believed it to be full of "hippies" (hi, Grandpa) and desired to distance themselves from that culture.

Commonality of belief: Includes presence of a Goddess / Mother / Queen / Lady in addition to a God or Lord; belief in fairies or "little people" as spirit beings or natural entities (the First Nations people call 'em "puck-wudgies" which is reminiscent of Shakespeare's Puck character!); a belief in descendancy from the Gods themselves, and thus ancestor worship; a belief in magick and the ability to use it or work with it, and a desire to use natural forces to create a beneficent environment for humans, such as using herbs to heal, and trancework or dreaming to achieve interaction with nature and spirits; a belief in reincarnation, a belief in spirits and the soul transcending death; and other practices that modern Pagans would surely recognize. In addition, there was / is a coexistence with Nature and self-sufficiency, as well as a severe pragmatism, that I find sadly lacking in Wicca and neo-Paganism. "Cursing" enemies or hexing for revenge was unfortunately common; following the "Wiccan Rede" was unheard of. Rituals nearly always included creating some type of sacred space (although NOT "casting circle"), summoning entities to help including Deity and minor spiritual beings, divination, celebration of seasonal holidays, performing ritualized dances, theatre and telling legends and lore, and the use of magick for attunement, healing or to create change. The latter included making potions, creating talismans, or "witching" a person to make them feel better, mentally, physically or spiritually, or "witching" a situation to achieve optimal results. However, the primary purpose was spiritual expression and yes, entertainment.

How does modern Wicca differ from oldline Witchcraft? Obviously the belief in "harm none" is important. I believe that the Wiccan Rede is the single greatest gift offered to the magickal community by neo-Paganism. It does not matter if it was Mr. Gardener's idea, or the invention of Lady Gwen Thompson or genuinely came from an older source, the Rede is crucial. It has probably prevented thousands of earth-scorching baneful spells from wiping out whole communities. No, really, I am serious. Cursing the neighbor's cattle and watching them all drop dead is not a diplomatic thing, nor is it nice when the neighbor's wife and kids have to go on Relief (before Welfare, there was Relief, and it was quite shameful to partake of it). The sense of community, of multiculturalism, of sharing beliefs and comparing traditions and merging cultures done by modern Pagans is wonderful. I really like that Wicca has become feminized and that neo-Paganism has gone political, fighting for our environment and for equality. Another thing that can be beneficial is the elements. Some older traditions have the same four or five as Wicca, and perhaps this derived from the First Nations (there's speculation that Mr. Gardner observed Native people on his trip to America, and compared their sacred directions to the elements and the Watchtowers of ceremonial magick). Recently, whole intensives have been given to immerse the soul in one particular element, to work with it until it's incorporated into the very fabric of ones' magick. Our tradition used the directions more as "wards" to guard us from harmful influences and to lend power. Earth is down. Sky is up. Water is Lake Michigan. It's great to find more ways to use, to integrate, to attune with the elements. Some modern scholars have argued that the elements are a recent invention of Wicca and ceremonial magick, but I disagree. The elements are pretty much universal to magick users and Witches. The Wiccan interpretation seems particularly useful.

However, the worst element of modern Wicca has been the frivolity, in my opinion. Magick and communications with the Gods and honoring Nature must be approached reverentially. We have food, and heat, and air, and our health, because of the beneficence of our ancestors, our Deities and the Earth. Modern Wiccans are neither satisfactorily awed nor thankful enough, in my observation. While oldline or meso-Pagans were often ridiculed as tree huggers, we were and are always a realistic bunch. We sometimes laugh at Pagans who attend festival without sufficient blankets and fire-kindling skills. (Yes, we'll help you. But we'll laugh at you.) Modern Wiccans and neo-Pagans could use a healthy dose of pragmatism. But please, keep your idealism, too. It's one of the coolest things about Wicca.

Today, when we hear about these big conferences on gender within Paganism, we snort behind our hands. Who cares? Can he milk a cow, can she dig a ditch? Equality, good. Rumination, not good. Of course, women and men are equal, and have different ways of approaching magick, and life. Yet so do individuals. Every ancient society always had one or two homosexual people, who were accepted just fine by others, usually the male school teacher or the spinster who made awesome soap or the two "maiden ladies" who shared a household. If they'd gone around "creating dialogue about gender", they would have been ignored or laughed out of town.

Handicapped people were found jobs they could do, making shoes, tending hogs, in the days before mandatory mainstreamed public education and our subsequent mollycoddling. Our society has completely debilitated our children, and neo-Pagans are some of the worst for extending adolescent dependency. And as Charlie Daniels sang, "A rich man goes to college, a poor man goes to work". My grandfather and uncles worked in the timber or mines from the time they were 14, and they were properly respectful of the boggins and knockers and gnomes and dirtkins and chrystal elves, who were offered whiskey, brack (not Obama, but bread) and songs to keep the excavation from caving in.

If we believed some neo-Pagan scholars (cough, Hutton, cough) we'd be under the impression that oldline magickal practices only survived as vestiges of ancient cultures, that Witchcraft had no connection to religion – let alone Goddess worship, and that all modern practices of Paganism came from either Gardner or ceremonial magick, were invented, or were reconstructed from ancient sources, primarily literature. I've been disputing this fallacy since approximately 1982, when I met and became involved with Wiccans and neo-Pagans – years before Hutton ascended his ivory tower and used working-class peoples' taxes to fund his badly-written theses coopting the text of his undergrads without giving them writing credits (shall I tell you how I really feel? LOL!) I've had this argument with Isaac Bonewits, who in his desire to debunk some of the myths surrounding Wicca with scholarship, threw out the baby with the bathwater and dismissed all surviving traditions of hereditary Witchcraft and folkloric magio-religion.

Since then, I've read several other accounts of the "Pow Wow" tradition, Appalachian Witchcraft, the Gullah practice of magick, Stregeria, the Curenderia traditions, generic European folk magick, family and hereditary traditions, and heard several other statements made by those who either discovered or practiced religio-magickal or folkloric traditions in America. Nearly everywhere I go, I find at least one other Witch, buying pretty rocks in gift shops for healing crystals, gathering herbs at highway rest areas, sewing magickal designs into quilts, murmuring prayers while knitting, doing spellwork as they garden. I've run into them at neo-Pagan festivals, and communicated online. There really are Witches everywhere.

Do I have any proof? Not really. My ancestors could've made it up. People who I talk to might be lying. It's been implied that I'm not being truthful, either, as many scholars view any hereditary traditions of magick or Witchcraft with skepticism. Let me assure you, my imagination is truly not that great. I've not documented my sources, as most of the individuals I've talked to prefer to remain anonymous, and not have college kids or magazine writers camped out on their doorstep, begging for scraps of lore and interfering with chores. Letters I received were wiped out with a computer crash, but maybe that's for the best. It's also been implied that since I went to work and had children rather than pursuing the futility of a college education, I am not qualified to write or lecture about folklore, magio-religion or modern-day Witchcraft. Y'know what? I don't care. Wanna hear some cool stories and rites, or argue about their legitimacy?

BIOGRAPHIES: PART ONE

by Don Lewis

The series of Biographies included in this book is based upon those used in the World of Witches Museum, formerly of Salem, MA. The series is by no means an all-inclusive, but many people relevant to traditional or contemporary Witchcraft are included. Many of the existing biographies have been reworked or expanded, and additional new biographies have been added especially for this project. This series has never been published in any book or magazine before.

APOLLONIUS OF TYANNA

Apollonius of Tyana was a wandering sage and magician in the early Roman Empire. Apollonius was famous for his psychic abilities, miraculous healings and physical apparitions.

Apollonius was born in Cappadocia, in what is now Turkey, during the reign of the Emperor Augustus. During his lifetime Apollonius wrote numerous books and letters, including a famous biography of Pythagoras. Almost all of these writings are now lost, though some fragments survive.

Apollonius is said to have traveled widely throughout the Roman Empire and beyond. Notably Apollonius is said to have traveled to India where he met his disciple Damis, who accompanied the sage thereafter and later wrote a biography of Apollonius, which is now lost.

Apollonius was especially revered by the Severan Dynasty, particularly the Empress Julia Pia Domna, who commissioned Philostratus to write a biography of Apollonius.

LYDIA BECKETT

Lydia Ann Beckett (nee Spurgeon) was born in on May 31, 1871, and lived most of her life in Indiana and Illinois, though she also traveled extensively. During her lifetime Lydia Beckett was well known as a painter of landscapes and Americana.

In her early life Beckett was a devotee of the Roman Goddess Venus, and established a classical revival Temple in honor of this Goddess.

In the late 1890's Lydia Beckett took a tour of Italy. One of her goals was to bring back a piece of marble from an ancient temple of Venus. Lydia was unable to find marble from a Temple of Venus however, and had to settle for a bit of marble from a Temple of Diana –which she would soon after regard as being an omen.

During her trip Lydia met and became acquainted with Charles Leland. Leland presented Lydia with a galley copy of the as yet unpublished "Aradia, or The Gospel of the Witches." After this Lydia adopted Aradian practice, a form of Italian Stregheria as filtered through Leland.

Back home in Indiana Lydia changed her classical revival Temple of Venus into an Aradian Temple of Diana, and introduced Aradian practices to the US Midwest heartland. Among those she influenced was her friend Caroline High Correll, who adopted Aradian ideas.

In addition to Leland, Lydia knew a number of other figures in the magical community of the day, including Aleister Crowley. Lydia was among those who helped support Crowley in his latter days when he was in straightened circumstances.

In 1937 Lydia Beckett and her daughter Athalo "Atsie" Lawrence opened the Lawrence Museum of Magic and Witchcraft, showcasing historical items as well as items from then-contemporary figures such as Crowley.

At first the museum was a small display within the Lawrence home —eventually it encompassed several rooms. The Lawrence Museum would remain open daily for over fifty years.

In addition to her Aradian practice Lydia and her husband, Rev. Henry C. Beckett, were also prominent in the Universalist Church. Universalism taught that all religions are valid paths to Deity and allowed for the expression of Pagan ideas in a low-key manner.

Lydia Beckett spent her last few years in deteriorating health. She died on December 21, 1953, at age 82.

ISAAC BONEWITS

Phillip Isaac Emmons Bonewits was born in Royal Oak Michigan on October 1, 1949.

Isaac first came to fame while at the University of California at Berkley. UC Berkley allowed students to create their own degree study program. This allowed Isaac to graduate Berkley in 1970 with the first ever Bachelor of Arts in Magic and Thaumaturgy. This was the first degree of its kind from an American university, and at the time and for some time after was a great embarrassment to UC Berkley. Today however, this is looked upon as the first ever degree in Pagan Studies.

While at Berkley Isaac became involved with the Reformed Druids of North America, becoming an initiated Druid Priest in 1969.

In 1971 Isaac published "Real Magic" a groundbreaking examination of magical ideas and practice from a modern perspective. In particular "Real Magic" expounded upon Isaac's understanding of the Laws of Magic, using a modern, systematized approach. The book was an immediate success and remains immensely popular to this day.

From 1973 – 1975 Isaac was the editor of Llewellyn's "Gnostica" magazine.

In 1979 Isaac created his "Advanced Bonewits Cult Danger Evaluation Frame" in which he outlined a checklist of items intended to determine whether a group was or was not a dangerous "cult".

In 1983 Isaac founded the Ar nDraiocht Fein, a Druid Fellowship more commonly known as the ADF. The first public announcement of the ADF was at the Winterstar Festival in 1984. The ADF is unique among Druidic organizations in that it focuses not only on Celtic religion but upon all Indo-European religions.

Isaac served ArchDruid of the ADF until 1996, when he stepped down accepting the title of ArchDruid Emeritus. The ADF focuses not only on Celtic but on all Indo-European religions.

On July 23, 04 handfasted fellow Pagan leader Phaedra Heyman Bonewits. The ceremony was presided over by Oberon Zell-Ravenheart of the Church of All Worlds together with an Arch Priestess of the Correllian Tradition.

Isaac was married five times, and has one child, Arthur Lipp-Bonewits. Isaac Bonewits died on August 12, 2010.

GLEB BOTKIN

Gleb Botkin was the son of Dr. Eugene Botkin. Eugene Botkin was physician to HIM Nicholas II of Russia and died with the Tzar at Ekaterinburg. Gleb Botkin grew up with the imperial children, and later would be a lifelong supporter of Anna Anderson's claim to be the Grand Duchess Anastasia.

Gleb Botkin was also the founder of the church of Aphrodite. The Church of Aphrodite was founded in Long Island, New York in 1938. One of the earliest Pagan Churches in the US, Botkin had to fight for the right to register the church legally, eventually arguing his case before the Supreme Court.

Botkin taught that Aphrodite was the supreme form of Deity, and that the creation of the universe was like a woman giving birth to a child. The Church of Aphrodite also taught that patriarchal civilization had created most of the world's problems, and that only a shift toward matriarchy could fix the world.

Gleb Botkin died in 1969, and the Church of Aphrodite did not long survive him.

RAYMOND BUCKLAND

Among the best known Wiccan authors, having published over sixty books. Raymond Buckland has written many books on Wicca, magic and the occult, as well as several novels.

Raymond Buckland was born into an English Romany family in 1934, in London, England.

Buckland was initiated into the Gardnerian Tradition of Wicca in 1963 by Monique Wilson, then Gardner's High Priestess. Buckland is credited with bringing Gardnerian Wicca to the United States, and at one time acted as Gardner's agent and spokesman in the U.S.

Buckland published his first book, "A Pocket Guide to the Supernatural" in 1969. He followed this in 1970 with "Witchcraft Ancient and Modern" and "Practical Candleburning Rituals". Also in 1970 Buckland published his first novel, "Mu Revealed", under the pseudonym of "Tony Earll".

Other works by Buckland include: "Buckland's Complete Book of Witchcraft": "Gypsy Witchcraft and Magic": and "Witchcraft from the Inside: Origins of the Fastest Growing Religious in America".

In 1973 Buckland opened what he termed "The First Museum of Magic and Witchcraft in the United States", a project he had been developing for some time. The contents of Buckland's museum are now in New Orleans.

Leaving the Gardnerian Tradition in the early 1970s, Buckland founded the Seax Wicca Tradition, which was intended to be more open and democratic in structure.

In the early 1980s Buckland and his then wife established the Seax Wicca Seminary, a correspondence school of Wicca which at one point had more than 1000 students. Buckland also practices Pecti Wicca, a form of Scottish Wicca.

In 1992 Buckland retired from active leadership and has since pursued a solitary path, but remains a prominent authority and lecturer. Buckland has also enjoyed some success as a technical consultant and script-writer in the entertainment industry.

DEENA BUTTA

Rt. Rev. Deena Celeste Butta was a Arch Priestess of the Fellowship of Isis. Lady Deena was born in Chicago as Deena Welgarz on June 1, 1950.

Lady Deena had a long and varied career in the Pagan community, ultimately achieving her most prominent role in the Fellowship of Isis.

Lady Deena became a member of the Fellowship of Isis in 1977, the second year of its existence. Lady Deena also belonged to Chicago's Earthstar Chicago Lodge from 1979 – 1984. She belonged to the Society of Janus from 1984 - 1987

Lady Deena took part in the Parliament of World's Religions in 1993, as part of the Isian delegation, taking part in the grand procession and the Isian Mystery Play, as well as hosting M. Rev. Olivia in her home. During the Parliament Lady Deena was created a Priestess Hierophant of Fellowship of Isis.

After this Lady Deena was charged with developing a Fellowship of Isis Convention in the United States, an event originally envisioned as being similar to the annual Fellowship of Isis Convention in the UK. From this was born the annual Fellowship of Isis Chicago Convention, beginning in 1994 the Fellowship of Isis Chicago convention would become one of the Fellowship of Isis' premier international gatherings. Lady Deena would lead the convention for eighteen years, until her death. The convention continues annually to this day.

For many years M. Rev. Olivia Robertson, co-founder and International Head of the Fellowship of Isis would travel annually to the United States, making many appearances including the Fellowship of Isis Chicago Convention. During her time in Chicago Lady Olivia would invariable stay with Lady Deena, and take part receptions, tours, and other events collateral to the Convention. Lady Olivia would later pay tribute to Lady Deena as having been "...one of my greatest friends..." on the Fellowship of Isis website.

The Fellowship of Isis Chicago Convention involved many conventional presentations and activities, but was particularly distinguished by the annual performance of an Isian Mystery Play, which set the theme for the year and served as the climax of the event. The Mystery Play is an important feature of Isian liturgy, but the way that the Mystery Play was handled in Chicago was said to be unique, in that they were mounted with the same level of detail and skill as full-blown theatrical productions, featuring elaborate costuming and choreography. Each year the Mystery play would begin with a ritual dance enacted by the Priesthood, which could often be strikingly beautiful. These magnificent productions were among the reasons that the Fellowship of Isis Chicago Convention was so successful.

Lady Deena was also known for a sometimes uneasy alliance with Rev. Don Lewis and Ed Hubbard, which resulted in the Fellowship of Isis Chicago Convention being promoted through their Round Table Magazine, Telepathic Radio program, and later Magick TV. Because of this many radio and video interviews exist with Lady Deena, Lady Olivia, and other prominent Isians attending the Conventions, as well as videos of many of the Mystery Plays enacted.

Lady Deena also edited the Isis Seshat Journal and held the standing of Dame Grand Commander in the Noble Order of Tara and Arch Druidess in the Druid Clan of Danu.

In addition Lady Deena was also a member of the Fellowship of Isis Arch Priesthood Union.

In her private life Lady Deena was a professional librarian from 1978 and a specialist in Genealogy from 1999. Lady Deena continued in her career as a librarian until shortly before her death.

Lady Deena was listed in the Who's Who of American Women in Year 2010.

Lady Deena died from Creutzfeldt-Jakob disease on January 27, Year 2013, just a few months before the death of M. Rev. Hon. Olivia Robertson.

LAURIE CABOT

Laurie Cabot was born March 6, 1933, in Wewoka, Oklahoma, while her family was en route from their old home in Boston to a new home in Anaheim, California.

In 1947 Laurie and her mother returned to Boston to further Laurie's education. Around this time Laurie was befriended by a woman she met at the library who encouraged her interest in psychic things and encouraged her to study alternative spirituality. The woman eventually revealed that she was a Witch. This Witch began training young Laurie, and prepared her for her initiation, which she received at the age of 16, in 1949.

In the 1950s and '60s Laurie pursued a career as a dancer. She married twice and had two daughters, Jody (B. 1963) and Penny (B. 1965). After the end of her second marriage, Laurie moved to the north end of Boston and made an oath that she would live thereafter as a public Witch, adopting ritual robes and stylized makeup as everyday-wear. Soon after, Laurie moved to Salem, already known as the "Witch City".

Laurie now began teaching classes in 'Witchcraft as a Science' as part of the "continuing education" program at the local Wellesley High School.

In 1970 Salem became the recipient of tremendous publicity as the "Bewitched" television program shot a number of episodes on location there. The following year Laurie Cabot opened "The Witch Shop", Salem's first metaphysical shop, located at 100 Derby St. She would subsequently establish "Crowhaven Corner", and her present shop "The Cat, the Crow, and the Crown" located on Pickering Wharf just up the street from the World of Witches Museum.

In 1973 Laurie Cabot established "The Witches Ball", an annual event she has hosted ever since.

In 1977 Massachusetts Governor Michael Dukakis awarded Madam Cabot the Massachusetts Patriot Award for her work with special needs children, and proclaimed her "The Official Witch of Salem".
In 1980 Madam Cabot became a member of the executive board of the Salem Chamber of Commerce, one of the first public Witches to hold such a position.

In 1986 Madam Cabot founded the WLPA, or "Witches League for Public Awareness." The WLPA was a civil rights group and media watchdog dedicated to advancing the Witch community, and for many years was one of the leading organizations in the World of Witches.

Laurie Cabot leads the Cabot-Kent Temple in Salem, and is Head of the Cabot Tradition of the Science of Witchcraft, a pre-Gardnerian form of Witchcraft based upon ancestral and modern practice and adhering to the Wiccan Rede and the Threefold Law of Return.

Madam Cabot is the author of many books including "Practical Magic: A Salem Witch's handbook" (1986), "Power of a Witch" (1990), and "The Witch in Every Woman" (1997), among others.

ONCE, LONG AGO...

by **Abby Willowroot**

Once . . .

Once my ancestors were
the people of the Mother Goddess,
the hungry gatherers of the fields
the fierce hunters of the beasts
makers of shelter from the elements
makers of talisman and charms
makers of clothing and tools

Once my ancestors were
the discoverers of fire
the painters of Caves
the walkers who migrated
wise shaman of distant times
children of the Mother Goddess
knowers of weather's secrets
listeners of the wind

My ancestors live in me,
the ancestors live in my children,
the ancestors live in my neighbors
they live in my friends and enemies,
deep within our DNA, our ancestors live,
we carry their ancient knowledge with us
mostly forgotten now, it is still there
they are still a vital part of who we are

Our ancestors are waiting to be remembered,
our ancestors are waiting to be honored,
waiting for us, to thank their Mother Goddess

> for our lives and our food, and our shelter,
> waiting for us to remember who we are
> deep in our cells, the ancestors wait,
> giving us strength and memories
> immunities, instincts, and skills
> we are our ancestors
> and they are us,
> Reborn

Our First Deity

> *Once our ancestors worshiped a Mother Goddess,*
> *and celebrated Her ability to create life and to sustain us.*

Nothing was considered more sacred than the power to create another living being. We honored the Mother Goddess for feeding and nurturing us. We celebrated Her miracles of birth, those births that created the animals we hunted, the animals who lived along side of us, the animals who fed ourselves, our families, and our tribes.

Our ancestors on the all continents made stone, clay, bone, & wood statues of the Great Mother Goddess. Their hands shaped Her ample form, She was the source, a divine, living source of food, protection and security. The Mother Goddess was the deity worshiped around the world, before history, before civilization, before cities, before Gods, and Shaman, before all others, we honored Her in ritual, song, and art.

We asked Her blessing to be upon our hunting and upon our gathering, She guided us.

Caves around the world are filled with images and symbols of ancient Mother Goddesses. Many painted and carved caves have been found in France, Italy, Africa, Spain, Australia, Yugoslavia, the Americas, Mexico, Switzerland, Russia, the Middle East, Greece, and Asia. Each year, more caves emerge from the long forgotten darkness of obscurity, revealing their ancient splendors. Animals were also depicted, as were human hunters, and the hand prints of the Cave painters and their family members.

Animals were the gift of the Mother Goddess whose miracle of Birth insured the herds would bring forth new, young animals each year. Men, women and children depended on the bounty of their Mother Goddess and fashioned images of Her in gratitude and to insure that the blessings of food and shelter would continue to be there now and in the future seasons.

In re-learning how to honor the Ancient Mother Goddess, we are reclaiming and honoring our own common human heritage. Moving into the future, we must come to understand that we are all of one origin, one family, one race, the human race. The commonality of our ancestors' beliefs and rituals for living, hunting, worshiping give us powerful clues to the universality of the human spirit. The ancient human knowledge and understanding of the divine centered on the miracles of birth and mothering. All over the world, similar customs, Goddess figures and praise of the Mother Goddess drew upon many similar beliefs and symbols.

The power of the Great Mother was alive in the ancient human heart, and it is still alive deep within your own DNA. Our ancestors saw Her in the world around them. She was all powerful, benevolent and fierce, She was both honored and feared. The struggle for survival of we humans has always been very challenging, and it still is today. Unlike our ancestors, we no longer fear the cave bear, lion or wolf, the dangers most of us fear are not usually posed by wild Nature, but the many threats and dangers of our modern world.

Learning to reclaim a reverence for Nature and our common human symbols will help us to reclaim sanity and a sense of security within our own culture. Honoring the Mother Goddess will lead us back to our most ancient roots.

We can begin this journey by listening for Her in the wind, the rain, and the rhythms, cacophony, stillness, and the many vibrant voices of Nature. Our ancient Mother Goddess lives in the forests, the desserts, the mountains, the ocean, the rivers, the cities, the fields, and in every cell of our bodies.

> We are our ancestors, all of our ancestors.
> Listen for the Mother Goddess . . . She is speaking

May the firelight rekindle our connection with the Mother Goddess
May we come to know the wisdom of our ancestors that live within us
May we understand that we humans are all related
through our ancestors
And will again be related through our children
and their children's children

> May you walk gently upon the Earth
> May your journey be long and joyous
> May it honor the ancient ancestors
> May it honor your own living spirit
> May it honor generations to come

http://spiralgoddess.com/OnceLongAgo.html

DEFINING THE SEA PRIESTESS

by **Stephanie Leon Neal**

Sea Priestesses/Priests are individuals that utilize all bodies of water on this earth and beyond. We divine with water, interpret dream symbols and give spiritual council through shadow work. We are Shamans or World Walkers of the all the seas, healing through working with our shadow self. Journeying, astral travel and dream encoding are our primary investigative modes. To sum it up in three words, we are explorers. The Correllian Tradition offers Sea Priestess training as well as training in World Walking and Correll Shamanism.

The following excerpt was taken from the Sea Priestess training

Introduction

Divination, confirms that we are being dreamt by a dreamer, as we too dream our creations into existence. We are a dream that dreams day and night. We are "the purpose" of a dreamer that dreams us, which lives within "Its" dream. That's right we were made on purpose, for a purpose. We were created as creators by a creator. How magnificent, how lovely, how powerful, that we are a loving, ever expanding dream. Within this dream, we are able to travel by many meridian types, the matrix, our, very core to find what we need to see for the so-called future. What does divination or dreams have to do with water? Divination, water and dreams are a clear looking glass to every "moment" which is found here, within this dream. One cannot study water or dreams very long, before seeing the so-called "future," clearly and begin to utilize our "third eye." Our inner sense becomes developed. As we look into our very own pool our eyes, there is no denying, our "future," because there it is staring right back at us. Know individuals can see further, utilizing water and dreams as your magnifier. Goddess/God desires that you know everything you desire; nothing is held back, for those that want to avail themselves to divinations skills; knowing it is a holy skill that carries much responsibility and diplomacy. Wisdom is found in water dreams, as both lie in your hands.

Divination or Attuning Wisdom

Individuals desire to find out what will be, as if their future has been already written by another entity. Our futures are written daily by our hands. Desiring to know what will come, so they may use that information to walk in wisdom. There are differing schools of thought on pre-destination that I do not wish to address. When people ask to have a reading, the main underlying reason, is, "Will everything be okay?" or "Will their family be okay?" Others want to have outside validation or confirmation, on what they have already done or have already decided to do, asking, "Is this the right decision or focus?"

Of course, some individuals want to know if they are going to meet someone special or if they are coming into money; both serious questions for the seeker. Everyone desires to know if everything will be okay, everyone needs wise counsel from the Living Springs of dreams and water. Wise spiritual counsel through divination and dreams are like a mother lovingly embracing her child and saying "I am here, with you always."

Seeing What the Water Sees

Water is always mentioned in almost every culture, when discussing dreams, divination, and prophecy, within most myths and traditions.

Nostradamus (1503-1566), renowned as France's greatest visionary, used water for divination. The following two quatrains are from his own hand, explaining how he would use water when seeing into the future:

"Gathered at night in study deep I sat,
Alone, upon the tripod stool of brass,
Exiguous flame came out of solitude,
Promise of magic that may be believed.

The rod in hand set in the midst of the Branches,
He moistens with water both the fringe and the foot,
Fear and a voice make me quake in my sleeves;
Splendor divine, the God is seated near."

One of Nostradamus's prophecies, that have not been fulfilled yet, is the Hall of Records prophecy, which explains that wisdom shall be found in an "Urn." In ancient times, it was the urn that would hold water and it was the urn that would be used as a measuring device. In the Vedas, we read that water holds wisdom. I.e. The Mesopotamia water god Ea, full of wisdom, dispenses counsel to the gods. The wisdom of water gods was the main function of their age. In the Hellenic world, the wisest were called "the old men of the sea." In Rgveda 10.125 says: "My origin is in the waters, in the ocean."

The Hall of Records Prophecy

"They will come to discover the hidden topography of the land (at Giza). The urns holding wisdom within the monuments (the Pyramids) opened up, their contents will cause the understanding of holy philosophy to expand greatly, white exchanged for black, falsehoods exposed, new wisdom replacing the established tradition that no longer work. (VII.14)"

I find it curious that this wisdom will be found in a water jug! How appropriate!

Another association to water wisdom and consciousness is the very ancient Manosaravar lake, which resides high in the gorgeous Tibetan mountains. A place where many believe this area is the very center of the world. Millions travel, every year, to this ancient lake to receive direction, wisdom and healing from the waters. Visiting the lake brings clarification to dreams, divination and deep enlightenment. The meaning of the word Manosravar is; "Lake of Consciousness and Enlightenment." We live in a moving, living energy ocean of consciousness, that quickens everything.

Hermes' Riddle, also supports the notion, that guidance is found in water. According to Shah and many other insightful writers, Hermes inscribed, on an emerald tablet, his riddle or "Key" that represents inner principles of alchemy, The Great Work. The following is Shah's rendering of the Emerald Tablet:

Emerald Tablet

> "The truth certainly, truest, without untruth.
> What is above is like what is below.
> What is below is what is above.
> The miracle of unity is to be attained.
> Everything is formed from the contemplation of unity, and all things come from unity, by means of adaptation. Its parents are the Sun and the Moon.
> It was borne by the wind and nurtured by the Earth.
> Every wonder is from it, and its power is complete.
> Throw it upon earth, and earth will separate from fire. The impalpable separated from the palpable.
> Through wisdom it rises slowly from the world to heaven.
> Then it descends to the world, combining the power of the upper and the lower.
> Thus you shall have the illumination of the world, and darkness will disappear.
> This is the power of all strength- it overcomes that which is delicate and penetrates through solids. This was the means of the creation of the world.
> And in the future wonderful developments will be made, and this is the way.

I am Hermes the Threefold Sage, so named because
I hold the three elements of all the wisdom."

I suggest you replace the word " IT," with the word "water" to Herme's riddle. What other element has been attributed to everything in this riddle, but water, thus rises through wisdom!

Divination Suggestions

All divination medians work essentially the same general way, as you would divine with a crystal ball. Go into alpha, consciousness in your own manner or deliberately enter into the sea of dreams, enter stillness then divine your tool or dream. The following list is just a small sample of water divination. It is also helpful to use your personified heart chakra for guidance, your Spirit Guides and power animals for guidance, in fact, that's all you need! Yet do not depend of them, depend on your own past experiences, lessons and knowledge.

Divination Methods

- Gaze into any body of water on the full moon. (There is always a full moon, somewhere in the universe)

- Gaze into a large dark bowl of water. (Adding a drop of oil into water can be read also.)

- Listen to a lake, pond, well, spring or any body of water. Listen to what the water is communicating. When listening to water, don't be hypnotized, stay focused and listen, to the answer to your question, the sounds of water heals also.) Meditation is not zoning out, it is zoning in, become more acutely aware of your surroundings.

- Waves vibrate with threefold harmony. Sound waves + our water filled cells + the universe's energies, all work together, providing a pathway to health, guidance and wisdom.

- Feel the water, either with your entire body or just a hand or foot. Allow water wisdom to come through touch, through your skin. The water ancients and World Walkers listen or sense for wisdom, through our skin.

- Dolphin divination is always at your call, by simply "seeing" a dolphin, finish your thought by thinking what you are dreaming for your immediate future. In other words think dolphin, then enter one of your dreams, then finish your dream in a way that is satisfactory to your life.

- Water stirring: Stir water and think what you want to bring into your life while asking, "What is coming into my life." Then wait for the answer. Some will ask and will not wait for the answer.

- Reading Waves, waves travel in threes, which are called a "wave train," the last wave of the train is the most powerful, for reading and receiving wisdom.

- Raising mist, sit quietly and see your hands over a quiet stream and watch for the streams of vapor rising from your hands. There is strong wisdom within this mist.

- Sea Salt has much wisdom locked in every grain, the Alchemists' say "Whoever knows the salt, knows the secret of the ancient sages." Salt is also a symbol of the soul.

- Us: yes we can be divined we are sea gifts of wisdom and divination too. Everything on our bodies reveals a story of our life, in both waking and sleeping dreams.

- Hold a shell close to your ear, in alpha, you will hear the ancient merfolk, tell you a story of old or they will tell your story. They always begin their muttering the same way, by saying, "Let us start a story, let us continue the dream." Shells like some trees are recorders of time.

- Studying "light" within the water is also an consciousness expander.

Divination and dream work are not for building ego, but for quiet soul growth.

Seth an incarnate ancient entity speaking through Jane Roberts reveals to us that when we see "It" we can see ourselves more clearly.

Seth speaking:

"When I speak of All That Is, you must understand my position within It. All That Is knows no other. This does not mean there may not be more to know. It does not know whether or not other psychic gestalts like "It" may exist. It is not aware of them if they do exist. It is constantly searching. It knows that something else existed before Its own primary dilemma when It could not express Itself. It is conceivable, then, that It has evolved, in your terms, so long ago that It has forgotten It's origin, that It has developed from still another Primary which has -again, in your terms- long since gone It's way. So there are answers I cannot give you, for they are not known anywhere in the system in which we have our existence. We do know that within this system of our All That Is, creation continues and developments are never still. We can deduce that on still other layers of which we are unaware, the same is true."

How does this quote relate to divination and dreams? Everything, because when we see the bigger picture, we begin to see "It," and when we begin to see "It" on many levels, we see us. When we start seeing "It," as not knowing everything and not perfect, then we begin to see how magnificent this plan really is! For some, divination and dreams will be the first time they truly begin to trust themselves. Trust your dreams, trust your divination, trusting yourself. Sounds like a simple precept, conversely for many individuals, have never spent one day trusting anyone, not themselves and most certainly not "It." For some this is a huge leap of faith, because they were subliminally trained not to trust their own self! Where does one go, when one does not believe in their self?

Some May Say

These are statements presented throughout the years.

- "I need proof, first, before I can believe I can hear through my skin!"
  Sea Priestess answer:
  "Okay, send that request out into the generous universe and you will receive your proof."

- "What if, I think I am not ready to learn water wisdom?"
  Sea Priestess answer:
  "Then you are not..."

- "Why is studying a single Element so important?"
  Sea Priestess answer:
  "Everything can be studied as a single subject, I chose water, because "IT" has chosen me."

- "I do not see why divination is important."
  Sea Priestess answer:
  "The ability to interpret, comprehend and attune with the cosmic mind, is more than seeing if you are going to win the lottery or find that someone special. Divining dreams is a nature skill a spiritual development, to see other dimensions, uncovering old and new truths. Let the unlearning begin, so that all our false conceptions and preconception are washed away."

Mutterings

~ Water activates everything.

~ Uncover hidden treasures that were buried long ago, with your help. You were so eager to please and assimilate, that you were willing to give away the best parts of you; giving up your power to Be what you were designed to do, from the beginning.

~ Dig in deep waters to regain your treasures; taking back what is rightfully yours. Reclaim your full emotions, so that you may fully operate your manifestation mechanism and may clearly see again.

~ Working with divination and dreams is digging for buried treasure that has your name on it. Why do you think so many hearts leap a little, when the words are just uttered, "Buried Treasure?" I believe that our DNA is deeply imprinted, collectively, we all know the truth; that there are buried treasures, and they all belong to us, treasures worth more than the money concept. Buried in the sands of time, and in the preverbal sea; they are living tools, yet know, if you are not going to use your tools/ gifts, then re-bury them, until you are ready to take on the responsibility and live in your own free will.

~ Beings that have an ego, with a capital E, will find it difficult to find their treasure, not that the universe is withholding a single gift, because "It" is not. Goddess/God is always with us, saying, "Here take all your gifts," Big E beings, are just too busy working something out in this life time. Outside validation is important to them; they need to feel important. They are already important and loved and validated! Big E beings just need much love, until they see Goddess/God in our Eyes, looking back at them.

~ Do you know there is a treasure, indeed, a promise that lives within you? Are you ready to approach the Holy of Holies?

Strong controlled emotion is the beginning of seeing that a tree is more than its color, shape and height that a bird is more than what we see with our physical eyes. We are beginning to experience our song, our love, our sixth sense. We are regaining what we have lost, long ago. We are returning to our Roots.

~ We already live in pure love we already stand together in Her wise bright light. We are already home; every one of us.

STORIES

There are glories in the universe that few can ever see
There are worlds within worlds within worlds within me
There are stories of the Ancient Ones inspiring us today
We are stories for the future ones in a future day!
-
There are glories in the universe that few can ever see
There are worlds within worlds within worlds within me
There are stories of the Ancient Ones inspiring us today
We are stories for the future ones in a future day!
-
There are glories in the universe that few can ever see
There are worlds within worlds within worlds within me
There are stories of the Ancient Ones inspiring us today
We are stories for the future ones in a future day!

THE FIVE MYSTIC SECRETS

by **Blv. LaVeda Lewis-Highcorrell**

With Introduction by **Rev. Don Lewis**

INTRODUCTION

Originally published under the cumbersome title "The Five Mystic Secrets of the Great Pagan Masters, or How to Live a Happy, Successful, and Truly Effective Life," and under the pseudonym of "Lady Elizabeth Greenwood," this is the only such booklet written by the Blv. LaVeda Lewis-Highcorrell, former Regent of the Correllian Tradition. Although she wrote a number of small articles and other materials, both published and unpublished, this is the only format in which the Blv. LaVeda set forth a comprehensive commentary on her metaphysical beliefs as a Correllian, and the first widely distributed exposition of Correllian ideas.

The Blv. LaVeda wrote this little booklet in the early '80s with the intention of its being a Pagan response to the Christian televangelists then popular in the U.S. Today many have forgotten how in the late '70s Christian televangelists, led by the likes of Jerry Fallwell, Jim Bakker, and Jimmy Swaggart, spearheaded the "New Right" political movement which was instrumental in the election of President Ronald Reagan. Dedicated to making the U.S. a "Christian Nation" and to eliminating the religious freedom of U.S. citizens, these televangelists were known for their extreme and hateful rhetoric, as well as for their skillful use of free-distribution literature.

Although President Reagan would repudiate them after his election, and they would ultimately be swallowed up by their own scandals and dishonesty, for several years in the late '70s and early '80s the televangelists were the cause of real fear among Pagans and other U.S. minority groups. Many people felt that they were in serious danger of loosing their religious and social freedom, because of very real attacks on these freedoms by the New Right.

It was in this mental and emotional climate that the Five Mystic Secrets was written. The careful reader will note that in many places the Blv. LaVeda has aimed her arguments directly at the assumptions and political/religious positions of the televangelists and the New Right.

A prime example of this is found in the section on the Second Secret; God. The televangelists were known for laying heavy emphasis on the idea that an individuals religious choices were of extreme importance to God, and that these choices potentially influenced the ultimate fate of the Universe —a point of view which the Blv. LaVeda and other contemporary members of the Correll Mother Temple flatly rejected. Statements made in the Second Secret such as "God does not require your validation to exist" or "God does not require your worship or your acknowledgement to exist and thrive," seem cold to many readers who do not understand the context in which the Blv. LaVeda was speaking. But when compared to the televangelical position they will be seen to illustrate Divine transcendence over temporal events and forms.

Another point which may require explanation for a modern Pagan audience is the use of the term "God" throughout the work. The Blv. LaVeda chose to use the gender neutral term "God" together with feminine pronouns to refer to Deity in the booklet, in part because she originally intended the work to speak to Pagan and non-Pagan alike and did not wish to alienate part of her intended audience from the start by using what to them would have been unfamiliar terminology. Also the Blv. LaVeda and many other Correllians felt that the gender/number neutral term "God" (as opposed to "The God" or even "The Gods") was an acceptable term for Pagan use, with a history of the neutral term going back to ancient Egypt and the dawn of written history. Today however most Correllians tend to use the gender/number neutral term "Deity" or "The Divine" in deference to the sensitivity which many Pagans feel toward the term "God" because of its misuse by the Book Religions.

Another change in terminology; Lady LaVeda makes reference to the Oversoul and the Undersoul, which in contemporary Correllian literature is more often referred to as the Higher Self and the Lower Self. This illustrates the natural changes in terminology which occur within a Tradition as one generation gives way to another.

The Regent LaVeda was born on 25 November, 1528 Pisces (1928 AD), when the power and influence of the High-Correll family were at their height. She was a child of privilege, who spent much of her youth on the Blv. Caroline High-Correll's estate Under-The-Hill on the banks of the Vermillion river. But by 1540 Pisces (1940 AD) the Blv. Caroline was dead, LaVeda's father had become a mental and physical invalid, crushed by prison and illness, and she had been removed from the custody of her divorced mother (the Blv. Mable, then Head of the Correllian Tradition) to briefly become a ward of the state because of the family's religious and social beliefs. These experiences, together with her Native American heritage and the issues that came with it, and the hateful acts which followed the early death of her only daughter, Linda, caused the Blv. LaVeda to live a very closeted life. In public she concealed her racial and religious identities, while in private she nursed a strong sense of the injustice done to non-Christian peoples and the need for action to change this —the same attitudes which had earlier motivated the Blv. Caroline High-Correll's teachings about the relationship of the

"Native Religions" vs the "Book Religions."

Although she made tentative steps out of the broom closet during the later '80s, the Blv. LaVeda preferred to write under a pseudonym, "Elizabeth Greenwood," inspired by the name of her home "Greenwood House."

The Regent LaVeda led the Correllian Tradition from 1566 Pisces until 1579 Pisces (1966 – 1979 AD). These were crucial years for the Correllian Tradition, which was then still known as the Nativist Tradition. During these years the original Correllian lineage and the Correll Mother Temple nearly died out, saving themselves only by union with the related Louisine lineage. During these years too, the Correllian Tradition came to identify itself strongly with the modern Wiccan movement. With its roots in Cherokee religion, Scottish folk-religion/witchcraft, and Spiritualism, as well as a strong association with Leland's Aradians, Nativism was arguably something apart from Wicca until the late '70s —depending upon the definition of Wicca one uses. Many members of the Correllian Council of Elders now define Correllian Nativism as having been primarily a Spiritualist movement until the '70s. The Blv. Caroline's original teachings were strongly Universalist and socially conscious, based upon the idea of pan-Pagan recognition and co-operation as the only salvation for the world's Native (ie; Pagan) peoples. The brand of Wicca popular in the '70s was strongly similar to this, and drew little distinction between Wicca and Traditional Witchcraft, leading the Blv. LaVeda and other members of the Correll Mother Temple to feel not so much that they were joining a movement as that they were acknowledging an association which had always existed. Contemporary definitions might challenge these conclusions, since many now define Wicca as created by Gardner, but this was not the case in the '70s.

The Blv. LaVeda was the Heiress of her mother the Blv. Mable, but did not succeed her —passing her claim after thirteen years of Regency to her niece Lady Krystel, the present First Priestess of the Correllian tradition. Lady LaVeda's son, Rev. Don Lewis, became First Priest and later Chancellor of the Tradition (in the Year 0 Aquarius / 2000 AD).

Lady LaVeda passed into Spirit on 13 September, 1589 Pisces (1989 AD), dying from complications of cancer. Her funeral, presided over by her son and niece, was low key but openly Pagan, in accordance with her declared wishes.

THE FIVE MYSTIC SECRETS

Behold 5 sisters. Their names are Knowledge, God, Life, The Soul, and Freedom. And in the love of these 5 sisters is the key to the Universe.

Foreword:

Greetings, my friends,

As I'm sure you know, there are dozens of little books like this one, all promising the keys to the Universe, inestimable power, and personal happiness.

It's a lot to ask, and for most, far too much to promise.

I make no such promises. I set before you five of the greatest secrets of life as conceived by my religion.

They alone can do nothing for you. It is what you do with them that matters.

The path to knowledge and a happy, effective life does not lie in what someone else does or does not conceive. They can tell you anything, however true or false —it is nothing. So long as it is theirs, it cannot truly affect you. To help your life or understanding in any way, the knowledge must come to dwell within your own heart, for only then are you truly free, and only then can you truly know.

Real knowledge is and must be more than repeating by rote, for the imitation of knowledge is not knowledge and will not give you comfort if prewritten words run dry.

There are many paths to knowledge, and much knowledge to be had, but none of it can do you any good at all if you do not come to believe and understand it for yourself.

Knowledge:

This is the first of the five sisters and the greatest secret I could give you if you listened to me for a thousand years —if you do not truly know them and accept them, all the secrets in the Universe are only so many mental knick-knacks.

So many people today say that they can give you true knowledge, as if it were a gift. Put your faith in them, send your money to them, buy their pamphlet, or do what they say, and for so small a price, you shall become wise, by osmosis.

Well, this is stuff and nonsense! No one can lead you down some primrose path to knowledge simply because it is convenient to them to do so. The path to understanding is a path which you must walk yourself, and of you own volition, not a celestial conga line open for the price of a $.30 ticket.

Other people can guide you; advise you; instruct you; aid you. But they can't believe for you. They can't know for you. In times of pain, they cannot be a strength within you, however much they may offer from without. And the strength within is the true comfort.

The people who tell you that all you have to do to possess the secrets of the Universe is to read a certain book, or buy a certain pamphlet, or watch a certain television program and send money - they are either simpletons or charlatans, for so much is not gained by so little.

To blindly accept the words of another is not to be loyal, or faithful, or pious – it is merely to be blind.

One must use one's own good sense and listen to one's own inner bell when one seeks a path to knowledge, for one is not simply drug along to peace and happiness no matter who promises to drag you. And so many make the promise, and so many shout along the way, that it can only be through discretion and inner guidance that one can possibly tell which paths have anything to offer, and which are merely meaningless diversions.

There is nothing you must know more than that a clever advertisement or a high production value has no relationship to the actual value of wisdom offered. A wise person may well investigate everything he or she encounters. But it is a fool who believes everything that is claimed merely because the claimant swears it is so.

Thus the first sister is not merely knowledge, but the knowledge thereof – the harder of the two, by far, to acquire.

As it is commonly said, there are no atheists in foxholes, (which isn't, however commonly said, as true as it is arrogant) so too it is one thing to claim knowledge and another thing to know.

Knowledge, as we discuss it here, is the knowledge of existence. Why we exist, how we exist; how we can affect our own existence and the quality of it. The knowledge of the nature of God.

There are many paths to such knowledge, many roads for many travelers. Just as many different roads once led to Rome from the many corners of its empire, so too, many roads lead to God from the many levels and corners of our existence.

A road which serves one well, may make another uncomfortable. A road which seems fresh to one, another may call lonely. A road which one finds familiar another may despise as common. Not all roads are the same length. Some are rocky, some are smooth. Some are narrow, some are wide and winding. All will ultimately lead to God, because God can wait for the last struggling traveler – God has time.

Some people think that God is in a hurry, but why would God hurry? God is an artist, and the best work always takes time.

All these roads which lead to God are equal. They all will deposit you at the same end. But some of them will take a lot longer, and may be significantly harder on your feet.

The second of the five sisters is the knowledge of God.

God:

Sooner or later, you will know God. You will choose your own way to get there, and no one can simply hand it to you. Again, its not so hard to encounter knowledge, but it only matters if you make it your knowledge – for anyone can say they believe, but if you don't really accept it, it can never help you.

And just as God can wait a million years for you to arrive, so too if it takes you a million years, well, that's all right. God will understand. God doesn't hate you. God wants you to find your way. God will wait. God isn't waiting for any excuse to slap you down –God is above that.

God did not make you to play hockey with. You are a piece of art in progress. God has spent good time starting you, and isn't going to botch it now just because you may take longer to complete than someone else.

At the same time, while all of this is true, it is also ultimate. There is no time limit; there is no deadline. God has all the time in the world and then some. When you arrive doesn't matter, only that you ultimately shall arrive.

You must go to God. God will not come to you. And when you do, you do so as a fulfillment of your existence, not God's. If you never did arrive, (though every by-road ultimately leads to the same place, after however much wandering) God would not be diminished by your absence. It would be your loss.

God is eternal. The actions of men and women cannot diminish God. God does not require your worship or your acknowledgment to exist and flourish. God existed before there was anything else, and will surely not cease to exist because of anything we could do or not do.

As a Pagan, I revere God as my Mother Who created all other existence out of Her own primeval existence, and shall hence forward refer to Her as such – though God is surely as much my Father as my Mother and Her existence cannot very well be limited by the names which we put on Her.

God is not an old man with a long white beard living on a cloud someplace. Nor is God a stately woman with oak leaves in Her hair living a sacred grove. These are our images, for our convenience. They do not matter in any wise at all to God.

God existed when the highest forms of life on Earth were dinosaurs and She existed in no less a stead than now, though dinosaurs built no temples to Her. She was no less a God for the lack of temples and altars, and She loved the dinosaurs no less than us.

They lived for a purpose, and their lives had meaning, and they learned the lessons of those lives as well as we do ours.

God existed when the only expression of immortal souls on Earth were microbes and amoebas. They offered Her no praise. They wrote no hymns or sacred books. Yet they lived and died and learned the lessons of their lives as well as we. And the Mother of all things did not whither and die because the tongues of men and women moved not in Her praise.

Her existence is independent and eternal. We do not influence it. We cannot bolster it. We cannot weaken it. God does not exist for us, or because of us, or for our sake. God exists because God exists.

Perhaps in some far off life, you were a dinosaur. Perhaps then you conceived of God as an eternal dinosaur, and the world Her egg. Or perhaps you were an ameba, or a giant fern. Someone had to be.

God does not require your validation to exist. She has no need, as some religious leaders suggest, to go running after worshippers begging for their allegiance and making bargains of what She will trade them for their worship.

It is the worshipper who requires God, not God the worshipper.

Though, it may be a blow to your ego, you are not the cog on which the wheel of the Universe turns. You are not a sale made in a celestial supermarket war between good and evil. Not a soldier in an army to protect God's throne. The Universe does not hang on the actions of your life. That is an appeal to your vanity. No matter what you do, the Universe will be just fine. It always has been. There is no Divine civil war. There never could be. The Universe is and always has been firmly under God's control and Her reign is no wise endangered, least of all by us.

Only the quality of your life is affected by whether you seek out God or not. Not even the fate of your Immortal soul is affected, for all roads will ultimately go to God, by however circuitous a path. Only the quality of this one life, and whatever effect it may carry over to the next life, is affected.

But isn't that enough?

If our first sister is the ability to know, and our second sister is the knowledge of God, our third sister is the knowledge of the nature and pattern of life.

Life:

God created life. Our life, and all life.
She did not mess up the job.
God does not mess up.
The first important point about life is that it is eternal. The body dies, the soul goes on. It is immortal.
This is no revolutionary idea. We have always believed it, even before we were us. The Neanderthals, a kind of being not quite the same as we, buried their dead ceremoniously, with a view towards afterlife, before what we today call "mankind" even existed as a species.

Yet to truly accept the concept of eternal life is such a release! One is freed from so many of the frustrations and sadness of life – not to mention the fears. Like putting a light on in the darkness, it changes everything. For, accepting life as eternal, what fear in this entire world is left to one?

Now almost everyone –particularly anyone likely to be reading this booklet – gives lip service to eternal life. But how many really believe it?

They say it because they are afraid no to believe it, but they do not really believe it either. They have not truly taken the belief into them.

In my family, it is said "send the dead forth in joy". A funeral is not the occasion of sadness and desolation. For if life is eternal, how can death hold either fear or horror?

Death, like life, perforce unites all living things. Can you imagine the difference it makes not to fear it?

What is it in this entire world which does not die?

Even the mountains rise up and fall down. The seas dry up as other seas begin.

Surely, you will die.

And yet the knowledge of eternal life cannot but invalidate the fear so many feel for death – if like our first sister they can truly accept the idea.

God did not mess up the world. And death is not a pathological condition. It is as it was meant to be. God intends for all living things to die. Death is meant to come – God planned it that way from the first. Death is not an end to life, it is a change, and all things must die. Without death there can be no rebirth. And just as the sun sets each night to rise again each morning, just as the trees turn brown and cast away their leaves to sprout again each spring, so too for us, rebirth invariably follows death.

There is no reason to live at all if one only lives once –for what can one do in one life that God our Mother would possibly have considered important enough to expend so much effort and care in our creation? Very few people (not even counting the millions who have died at birth, in infancy, and childhood) do anything in their lives particularly good or bad – leastwise on a scale to impress God. Most lives are very humble compared to God. A Hitler or Ghandi might have a life meaningful enough to impress God if the purpose of life were really a pass/fail test of the quality of a soul. But what about a woman who spent her life in a nineteenth century cotton mill? A man dead at nineteen in Vietnam? An Amazon Indian who never lived above subsistence level? Are any of these really worthy of eternal damnation for the petty acts of underprivileged lives? Could any of them even have the opportunity to be really evil? And by the same token on such flimsy grounds which of them could be truly said to be worthy of eternal paradise?

One life is not enough to do or be anything for the vast majority of people. If God were going to judge them on it, how many of them would be any use to Her at all? To sit in a heavenly choir all day and so nothing but sing Her praises maybe, but that is a remarkably trivial excuse to have gone to so much trouble for, isn't it?

But after many lives a soul could be well educated for eternity, and a credit to God, as well as useful to Her, truly deserving of an eternal existence as a single life could hardly make it.

And an end product worth the effort.

The God Who created this Universe was a practical, thoughtful God. Not a vain, self indulgent, dreamer.

As God is our Mother, so life and death are Her right and left hands. Her two faces. An eternal cycle in this world.

To Pagans, the forms of God are never literal. They are to help us understand the complex nature of God.

God is like a diamond, and all Her different forms in all the religions of man are the glittering facets She wears.

Life and death are two of the most important of these facets in our religion. They have always been enshrined and honored by us through many eras and cultures.

In Egypt, they were the lovers Isis (life) and Osiris (death). Also the combatants Horus (life) and Set (death), and Ra (life) and Aapep (death). To the Aztecs, Quetzalcoatl (life) and Texcatlipoca (death). They were Ishtar and Tamuz, Persephone and Hades, Apollo and Diana, forever loving. They are Apollo and Pan, St. George and the Moor, eternally at odds.

We live, we die, we live again. For centuries. Millenia. Now that is an excuse to create a Universe.

And whether shown as lovers or combatants, the dance of life and death is the dance of forever, the dance of the soul, stepping lightly between this world and the Other.

The Soul:

Now for the fourth sister.

They fourth of five secrets to a happy and effective life is the knowledge of the soul.

What I have heretofore said about God, and about the cycle of life and rebirths, has also largely explained the nature of the soul.

That it is eternal, not temporal. That it lives many times in this world, in many forms. And that the purpose of its entering this world is for experience, and not as some sort of punishment.

God desires to build up, not to tear down. For it is easy to tear down. There is no honor, no accomplishment, and no satisfaction in destruction. Creation, not destruction, is the true joy of existence.

Having reiterated this let us look upon our fourth sister who is, not the nature of the soul, but its function in everyday life.

You, as a living thing, and like all living things, have two parts.

An oversoul, or soul proper, which can be though of as being like a diamond. And an undersoul, one of the diamond's many facets.

The oversoul is the total of all your soul's experiences, in this world and on the Otherside, since it came into existence.

The oversoul includes all of the innate abilities of the soul, as well as all of its acquired knowledge.

All of the so-called paranormal abilities – clairvoyance, psychokinesis, astral travel, and all of the hidden abilities – reflect the powers of the oversoul.

If the oversoul can be said to be the hidden part, then the undersoul is the part which is visible.

The undersoul begins with birth and builds throughout one's life, but it does not cease with death, it is forever a part of the oversoul. Just as the experiences you had as a child are still a part of you, so too, and in the same way, every life remains with the oversoul.

The closer the undersoul is to the oversoul, the more of the oversoul's abilities will be available to the individual – this is why the fourth sister is important.

In many Pagan religions, the undersoul and oversoul have been portrayed as lovers -Siva and Sakti, in Hinduism, Apollo and Diana, in Mediterranean and modern Paganism, Adonis and Venus.

There are the same two lovers, Life and Death, Whom I have discussed applied on an individual theme. Life is the undersoul. Death, or eternal life, the oversoul.

Some people are born into this life with these two forces in close contact. This has to do with previous lives they have led and the amount of experience their souls may have had. Sometimes such people are said to have been Born Old. Such was the phrase which was used in my family.

For these people, the veil is thin, and they may manifest great psychic or other abilities from an early age, seemingly uncalled for.

This is not always a blessing, for such abilities can be very powerful, and difficult to handle. Very much like an electric current the powers of the soul can be unpredictable and dangerous, as well as beneficial. And for this reason the images which represent them, such as Loki, the Coyote, Set, or Hecate, are complex with both positive and negative sides.

One Born Old may never need instruction, but seem merely to reach out for what is already there, within them. Even if they seek to ignore or deny their abilities, these remain with them, sometimes quite obstreperously.

They cannot simply be shrugged off.

Other people —most people— are born with a much greater distance between the undersoul and oversoul, and must work to bring them together. They must seek and apply knowledge if they are ever to know the abilities and wisdom which dwells within them.

Most people realize that there is an understanding that they are lacking in their life, but they do not realize that they can find it within themselves. Instead they look for someone else to give it to them, as if another person could learn, understand, and believe for them.

This lack, this barrier between the under and oversoul, is linked to the abilities of the present physical body. Limitations may be placed upon the undersoul by the circumstance of this life, but they are not insurmountable.

The undersoul, you see, acts as a blinder on the oversoul. It shuts out many, and sometimes all, of the oversoul's abilities and memories. But this barrier is a curtain, not a wall, and can be seen through, or even drawn aside.

Everything which is alive has a soul. And all souls are the same – in essence, if not always in experience.

If a child is born with a mental disability it is not because his or her soul reflects such a disability. It is the undersoul, the personality intended for this life, which is different, the oversoul having the same capabilities as any other.

If a person is in a car accident, and afterward, he or she no longer has the same mental ability as before, or even retains the same memories as before, does it mean that something has changed within the soul? No. It is the outer face, the undersoul, which is affected. The oversoul remains as it has ever been.

And just as the gap between the undersoul and the oversoul can shut out many of one's true abilities, so too can the gap be bridged and these abilities tapped.

Just because Joe Psychic can do things you cannot does no mean he has powers you do not. It means that Joe Psychic has a narrower gap than you do, because – in this life or another- he has worked to narrow it.

Similarly, because sister Jane is a Rhodes scholar while brother John suffers from Downs Syndrome, it is not because there is a difference in their souls, but because there is a difference in their undersouls. Each soul has the same abilities, but expresses itself differently in this world.

There is a reason for this; a reason that we are in this world at all.

And what other reason could this be than to learn?

Some say to decide an eternal fate – to choose between good and evil.

But how many people in their lives do anything either good enough to deserve eternal reward, or bad enough to deserve eternal punishment?

I dare say few.

The average life is not lived on a scale grand enough to edify or offend the public general, much less God – Whose standards one would assume to be higher, what with eternity and all for reference.

To be a marker in a paper war between good and evil, one to be the victor?

Such an existence would be remarkably little cause to have created such a Universe. And it would be a remarkably unimpressive God Who would have to fight a numbers war for dominance in a Universe It created in the first place.

Besides, a God unable to foresee such a battle, unable then to avoid it, and finally, unable to end it quickly, would hardly have been capable of weaving the very complex and lovely web of this world in the first place, the excellence of the latter precluding the ineptness of the former.

No. As I have said before, God is not deposed or embattled. The Universe is exactly where and how it should be. It is just as God meant it to be, and our lives fulfill the purpose for which they were intended- experience.

What better way to lean than by experiencing every situation in every way? Every emotion, good or bad. Every level of existence from ameba, to dinosaur, to man, and beyond.

Now that is and education!

And that is a soul that would be truly pleasing to God. A truly excellent end product, which justifies the creation of the Universe, not as some half-baked whim, but as a thoroughly practical and thoughtful act.

And now at last, we are ready for the fifth sister and her name is Freedom.

Freedom:

This sister tells you that you need not be shackled in place, and that if you are, you yourself possess the key.

Her's is a secret to take to heart. Her's is the secret of action.

If there is anything in you life you do not like, you can change it — try!

If there is anything not in your life that you desire, you can have it — reach!

You hold yourself back! YOU are the master of your own fate, and alone the responsibility is yours alone.

Scary, isn't it?

If you reach for something, you may not get it. But if you do not reach, then surely you will not get it. It's your choice, every time — and a choice, to be sure, to be made with good sense and intelligence. But still, your choice.

It is a choice you were created to make, not give away or hang about the neck of a scape-goat.

Taking responsibility in your life is not disobedience to God. God gave you the responsibility in the first place. If God wanted you to be unable to make choices and stand on your own feet, She would hardly need have created you, now would She? Why would God go to the trouble of setting all this up just so She could spend her time matching a hundred billion people's socks for them?

Making your own mistakes is the point of existing at all — so that you can learn from them.

So you are making your own successes.

God doesn't need you to build Her sandcastles for Her. Nor does She need to build sandcastles "through you". God can build Her own sandcastles. Don't take my word for it — have a look at the Mojave desert, or the Grand Canyon. When you build a sandcastle, it's there for you to enjoy and take pride in. God doesn't need the credit for your sandcastles, as some people suggest She does. She gave you the ability so that you could build it to uplift yourself.

When you do something good, you deserve the credit for it — God rejoices over your sandcastle, She isn't jealous of it.

And when you do something bad, you must take the responsibility for that too. The devil didn't make you knock over Billy's sandcastle, you chose to do it. If you want to make it right again, then you must do something as nice as that was mean to make up for it. That is Karma. And until you make up for the bad things you've done by doing good things, you'll just get more and more lost on the road to God.

But God will wait for you.

Freedom is responsibility.

God doesn't want you to be intelligent and creative. She wants you to be worthy and useful. And She can wait for however many lifetimes it takes for you to become that. After all, She's already waited this long.

If God just wanted a bunch of sheltered, inexperienced servants, She would never have had to create a whole Universe to get them. And if She needed a bunch of sheltered, inexperienced servants, well then She would have floundered at the start when She was on Her own.

God wants variety! Open your eyes and see it about you!

What is the hallmark of Nature if not variety? God loves things that are new and different. She likes bright colors and original ideas.

God doesn't' want everyone to be the same. If God wanted homogeny you'd see it in Nature –surprise! It isn't there.

God doesn't want to put you in a pigeonhole or a bracket. She doesn't want you to walk on a straight and narrow path either – She wants you to look to the sides and see the flowers! Look above and see the clouds! Walk in the grass and explore!

This is God's real will.

She wants you to be free. To be happy. And to succeed. She is a helping hand, not an obstacle, on your path.

There is nothing to hold you back, not even death for death is not real, only a temporary rest on the Otherside between lives.

Only your own fear can hold you back. Fear, or bad planning, self-doubt, and ill will towards others.

So be free, and take advantage of the world that's been created for you! For your only gaoler is yourself.

So be it. These are the five. The secrets to a happy and successful life. Those who believe them are without fear. For what is there to fear when you know in your heart that life is eternal. That God is nice, and likes you, and wants to see you do well. And that within you awaits the peace and serenity you seek, waiting only for you to look inside, and truly believe what you say you believe.

With that knowledge, truly believed, you can pursue anything, without fear. You can develop the powers within, or go bravely into the world —what could hold you back?

But none of it can help you unless you come to truly believe it, for if you do not truly accept any belief you lay claim to, it will leave you wanting in the lurch.

All this being so, I say "May the blessing be and may you succeed in all you do. Whatever you do, do it with love, and good things shall be yours."

        Thank you,

        Lady Elizabeth Greenwood

GRANDMOTHER'S WISDOM
Reflections on a Correllian Vision for the Future

A Commentary on the 5 Mystic Secrets

by **Colin A. Keller**

    <u>The Five Mystic Secrets,</u> by LaVeda Lewis High-Correll can be considered the founding philosophical statement of Modern Correllian Wicca. This Treatise was composed at a time in the late 1970's/early 1980's when the Correllian Nativist Tradition (a familial Tradition) transitioned to open public membership, and by the late 1990's /early 2000's would include a comprehensive Correllian Clergy Degree System, and a Internet based educational platform, Witch School International. With these two programs, the once familial nativist tradition became one of the fastest growing Wiccan traditions in the World.

    "Grandmother's Wisdom" is passed by storytelling around the Kitchen Table, telling stories around the campfire, or sharing a cold drink reclining in your favorite Rocking chair on the Front Porch. The **<u>Five Mystic Secrets</u>** is more than an earth based nativist philosophy; it is a prophetic teaching divined for a future family, the Modern Correllian tradition. More than a response to the Conservative Right movements of the 1980's , the Secrets reflect personal "Wise Woman" ethics and philosophy, based on years of soul searching and personal reflection. The Five Mystic Secrets represents a theological and philosophical "bridge" of growth from family to worldwide tradition, in ideas easily understood and communicated in the framework of an oral storytelling tradition. The Secrets are the connecting document of growth, philosophies past on and reflections instilled in new hearts and minds of a soon to grow Wiccan Tradition. A look at the Divine, the Soul, freedom, life and knowledge, **The Five Mystic Secrets** reflects (at the time) an undiscovered and alternative worldview, very much foreign to conventional and mainstream religious thought of the time. Blv. LaVeda sits us all down at the Kitchen table and shares with us what she has learned and come to experience. This is the Magic of the Five Mystic secrets. Please share in this wisdom by reading and sharing in this most wonderful document, Blv. LaVeda Lewis-Highcorrell's, **The Five Mystic Secrets**.

An Essay On
THE FIVE MYSTIC SECRETS

by **Melissa Brown**

The Five Mystic Secrets

The Five Mystic Secrets is a wonderful testament to the faith and beliefs of all who follow the Wiccan path. It also addresses the public very well. Because this pamphlet was written during a time of common public religion, Lady Greenwood used terminology that anyone could relate to on a personal level. At the very beginning of the pamphlet she explains that she does not offer the keys to the Universe, inestimable power, and personal happiness. She explains that she offers five of the greatest secrets of life as conceived by her religion. This statement in itself shows that she is not looking to lead people down a path for personal profit, but rather to help them on the path enlightenment. One of the most important things about this work is that she makes clear at the beginning that it is not about the knowledge she is giving you, but rather about what you do with this knowledge. Intent is one of the most important parts of the Wiccan Path.

The first of these great secrets is Knowledge. Lady Greenwood explains that this can be one of the most important secrets that one is given. If a person does not gain a testament of the knowledge they have found for themselves, this knowledge turns into nothing more than "mental knick-knacks". She explains that blindly accepting others words, is to simply be blind to the truth. We all must search and understand truth for ourselves. She explains that it is important to listen to one's conscience and good sense. By doing this we will find the truth that is right and works for us. She explains that there are many roads to the same end but some may be significantly harder on your feet. She also explains that only fools take the words of people to be true just because they swear it so. For what is a stranger's word more than just that, words. We must search and ponder on truths before we decide if they are right.

The second secret that Lady Greenwood talks about is God. Lady Greenwood explains that God can wait for each of us. God isn't vindictive and God does not look for a chance to smite us down. God is an artist and every great piece of art wasn't finished in a day, just as all knowledge cannot be gained in one lifetime. She also explains that we must go to God. God will not come to us. It takes effort on our part to find God. She also explains that our actions cannot diminish God. She explains that God is our mother and we all came from her. God cannot be limited to the names we put on her. She also explains that God is just as much our father as our mother and because God is above our understanding many of the images we have for God are for our own convenience and do not change God. We are not part of a big war between good and evil. Our souls are not bargaining chips. As God is our parent, we are her children. That is the relationship. Only the qualities that we have gained in this life affect our immortal soul.

The third secret is the nature and patterns of life. God created life. God created all life. Many people think that God made mistakes in creation but this is untrue. Though we cannot see much of God's plan there are no mistakes. Everything is how it should be. Like Lady Greenwood said at the beginning of the pamphlet, it doesn't matter how long it takes us to get to God. God has time. She tells us to accept the concept of death with joy. Death is a release from the burdens of life. She explains it as turning a light on in the darkness. What joy this should bring us! Death brings us a new beginning and a new chance to live to the fullest! Many people fear death because it is not comfortable for them. They are used to life. A parable I heard is a great way to explain people's fear. "Life and death came together. Life asked death 'Why do people love me and hate you?' To this death replied 'Because you are a beautiful lie and I am a painful truth." This holds true to many people. Life is a wonderful gift because it allows us to learn and grow. But death is inevitable and death was meant to be.

The fourth secret that Lady Greenwood spoke of is the Soul. Many people seek eternal life without realizing that they have it already. For as a body is meant to die, a soul is meant to live on. The soul is eternal. It lives through many lifetimes and takes many forms. Each person has an oversoul. The oversoul contains all the experiences and knowledge of each lifetime. She explains the concept of being born old. This is to say that someone has gone through many lifetimes and learned many things. This person may never need instruction but has the answers they seek within themselves already. As there is an oversoul, there is an undersoul. Lady Greenwood explains that the undersoul is the aspects of the soul that are supposed to manifest themselves in this lifetime. The undersoul is not a direct relation to the oversoul as the oversoul is the accumulation of many lifetimes. While pieces of the oversoul manifest themselves sometimes in our undersoul, as with the case of psychic abilities, the undersoul is not how the oversoul looks. Lady Greenwood uses the example of Down syndrome in the pamphlet. Just because someone has Down syndrome in this lifetime does not mean that the oversoul does, it is just how the soul was supposed to present itself in this lifetime.

The last secret is Freedom. This secret is to show us that we have no need to be shackled in place. If we are indeed shackled in place we ourselves possess the key to freedom. The purpose of this secret is to show us that we can obtain whatever we want! If we have something about us that we do not like we, ourselves can change it. If we want something we can have it. While we may not have exactly what we thought we wanted, if we never try, we will never succeed. Many people try to avoid mistakes, but mistakes help us to grow and learn. Learning and growing is the point of our existence. Another part of freedom is the freedom to take responsibility for our own mistakes. Many other religions blame our mistakes on the temptation of an evil force. This is not so. God wants us to take responsibility. She goes on to say that God is there to lend a helping hand not to be an obstacle. God rejoices in our successes just as we should rejoice in them.

These are the secrets to the Universe. The important thing that Lady Greenwood was trying to get across is that it does not matter how much knowledge you gain, if you do not come to the understanding of such knowledge yourself and gain a testament through this understanding it does not matter how much knowledge you gain. Life is about what we do. The intent of our actions and how we handle not only successes but our mistakes defines who we are in this life. God is there to be a helping hand. God doesn't need us, we need God.

An Essay On
THE FIVE MYSTIC SECRETS

by **Rev. Daniel S. Seneker**

To all who shall see these presents, greetings. My name is Daniel S. Seneker, and I am currently a Second Degree Priest with the Correllian Nativist Tradition. Through this work I wish to expound upon, rather than alter, the Wisdom found in the "Five Mystic Secrets". The original work was intended to be a brief introduction to the topics therein broached, if my understanding of it is correct, so I will endeavor to add some additional insights as Goddess inspires.

─ ─ ─ ─

In the forward to the "Five Mystic Secrets" is the following:

> "As I'm sure you know, there are dozens of little books like this one, all promising the keys to the Universe, inestimable power, and personal happiness."

Lady LaVeda added to this that she made no such promises, which was for good reason. The results of reading a work being dependent upon proper understanding, integration, and application of the knowledge therein contained. Lady LaVeda, in essence, conveyed that you must make the knowledge yours by truly understanding it. Making knowledge one's own can be a daunting task, for it often requires not only ingesting that knowledge, but digesting it and integrating it into one's being. Such a process can, in most cases, only occur through experience, which is why the Goddess brings many and diverse events into our lives. The need for experience and the integration into our true beings of such knowledge is the reason for the "year-and-a-day" requirement that is imposed upon aspiring Clergy in our Tradition. As to "personal happiness", this can only occur when one learns to accept "life on life's terms". All of modern man's many innovations cannot erase the foundation upon which this world and Her inhabitants is based: that foundation being, namely, the natural order of things. Modern societies, communities, etc. all function based upon certain natural principles. The foremost among these principles is that of balance. To attain happiness, a person must learn to accept all of life's events: both the "good" and the "bad" as essential components to what I call "the tapestry of life". Life's tapestry exists as a means to facilitate learning, and only through such learning can one expect to rise above the tempest and reach calm, sane, space. As to balance, this is a Universal principle based on the concept of give and take. When a person eats food, for example, she/he is taking. In the same vein, when one is eaten, fed upon, etc. that person is in the mode of giving. This "giving" is the essence of what it means to pray for someone, for what it truly means is that you are acting as prey for that person so that she/he can gain strength, etc. If a person gives continuously without taking, then she/he will quickly run out of things to give. To "take" has gained the attached connotation of "evil" and to "give", "good". The answer to personal happiness lies in achieving balance. A common theme in the mythoi of many of the world's religions is that of the struggle between order (good) and chaos (evil), this struggle being a way of conveying the natural principle of balance. In one myth of Ancient Egypt the champions of order and chaos fight (symbolizing this struggle) and the god Thoth alternately heals whichever of the champions is currently being overwhelmed to ensure that neither side gains victory. Pharaoh had both crook and flail, which is echoed in the Hebrew god's rod and staff: a rod to discipline and a staff to comfort. Either rod or staff alone can destroy a person. Too much comfort and easy life can spoil a person rotten, while too much discipline can turn a person into a monster. The real Truth, therefore, lies in balance between the two sides. Personal happiness can only come after realizing that one exists as part of a larger tapestry: the Universe, and exists as but a small portion thereof. Once one ceases to struggle and embraces all that life has to offer, having learned that all of it is to her/his benefit whether perceived as "good" or "bad", then, and only then, can personal happiness be achieved.

> "The path to understanding is a path which you must walk yourself…"

No one can walk your journey for you, for by this you would not learn. There are times, as a Wiccan Priest, when someone may ask you to perform some spell work for them, which can at the time seem like the beneficent thing to do. There is, however, an old adage:

> "Give a man a fish and you feed him for a day. Teach a man to fish and you feed him for life."

Such things as doing spellwork for another, thus, amount to giving that person a crutch rather than healing them. At a certain point in a young lion's life it must learn to hunt for itself. Training in spellwork is, therefore, the real prize, and such training can only be integrated through experience. Power cannot be given by "osmosis": it must be earned. Knowledge, it is said, is power, but I might add that knowledge is only power when properly integrated. As Lady LaVeda said "you must understand it for yourself", making the knowledge your own, which is the essence of integration.

> "Thus the first sister is not merely knowledge, but the knowledge thereof…"

The "knowledge thereof" is Wisdom, or the ability to put knowledge into practical use.

> "The second of the five sisters is the knowledge of God."

Perhaps the most poignant phrase in all of the document is, "You are a piece of art in progress". God, you see, is the Master Craftsman, and all of us who are on the journey are in a constant state of refinement. Just as dross is removed from gold as it is refined, so too do outmoded portions of our makeup become "refined out" and discarded when they are no longer of utility. Such parts, however, are useful until the lesson they would teach has been learned, which is another reason why each must walk her/his own path.

> "Only the quality of your life is affected by whether you seek out God or not."

When a person reaches the point in her/his life when she/he chooses to seek out God/dess it is often because she/he needs more from this life than what the merely mundane has to offer: a sense of the Ultimate and a meaning of life. According to Correlianism, the purpose of our lives is to learn so that we can eventually become reunited with God/dess. The way in which we learn is by the journey and the experiences that life has to offer. The true meaning of our experiences, and the purpose, generally only become evident when a person chooses to seek out God/dess.

> "...all roads will ultimately go to God..."

Seeking out God/dess, thus, is a means to secure help in the journey, but the journey must still be traveled by the seeker. The mother lion can teach her cub how to hunt, but she will not hunt for the cub beyond what is necessary in rearing it. You must make the journey your own, no one can travel it for you. The good news is that the Ultimate is at the end of the journey waiting for you to come to Her. God/dess can be reached by every path known, but some paths, namely those that choose to ignore God/dess, are particularly long and painful.

The third of the Five Mystic Secrets is Life. Lady LaVeda wrote that "life is eternal", which means that the immortality of the soul is secure regardless of our actions. One of the most despicable means to secure followers is to appeal to a person's fear of death, and even more to threaten the person with eternal torment in "Hell". Such a person, having been so threatened, would come to God/dess out of fear rather than Love, setting her/him back light years on the journey. Fear is the illusion, but Love is the Ultimate.

> "Yet to truly accept the concept of eternal life is such a release!"

I find that the fear of death is paramount among the woes of (most of) mankind, for what has one gained from a lifetime, regardless of actions "good" or "bad", if she/he becomes "erased" upon death. "Vanity of vanities, all is vanity" is the conclusion reached by Solomon, who is said to have been the wisest man to ever live. Yet all is not vanity, for life is eternal! Every action we perform, every word we utter is stored in what is called the Akashic record. The Akashic record is like a Spiritual supercomputer that remembers all things. The events of one's life, therefore, are not lost after death, but are remembered in the Akashic record and also by the person's oversoul. An oversoul consists of the parts of a person that have transcended life in the flesh and live upon a higher plane, assisting the incarnation through the journey.

> "One life is not enough to do or be anything for the vast majority of people."

Death is a natural part of life, but it is not the end. Death is a period of transition between one life and the next in an endless cycle until one becomes reunited with Deity. The cycle of life, death, and rebirth is the significance behind the "infinity" symbol, which is a sideways 8:

The cycle of life, death, and rebirth is also evident in the Wiccan Wheel of the Year, with our 8 Sabbats, which are divided into a light half and a dark half (order and chaos). The journey, thus, consists of a series of lives, each one adding to what was learned in the previous lives in a gradual process of refinement leading, eventually to reunion with Deity.

> *"God is like a diamond, and all her different forms in all the religions of man are the glittering facets she wears."*

We are all, therefore, a part of the Ultimate, but existing in the material world is existence on a lower plane than that of the Ultimate, for the Goddess chose to descend into matter to reunite with the God. In so doing she separated Herself into the many incarnations now evident in the world with the eventual goal of reuniting all within Herself after having gained the knowledge that can only be learned by physical existence. This is not meant to imply a lack of knowledge on the part of the God/dess, but rather that God/dess desired to enjoy the journey with us, for she is with us through every trial and tribulation: all working toward the greater good.

The fourth of the five sisters is the Soul. The Soul is basically divided into two parts: the Oversoul, which consists of those parts of us which exist on a higher plane than the temporal, and the Undersoul, which is the current incarnation. The totality of the structure is divided into seven parts:

Physical
Emotional
Mental
Astral
Egoic
Monadic
Divine

The Undersoul consists of parts 1-3, while the Oversoul is parts 4-6 with part 7 being the Ultimate. The physical is pretty much self-explanatory: it is our bodies. The emotional is the world of contrasts: Love, Hate, Patience, Hastiness, etc. The mental consists of logic and rationality. The astral is the plane wherein we create our reality. The Egoic (or Soular) is the part of us that exists as a unique part of Deity, it is what is under construction through our various incarnations. The Monadic consists of 9 parts of the Goddess that she separated out of herself to begin the descent into matter. These 9 parts represent basic personality types. The Divine is the All-in-All: the Ultimate. The Ultimate, thus, exists at the center of all things and branches out into every direction into more and more differentiated forms, which result in the individual incarnations we experience as people. In modern Correllianism, we refer to the Oversoul as the Higher Self and the Undersoul as the Lower Self.

"Life is the undersoul. The oversoul is death, or eternal life."

Otherwise said, the Oversoul consists of the parts of us that persist from lifetime to lifetime. When an incarnation passes from this life, beyond the veil that separates the carnal from the Spiritual, she/he becomes a part of the Oversoul. In some people the veil of separation is thin, allowing them to manifest the abilities of the Oversoul in the incarnation. Such abilities include clairvoyance, clairaudience, astral travel, etc. People in which the veil is thin are said to have been "born old", meaning they have lived many lives before and are closer to eventual reunion with Deity. The Undersoul and the Oversoul could be thought of as the contrasting qualities of order and chaos. We, therefore, each have these two qualities present within us and these vie with one another at times to produce reality as we know it much like a blacksmith shapes work between the hammer and the anvil. Living a happy and fulfilled life can be achieved by developing a third quality: that of balance. Otherwise said, the mundane must be balanced with the Spiritual. It is perfectly fine and good to take enjoyment out of mundane things, but one must not become obsessed and thus controlled by the mundane. The reciprocal is also true: a person who constantly has her/his "head in the clouds" is not of much practical use to society. Yet it is this very dichotomy between order and chaos that allows for the Universe to exist at all! These forces are made manifest, on the physical plane, as the subatomic particles protons, electrons, and neutrons of which all things are comprised. Thus, it can be seen, that these forces are good and necessary and a part of a larger Harmony.

> "What better way to learn than by experiencing every situation in every way, every emotion, good or bad, every level of existence from ameba, to dinosaur, to man, and beyond."
>
> "Now that is an education!"

The fifth, and final, sister is Freedom. Lady LaVeda wrote that "YOU are master of your own fate" and "you yourself possess the key." If your life is a mess YOU must take responsibility for that mess and work to set it in order. A life that is a mess is an example of a person that "has their head in the clouds" and is, therefore, of little or no practical use or it is an example of a person that is obsessed with the material, which often takes the form of such things as alcohol and/or drug addiction or placing too much value in material possessions, which can lead to rotting of the soul. All of these things are an example of a life that is out of balance. As I wrote in the beginning of this work, all of mankind's innovations do not place her/him above the principles upon which this Universe was founded: namely the Harmony between the three concepts of order, chaos, and balance! All three are necessary and good, but balance must be foremost for it is in balance that peace can be found. This cosmic balance is the primary reason and function of karma. Otherwise said, if you perform an action to harm a person and fail to right the wrong by making amends, then karma will bring misfortune your way. Karma is not a Divine flyswatter, but rather a basic principle of the Universe that exists to maintain the balance.

> *"What is the hallmark of Nature if not variety? God loves things that are new and different. She likes bright colors and original ideas."*
>
> **LIVE!**

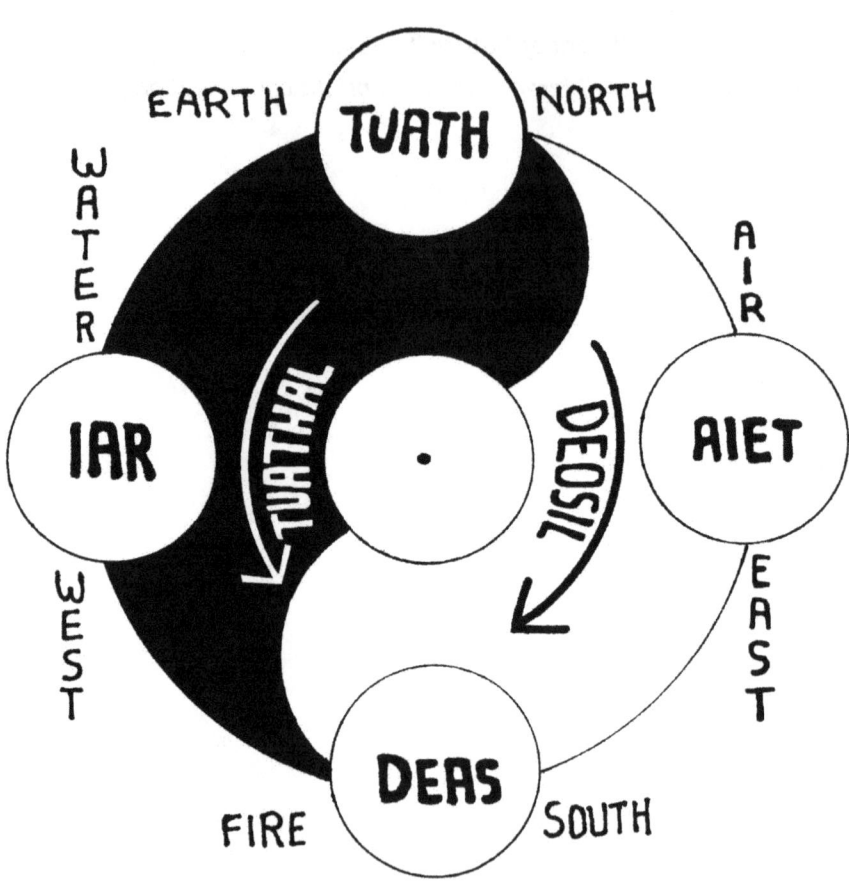

BIOGRAPHIES: PART TWO

by **Don Lewis**

DOROTHY CLUTTERBUCK

Dorothy Clutterbuck Fordham was born on January 19, 1880 in India. She was the daughter of Thomas St. Quentin Clutterbuck, a British military officer.

As an adult Dorothy Clutterbuck came to live in England, where she spent many years as an unmarried woman of independent means. In 1935, at the age of 55, Clutterbuck married Rupert Fordham. Fordham died in a car accident in 1939, and it was subsequently revealed that they were not actually legally married at all, which began a highly publicized fight over Fordham's estate.

Dorothy St. Quentin Clutterbuck died on 12 January 1951.

A figure surrounded by tremendous controversy, Dorothy Clutterbuck was identified by Gerald Gardner as the High Priestess who taught and initiated him as a Witch in the 1930s. Gardner also claimed that Clutterbuck's materials were "fragmentary" and that he had found it necessary to augment them with more Ceremonial elements —which if true suggests that her practice may have been closer to eclectic Wicca.

For many years Gardner's detractors alleged that Dorothy Clutterbuck was in fact an entirely fictitious creation – but in the 1980s Doreen Valiente successfully proved that Clutterbuck was indeed a real person.

It has since been alleged that Clutterback could not possibly have been what Gardner claimed she was – that she was in fact a devout Christian of the most conservative sort. However she lived for

93

years with a man to whom she was not actually married which seems an unlikely thing for a devout Christian of the most conservative sort to do. Moreover her "diaries" have been shown to contain highly Pagan themes, including overt devotional references to Classical Pagan Deities as well as to the Fairy Queen, which would seem to be the Smoking Gun.

As for Clutterbuck's coven some have suggested that it was connected to George Pickingill, while others suggest that Clutterbuck was inspired to found it by the writings of Margaret Murray.

SCOTT CUNNINGHAM

The most popular of all Pagan authors, Scott Cunningham's short life established a remarkable and enduring legacy in the world of Witches.

Scott Douglas Cunningham was born on June 27, 1956, in Royal Oak, Michigan.

Scott was introduced to Witchcraft by a classmate in High School, and would go on to become a member of the Serpent Stone Family, receiving his Third Degree High Priesthood through them. Later Scott would also study under Raven Grimassi.

A prolific author, Scott would write a total of twenty-two books on Witchcraft and magic —several of which were published posthumously. His book *Wicca: A Guide for the Solitary Practitioner*, is considered the definitive treatise on Solitary Witchcraft by many, and is among the most popular books on Witchcraft ever written.

In addition to his works on metaphysics, Scott also published a number of romance novels, writing under his sister's name.

Scott Cunningham died in 1993 at the age of thirty-six from AIDS related cryptococcal meningitis.

Some of Scott Cunningham's many books include: *Earth Power: Techniques of Natural Magic* (1983). *The Truth About Witchcraft Today* (1988), *Living Wicca: A Guide for the Solitary Practitioner* (1988).

DR. JOHN DEE

Born in 1527 Dr. John Dee was one of the leading magicians of the Elizabethan age.

Dr. John Dee was the royal astrologer and magician to Queen Elizabeth I of England. Dr. Dee cast the horoscope for the Queen's coronation and served her in both magical and political capacities, including espionage. Dr. Dee also taught the Virgin Queen astrology so that she could practice it directly.

Dr. Dee had been imprisoned under Mary I because of his magical practices.

In 1581 Dr. Dee began to work with Scrying – receiving visions through crystal balls and similar media. Finding he had no talent for scrying, Dee sought out an assistant in the form of Edward Kelly. Thereafter for many years Kelly would scry for visions which Dee would interpret and interact with.

Dr. Dee and Kelly worked with "Angels" who instructed them in the secrets of high magic.

Together Dr. Dee and Kelly brought through a huge body of channeled work which forms the basis of "Enochian" or "Angelic" magic. This included a large number of rituals, magic squares, descriptions of the spirit world and magical beings, and even an Enochian alphabet for magical use. From this material Dr. Dee wrote the Book of Enoch and the Forty Eight Angelic Keys.

After traveling through Europe Dee and Kelly eventually fell out, and Dee returned to England. In his latter years Dr. Dee fell into financial difficulty which prompted his old Patron Queen Elizabeth to appoint him as Chancellor of St. Paul's Cathedral and later Warden of Manchester College.

Dr. Dee died in 1608.

ED THE PAGAN

Ed Hubbard, better known as "Ed The Pagan", was born February 10, 1963, in Chicago, IL. Ed is among the most prominent Pagan media people in the World of Witches today, and a leader in the Pagan business community.

Perhaps most notably Ed founded Witch School (WitchSchool.com) on September 4, 2001, along with Don Lewis and Lisa Tuit. Witch School was a revolutionary education system utilizing peer-to-peer teaching and the power of the Internet to bring Pagan religious and magical education to people around the globe. The Witch School system was able to reach people in remote geographical areas who were otherwise unable to connect with teachers, and to provide training in an extremely flexible and effective way that is today providing a model for educational systems in lesser-developed countries.

Today Witch School has over 200,000 students in more than 180 countries around the world.

Ed has been a High Priest in the Correllian Tradition since 1990. Ed served as First Director of the Tradition from From 1992 – 2010. Subsequently Ed served as First Elders of the Correllian Tradition and from 2011-2012 Ed. Ed has also served the Correllian Tradition as Paladin General and has been awarded the Order of the Round Table, one of the Tradition's most prestigious awards. Ed currently holds the title of First Elder Emeritus.

In 1994 Ed also received a Gardnerian initiation through Donna Cole Schultz of Chicago's Temple of the Sacred Stones.

Ed served for several years as Head of the Newcastle Society, a utopian social group with a strong emphasis on the use of magic and technology to build a better world. The Newcastle Society united with the Correllian Tradition in 1992 AD after a series of joint projects. This union set the stage for the Tradition's modernization and expansion. At this time Ed was made a member of the Correllian Council of Elders. Ed also served as First Director for the Correllian Tradition from 1992 – 2005.

Ed is also founder and First Officer of the Pagan Interfaith Embassy, an organization dedicated to promoting communication and co-operation between Pagans everywhere.

Ed founded the Pagan Interfaith Embassy after being involved as a staff member in the second Parliament of World's Religions, held in Chicago in 1993. Ed found the Parliament to be a deeply inspirational and life-changing event. The Pagan Interfaith Embassy went on to sponsor Chicago's Pagan Leadership Conferences in '94, Pagan Unity Night ('94), and Pagan Expo '97, 2000, and 2001.

Ed has an extensive publishing background, having published Psychic Chicago Magazine (1990-1992), The Round Table magazine (1994 – 2000), and The Daily Spell E-zine (1998-present), as well as many books and pamphlets through Witch School.

Ed has hosted several radio programs including Psychic Chicago Radio and Telepathic Radio. Currently Ed is hosting the Pagans Tonight podcast.

Ed is the author of Principle Prophetica, Pagan Cyber-Ministry, and The Witch Wars Defense Manual, among other works.

Ed is known for his innovative ideas and forward-thinking projects, particularly in regard to community building and infrastructure. Ed is known for seeing and finding solutions to problems others miss. He is also known for an emphasis on the importance of involvement of Pagans in the wider world.

ELLEN DUGAN

One of the hardest working women in the world of Witches, Ellen Dugan has been a practicing Witch since 1983.

Lady Ellen is Co-Head of the Greenwood Coven in St. Louis, and offers classes locally in Witchcraft and Magic.

Author of twelve books on Witchcraft, Lady Ellen makes appearances at many festivals and events each year.

A master gardener, much of Lady Ellen's work focuses on herbalism and Natural Magic – so much so that she has become known as the "Garden Witch".

Some of Ellen Dugan's many books include: Garden *Witchery: Magick from the Ground Up* (2004), *Cottage Witchery: Natural Magick for Hearth and Home* (2005), *Natural Witchery: Intuitive, Personal & Practical Magick* (2008)

GERINA DUNWICH

Gerina Dunwich is a Wiccan High Priestess and a member of Circle, the Fellowship of Isis, and the Universal Life Church. Lady Gerina is the author of twenty-eight books on Witchcraft, magic, and paranormal activities.

Born on December 27, 1959, in Illinois, Lady Gerina was introduced to Witchcraft at the age of ten by an older member of her family, and has been devoted to the Old Religion ever since.

In 1980 Lady Gerina began publishing Golden Isis, a magazine dedicated to Pagan poetry and fiction which was to become a staple of the Pagan Press.

In 1996 Lady Gerina established the Mandragora Coven, serving as its High Priestess. She also established the Wheel of Wisdom

School that same year, a correspondence school dealing with the Wiccan Sabbats. Also in 1996, Lady Gerina also founded the Pagan Poets Society, a literary circle for poets of the Pagan persuasion.

Lady Gerina is also the founder of the Paranormal Animal Research Group, a paranormal investigation group that investigates cases of hauntings by animal spirits.

Among Gerina Dunwich's many books are: *Candlelight Spells* (1988), *Everyday Wicca* (1997), and *Your Magickal Cat* (2000)

ENHEDUANNA

EnHeduAnna is the first author in human history known by name. She is also the first known author ever to write in the first person voice.

EnHeduAnna was an Akkadian Princess, daughter of Sargon the Great, ruler of Mesopotamia, and Queen Tashultum. EnHeduAnna was the High Priestess of the Moon God Nanna, and may have been regarded as His consort. She was also a devotee of the Goddess Inanna.

As High Priestess EnHeduAnna wrote a huge corpus of religious literature, most of which was in the form of hymns, paeans and prayers. The liturgical pieces she created continued to be used for hundreds of years after her death. Her most famous hymn is the NinMeSara, or "Exaltation of Inanna."

Many of EnHeduAnna's hymns to Inanna celebrate her personal relationship with the Goddess, and constitute the first time a human being ever set down details of their inner spiritual life in writing.

A syncretist, EnHeduAnna worked to merge the identities of the Sumerian and Akkadian pantheons. EnHeduAnna's writings particularly helped to identify the Sumerian Inanna with the Akkadian Ishtar.

The ancient Sumerians considered EnHeduAnna's prayers extremely magical, and revered her highly for many hundreds of years.

STEWART FARRAR

Stewart Farrar was born on June 28, 1916, in Essex, England, and had an extensive career as a journalist and as the author of detective novels, but he is best known for his role in and writings about the Alexandrian Tradition of Wicca.
It was in his capacity as a journalist that Stewart first met Alex and Maxine Sanders, founders of the Alexandrian Tradition, and he quickly became interested in Wicca.

Stewart was initiated as an Alexandrian Witch on February 7, 1970, and achieved his second Degree in October of 1970, on the same day as his future wife Janet Owen Farrar. Together Stewart and Janet formed a coven at Yule of 1970, under the imperium of the Sanders.
In April of 1971 Stewart and Janet achieved their Third Degrees and their coven became independent, in accordance with Alexandrian usage.

Stewart and Janet Farrar were handfasted in 1972 and legally married in 1975. Together Stewart and Janet Farrar co-authored some of the most influential books on modern Wicca, including Eight Sabbats for Witches, the Witches Way, the Witches Bible, and the Witches Goddess among others.

Stewart Farrar died on February 7, 2000, at the age of eighty-three.

DION FORTUNE

Dion Fortune was born Violet Mary Firth on December 6, 1890, at Bryn-y-Bia, Llandudno, Wales.

Violet showed signs of psychic ability at an early age, and began actively developing her psychic skills at age twenty. Violet believed that she had lived as a Priestess in Atlantis, and has visions of this as early as four years of age.

As an adult Violet studied many metaphysical disciplines, becoming a Theosophist, Freemason, and a member of the Order of the Golden Dawn. She ultimately founded her own order, the Society of the Inner Light which remains active to this day.

In 1919 Violet began writing on metaphysical subjects and took the pseudonym "Dion Fortune" based upon her family's motto "Deo Non Fortuna" meaning "God, not fortune."

Among Dion Fortunes most famous books are *The Cosmic Doctrine*, *Mystical Qaballah*, and *Psychic Self Defense*.

Many of Dion Fortune's works, notably *The Sea Priestess*, *The Goat-Foot God*, and *Moon Magic*, deal with themes of religious Witchcraft/Wicca.

Dion Fortune participated in the "Magical Battle of Britain", which was an attempt by British occultists to magically aid the war effort and which aimed to forestall the impending German invasion during the darkest days of World War II. Her efforts in regard to this are recorded in a series of letters she wrote at the time. The effort involved in this endeavor is said to have contributed to her death shortly after the war ended.

Dion Fortune died in 1946.

SELENA FOX

Among the most prominent of all contemporary Witch Priestesses, Selena Fox is the founder of the Circle Craft Tradition of Wicca. Born December 20, 1949, Lady Selena has been in the forefront of the Pagan Press and Pagan civil rights activism for over thirty years.

Lady Selena's publication, Circle Magazine, is perhaps the most influential of all Wiccan magazines and has played a formative role in the development of the Wiccan community in the US Midwest.

In 1974 Lady Selena founded Circle Sanctuary, one of the oldest Wiccan churches and centers in the U.S. In 1983 Circle Sanctuary established its Headquarters on the 200-acre Circle Sanctuary Nature Preserve.

In 1978 Lady Selena began her magazine, Circle Network News. One of the most important magazines of the Pagan Press, Circle was immensely influential in the Wiccan/Pagan community of the US Midwest especially. In 1980 Circle Network News adopted a newspaper format, and in 1997 it took on a magazine format, changing its name to Circle.

Lady Selena is the founder and executive director of the Lady Liberty League, an organization dedicated to advancing the civil rights of Witches and Pagans.

The Lady Liberty League has been involved in many important civil rights cases, most notably the Pentacle Campaign – the long legal battle to win for Pagan service people the right to have the pentacle as the emblem of faith on their tomb stone if they were buried in a national cemetery.

SURVIVING THE HOLIDAY SEASON

by **A.C. Fisher Aldag**

Part One: An overview, and surviving Thanksgiving

Let's face it, the holiday season can be difficult for Pagans, Wiccans and Polytheists. We might enjoy the idea of Thanksgiving and Christmas – the notion of good cheer, family togetherness, a wholesome dinner, and merry tidings of joy. We may even like certain aspects of the celebrations, such as the decorations, the shopping, the music, and the food. However, we might dislike the "Christmas fever" that overtakes American society, which seems to begin earlier every year. This year, it seemed as if the minute the pumpkins came down, the plastic trees and ornaments went up. The commercialism may be bothersome. The religious overtones might be hard to digest. Some of us might be facing economic troubles, and can't afford to buy everyone presents or purchase a fifty-pound turkey. We don't all have a great relationship with our biological families. There may be political, ideological, and religious differences between us and our kinfolk, which can cause arguments during a prolonged visit. We might even have serious emotional wounds left over from abusive childhoods. While this article cannot replace psychological counseling, it may be able to offer some help and advice for coping during the mainstream holidays.

Before we begin, think of five things you like about the holiday season, and five things that are problematic for you. Some of us may truly enjoy watching parades or football games, others might find it excruciating. We might want to cut a live tree, while others can only think of the death of the environment. Others might really like Christmas carols on the radio, while for some, it's auditory torture. What events can we participate in that bring us pleasure? Baking cookies, going ice skating, watching movies on T.V., driving around and looking at light displays are activities that are "religious neutral" and fun. What holiday things that we dislike can we avoid? And what must we participate in, and how can we make the best of a bad situation? We may have to attend the obligatory office party, but we can duck out of the neighborhood gossip fest. Or we can bring our own traditions to the gathering – see if you can engage your co-workers in Wassailing the Trees or creating handmade ornaments. Suggest alternatives that work for everyone – how about a cooking party? Attending a concert with a neutral holiday theme, such as "The Nutcracker Suite", or a restaurant, or walking through a decorated park, might be much more enjoyable for everyone concerned.

Those of us with children may have to compromise – allowing the young ones to watch three pre-selected Christmas specials on T.V., finding programs that emphasize our own values, such as tolerance and sharing. One mother was appalled by a cartoon that showed a "good" kid receiving lots of presents from Santa, when her family was financially strapped and unable to afford more than one pair of mittens and one small toy per child. We may have to explain that rewards aren't always material. Others may feel overwhelmed by images of baby Jesus and songs that proclaim "He rules the world". During Thanksgiving, we might be upset by revisionist history that shows Indians eating happily with tolerant Puritans, when we really want to participate in the First Nations' "Day of Mourning". We may have to simply turn off the television and radio and play DVDs of our favorite movies. Or take out a wheelbarrow-load of library books. If we can't avoid it – attending the annual school Christmas program, where your child is the lead reindeer – we can try to make the best of it. Sing songs with traditional meaning, such as "Deck the Halls" or something without religious overtones, like "Frosty the Snowman" and sit stoically through "Silent Night". Or hide your earbuds under your hat and listen to Pagan music or your favorite podcast. Learn about another culture's harvest holidays, or if you can afford it, go to a place like Chinatown, or stay in a motel owned by a Hindu family – someplace where Christmas doesn't exist. Many theaters show movies on Thanksgiving Day and Christmas, where you can escape the holiday hassle for a couple of hours.

Then there's family visits, Thanksgiving dinner, Christmas presents around the tree, a dinner with your entire clan. All of them. Even Uncle Ralph. If these scenarios make you grit your teeth, just thinking about them, you might want to propose some activity that is much less stressful. How about holding Thanksgiving at a favorite family restaurant, where everyone chips in for the bill? Or a Thanksgiving potluck on neutral ground? On Christmas, you may be expected to come to an extended family get-together. This can be difficult if your loved ones are in denial about your sexual orientation, angry about your religion or lifestyle, or disappointed about some other expectations that they feel are unmet. You may need to propose a compromise here, as well. Tell your family members that there are certain topics that you will not discuss, and ignore any attempt to draw you in. Remind yourself that your life is one that you chose and recall the reasons that it makes you happy. And also, remind yourself that your family is entitled to their opinions, and you are not responsible for their choices. Release karma. Perform shielding and grounding rituals to magickally protect yourself from baneful glares and hurtful words. Go to your family's Christmas extravaganza for a few hours, bring the materials to bake a Yule log or homemade cookies together. Bring crafts items to construct nut cups that resemble turkeys, or make construction-paper chains with the younger relatives. Go outdoors and create snowmen, dance in the piles of leaves, make snow fairies, or just go for a walk. Volunteer to haul youngsters around the block on their sleds. Help the teens to hang lights or do other activities that take you out of the house, away from the relentless holiday spirit.

Or, don't go. That's right, do not go to your family's celebration, if you'd really rather not. So often, we hear people say that they "Have To" go home for the holidays. Grown adults do not "have to" do anything but pay taxes and breathe. It is your choice. If returning to your family household for the holidays is going to send you into therapy, you do not "have to" do it. You do not have to subject yourself to verbal abuse or painful situations. You may be able to communicate by phone, or Facebook, or write a nice non-religious holiday greeting... or not communicate at all.

Okay, so your family isn't really all that bad, just mildly annoying. Your grandma insists that when you just met the right girl, you'll decide not to be Gay. Or your mom really wants you to raise your children as Episcopalians, if you'd just get over this "witchcraft phase". You may have to establish certain ground rules, by phone or email before visiting your family. "I am bringing my significant other, and you will be nice to him throughout the day." "Sally and I cannot afford presents for everyone this year. You know that I am laid off. Let's pull names out of a hat, or make presents, or have a spending limit of ten dollars." "Mom, I know your religious traditions are important to you, but the kids and I are not going to church for Christmas Eve services. How about you explain to your grandkids about the Christmas story?" You can prompt your children in advance that some people believe XXX, and other people believe YYY, and that you believe in the Goddess and magick. "Every path is wonderful and has validity, but Grandma's way doesn't work for me. How about you listen to her, and learn about her religion?" Hopefully, compromises can be reached.

Younger people in college or working a seasonal job might not have any choice about going home for the holidays. Or you may live at home, for whatever reason. If you're somehow dependent on your family – economically, or for living conditions, or emotionally ... you truly want to maintain a good relationship without upsetting them over your religious or social life – then you may have to put up with their well-intentioned yet irritating holiday celebrations for a few days. Think about what is worth a confrontation and what is not ... can you tuck your religious jewelry under your shirt, or will this make you feel emotionally uncomfortable or dishonest? Can you endure a prayer over dinner? Can you keep silent while certain topics of discussion are brought up? Can you redirect conversations so as to avoid an argument? Consider ways to balance your religious needs with your family life. Will offering your own libation cause a fight, and if so, can you do it later, in silence? It may help to make your needs known beforehand. "Mom, I'm a vegetarian. Gravy contains meat juices, so please don't put any gravy on my mashed potatoes." "Dad, I really appreciate the presents that you buy, but please don't purchase anything from that company, because their products are made by slave labor." They might have perfectly legitimate requests of you, as well. Try to reach an understanding.

You may want to sit down with your loved ones, tell them that they are meaningful to you, but that you do not share the same religious views, and therefore, you do not wish to attend Mass or light the Menorah or sit through another church meeting where the preacher shouts that non-believers are going to hell. If they remain unyielding, you may have to bite the bullet, attend the religious services, and count light bulbs or red panels in the stained glass. Silently say prayers to your own Gods. Touch the wooden church pews and invoke the tree spirits laying dormant within. Remember to ground, center and shield yourself. Or you might suggest alternatives, such as staying home and cleaning the house, shoveling snow, or participating in a charitable event, instead. Dad probably has a good point if you're sleeping in until three and playing video games throughout the holiday week, when he'd rather you go to church. It may be more difficult for parents to argue in favor of religious rites if you're spending Christmas morning serving breakfast at a soup kitchen or delivering presents to needy children. And pray. Pray to your Gods for tolerance, fortitude, and patience.

In the next edition of Magickal Media, we'll discuss more about surviving Christmas. This time, we'll concentrate on getting through Thanksgiving with the family:

- During the prayers before dinner, think of things, situations and conditions that you are truly grateful for: the public library, air, a new sweater, a wonderful friendship, finding the perfect Pagan book, food, music, the path that led you to the Gods. Thank your own Deities, guides and spirit helpers for their contributions to your life. Silently honor them.

- Bring a cornucopia to use as a centerpiece, stuffed with fruits, nuts, and vegetables. Ask each person to write something they are thankful for on a piece of paper, and put it into the horn of plenty. Later, at home or in private, place the offerings outdoors, or put them into a compost bin. As they decay, they return to the Earth. You've just performed a Pagan ritual with your family.

- Look up Gods and Goddesses that represent the harvest, gardening, the hunt, grain, fruits and abundance. Find out more about the Deities in books or online.

- Make a collage of things and conditions that you are thankful for. Cut pictures out of magazines or newspapers and glue them onto a cardboard backing. Add glitter glue, color with markers, write blessings in the margins. Use copies of photographs that are important to you. Your family may want to participate. It doesn't matter if they are thanking Jesus or Allah, and you are thanking other Deities. The point is gratitude and sharing an activity with loved ones.

- Thank the people who helped or influenced you. Write them letters, drop them an email, tell them in person, or if they've passed away, speak it aloud outdoors or write a private note to them.

- Perform a Ritual of Thankfulness. Light a candle in harvest colors – yellow, orange, tan, or a scented candle such as pumpkin pie spice. Fill a bowl or cornucopia with fruits, nuts, vegetables and things that symbolize grain, such as bread or a granola bar. Place a slice of bread, muffin or cookie on a plate. Fill two glasses, one with water, and one with beer, wine or fruit juice. Summon guides, elements or helpers and Deities as usual. Create sacred space by casting circle, hallowing or as according to your tradition or will. Speak words of gratitude for people, situations, material things and conditions that are beneficial to you. Drink half of the beverage, and eat half of the bread, while mindfully contemplating abundance, the harvest, and the gifts of the Gods. Then take the remainder of the beverage and bread outdoors for a libation. (Some prefer to thank and dismiss the elements, Gods and other helpers, and de-sanctify the sacred space before going outside). Pour the beverage onto the ground, tear up the bread and scatter it, while looking at the sky. Notice the clouds or stars. Say three times, "I am thankful" and offer a blessing.

- If family members seem receptive, you may wish to include them in these rituals. If they use words like "abomination", it may be best to keep it private.

Next time, we'll discuss how to endure the rest of the holiday season, and how to survive Christmas with non-Pagan relatives.

GROWING SACRED SPACES

by **Abby Willowroot**

Healthy communities grow organically like any other living thing. New additions fit in to existing spaces or flow easily out from the edges, ever expanding the whole. Steadily, like attracts like, and the community shifts slightly with the addition of each new individual, each new skill, and each new facet.

Earth-Spirit Faiths are growing and shifting and finding a voice. We are beginning to recognize ourselves as a Sacred People of many Tribes and beliefs. In our diversity we creating connections without homogenization; Religions without dogma or exclusion. Now, we are growing organically and quickly as we begin to create our own permanent places of worship.

Labyrinths and Earthworks are springing up on land, in parks, nestled in the hills, on beaches, and a hundred unexpected places. Grottoes, Groves, and even Temples have begun to appear. With each new space the fabric of the Earth-honoring Communities grows stronger, more diverse and more vibrant.

What is necessary to create a public worship space? It can be as simple as using the same place over and over again for open rituals, or renting the same land each year for festivals or gatherings. It can be making a Labyrinth in your yard available for others in your community to use for rituals. It can be gathering together at the ocean, river or lake for an open ritual, inviting anyone who is interested in celebrating the Goddess.

Sacred Worship Spaces appear when we reach out and include those we do not know yet in our Rituals and celebrations. When we share Sacred space with others who share different beliefs than our own.

The Universe always fills a void. When we plan to gather and embrace all who seek to join us, the Universe is signaled that new places for meeting and worship are needed. The Universe then moves quickly to fill these needs. The more we celebrate our Spirits, the faster our network of public Sacred Spaces grows.

If we stay to ourselves and practice our spirituality only with those we already know, we cease to create new connections and Sacred Space in the world.

Do you dream, of a Sacred Space? ... Begin to create it with the Universe.

http://spiralgoddess.com/Tomorrow.html

WHAT IS A COVEN?

by **William Halstead**

One of the more interesting experiences that I have found that I have had on the internet was looking up the definition of the word "coven" on the net. We got a lot of pages regarding covens, ranging from Polish rock and roll music, to a witch role playing game, to a small sampling of on-line covens. This is after I narrowed my search criteria down to "what is a coven." Only two sites offered a brief blurb on "what is a coven" out of some of the pages that I saw!

So, I am offering my own brief definition of what is a coven. A coven is a collection, a group, of three or more witches or Pagans that share a common interest and goal. In other words, a coven is not simply a gathering of people who elect to get together just because they are all non-Christian; they need to have a common purpose in order to attempt to work together as a coven!

Now, in my view, what may be some of the qualities of a working coven? I came up with some of the following points that I feel are important in a working coven. They are that a coven should have:

- A group of practicing witches
- Generally have a decent number of members (Tradition says 13, but that is not engraved in stone)
- The ability to function as your chosen family
- Tradition
- Loyalty and commitment
- Regular meetings
- Goals
- Purpose and intent
- A High Priestess and/or a High Priest
- Ethics

- Beliefs
- Safety
- Trust
- Confidentiality
- Honesty
- Conviction
- Follow through

A group of practicing witches

A coven is a group of practicing witches! It is as plain and simple as that! Despite the page that I saw on the web about Polish rock bands, a coven (for the purposes of Wicca) is a collection of witches. It is not a group of Sunday school teachers. It is not an insurance salesmen convention. It is a group of witches working together, celebrating together, and worshiping together AS WITCHES!

Please note that I say a coven needs to have a group of practicing witches. I was once part of a coven that met on a regular basis -- at a local Denny's! While we had fun conversations and a lot of food and coffee, we were not working together. We were a coffee klatch, a social gathering, not a coven!

Generally have a decent number of members (Tradition says 13)

I have seen some small gathering of witches, two or three witches, working together. Now, is that a coven?

Actually, I would have to question that. A coven should be able to be self-sustaining. If a member has to leave the coven (let's say that this member had to move across the globe), then the coven should still be able to function despite that loss! Worse yet, if a member leaves the coven because of internal politics, then the coven should definitely be able to function after that loss!

In this light, it would seem that a gathering of only two or three witches is not a coven! Why? Well, if just one of those members has to leave -- no matter the reason -- the coven, the odds are pretty good that this "coven" would not be able to survive. It could not be self-sustaining.

The ability to function as your chosen family

Your coven is your home away from home, your family away from family! This is the family that you choose. It is your logical family rather than just your biological family!

When you coven with a group of people, you expose yourself to a group of people, telling things about yourself, sharing some of your needs that you may want help with from your coven. This quickly dissolves the notion that your coven is just a group of strangers that you get together with from time to time! If it doesn't, then you may be in the wrong coven!

Doing this kind of intimate work can quickly dissolve the barriers between strangers. It seems that it is better to do this with people you feel a "family" connection with rather than just a group of clinical or disinterested strangers!

Tradition

One of the things that I believe is that a coven needs to have some sort of Tradition, rather an already established British Tradition, the Correllian Nativist Tradition, or a newly created one for that specific coven! This concept of Tradition (the way of practicing and believing) helps to define for the coven who they are and what they are. An eclectic group, one in which everyone does their own thing, practices their own practices, does not offer this sense of identity or definition. It may be fun to attend such a group, but, since no one is on the same page, how can such a group be categorized or defined?

Loyalty and commitment

Covening is hard work! You may have ritual to attend even when you would rather stay home and just pop in a videotape! You may have a class to teach, even when you would rather go hiking in the mountains!

Loyalty and commitment is sticking to the planned schedule, even if you do not want to. It is studying, even when your favorite movie is playing on cable. It is going to ritual, even when a car show is in town. It is staying together and getting done what you have promised and pledged to get done!

Now, even though this is not actually a part of the above issue, commitment should also include punctuality. In simple terms, this means being on time and not running on Pagan Standard Time!

This type of loyalty and commitment also indicates, since not everyone can be in attendance or punctual 100% of the time, having the courtesy to call your coven or High Priestess or High Priest if you are going to be late! It is inappropriate to have everyone waiting for you, not knowing where you are! Poor excuses, such as "My dog ate my magic wand" may not be accepted by your coven mates!

Regular meetings

Covens are not a spur of the moment thing. They happen on a schedule! Why? Well, regular meetings help to keep everyone on the same page, rather than just having some people show up today and, what the heck, someone else show up three days later for the same class! Also, regular meetings help others know what is expected of them: what outside events I can schedule that won't interfere with my coven responsibilities!

Some groups seem to feel whenever they get together -- at the drop of a hat -- that it is a coven activity or event. Sorry, but a coven cannot identify itself if it doesn't know if it is a coven event tomorrow night or is that six months from now?

Goals

A coven needs to have goals. It needs to see the future of where your group is going to go.

Setting goals is important. Its purpose is to let you know [a] what your groups wants to do and [b] what it may need to accomplish this goal. Goals set a direction! Goals will more accurately reflect what the actual values and ethics of a coven are than a mere mission statement.

As I mentioned earlier, our groups used to get together and just talk. That was all that it did. It completely lacked a direction and a goal. Without such a goal, the group was destined for failure. And, surely enough, the old group died a quiet death.

Purpose and intent

Now, this is closely related to your goals. Your goals give a destination. Your purpose and intent say why your coven exists. Your goals may change, but your purpose and intent will remain pretty much the same. As one member of my old Circle points out, "for me, my intent is to learn and live something!"

A High Priestess and/or a High Priest

Covens need structure and they need some type of leadership. They need someone they can look to, when all else fails, to cast that final deciding vote, to speak the mind of the coven members. We do not mean that a coven needs its own version of the Pope, but it does need a final person to act as arbiter to help the coven keep on its appointed direction.

Others may lead some of the rituals, but there has to be someone responsible for and to the coven! You cannot have an anarchy in a coven. This just means that everyone will leave once they do not get their way. A High Priestess and/or a High Priest is there to keep everyone ultimately on track and to provide that sense of organization and structure.

Ethics

Ethics are key to a coven! What does the coven believe? What are its practices? Ethics exist to keep the coven acting in ways that responsible ways and that point out the actual foundation of a coven's belief system!

I actually studied with a coven that, while it had a good curriculum, did not teach ethics to its students for months on end! Honestly, I feel that ethics should start being taught from day one -- even if not in an actual topic that first day. Ethics are the things that establish what the coven's actual values and beliefs are, more so than pretty language in a ritual or remembering Gerald Gardner's date of birth!

Beliefs

Along with ethics, a coven should have a set of established beliefs. It must be hard to identify and define your Tradition when one member of your coven practices Druidism and another in your coven is Asatru while you practice Christos Wicca. A coven should have members that pretty much agree on the same mythological basis for the group, the same practices, and other beliefs rather than just having a spiritual free for all!

Safety

People in a coven need to be able to feel safe. They need to feel secure. They need to know that they will not be abused by their coven. We have actually heard of one coven in this town where a member forgot to bring in her homework assignment one Sabbat (while another coven was visiting). This unfortunate young lady's High Priestess actually ordered her to act as the footstool for the visiting High Priestess. Worse yet, the young lady's boyfriend was also visiting this Sabbat. She definitely did not feel safe after this incident!

Safety is a group effort! We all, as a family, have to look our for one another. If someone is acting inappropriately, then you need to let someone else in your coven know! Your safety is important!

Trust

One of the lines in the Wiccan Rede is "in perfect love and in perfect trust." A coven needs an atmosphere where each member can trust another member. Additionally, each person should be able ascertain just how far he or she can trust another member, rather than just expecting the other member to be Superman. We each need to know each other's inabilities so that we do not overburden another member because "we trust them perfectly!"

Part of trust is respect! If a member cannot show respect to their coven mates, it is harder to trust that member! If a member is always rude to their fellows, then the others will avoid trusting the rude member ... And possibly avoid respecting the rude member!

Trust also means being honest with your coven mate. When you have an issue with another member, such as the above described rude coven mate, then a good idea might be to walk up to that person and be honest enough to tell them your concerns about them! Some of us may only have a million more incarnations to try to get it right!

Confidentiality

Close to trust is the issue of confidentiality. We have people in one group rush right out of their Wiccan group to tell their friends in another Wiccan group just what happened at their last ritual! We have heard of people visiting one group's public events just so they can go tell their friends everything "wrong" that this public group did.

Things that are done or discussed in a coven should stay in a coven. They are not meant to be public news. If they were, then let that coven hold its own press conference. We don't need to hold it for them!

Honesty

Honesty is the best policy! We have all heard that saying. Guess what! It's still true! If we cannot deal in the reality of honesty, then what reality are we dealing in? Certainly not the one that will help you to succeed with your magic and certainly not the one that will help you effect whatever needed changes in your life that you may need to spiritually evolve!

Be true to yourself, then you can be true to others!

Conviction

Conviction and commitment go hand in hand. If you make a commitment to your coven to do something, you should have your convictions, your principles, to make you stand up, be counted, and to do it! You should not be in a coven or do something for you coven just because it may be "cool," you should do these things because you believe in them.

Follow through

Last, but not least, is the commitment to follow through with things! We have seen many groups start out with enthusiasm, get tired of it after a while, and never follow through with what they promised or with what they started!

Don't suggest ideas or start things unless you are willing to follow through! Talk the talk and walk the walk at the same time!

SOME THOUGHTS ON SOULS AND TREES

by **Don Lewis**

I tend to think of the Higher Self as being like the branch of a tree, which arising from a single point forks and splits many times as it grows. We might think of the tree trunk as being God/dess, and each branch coming off of that trunk as a Monad. The forks in the branches are Souls, and the twigs coming off the forks are Lifetimes –which themselves may fork into differing probabilities. The leaves on the twigs are experiences. As with a tree whose leaves obscure the branch structure, our many experiences obscure our view of the Higher Self.

When we work with our Higher Self, whether through meditation, soul retrieval, energy work, past Life work, etc... we are like a squirrel running up the branch from the leaves toward the trunk. Doing such work takes us from twig to fork to branch and ultimately to the trunk where all connects. Perched on the end of a twig we might well think that it is all there is, a thing in itself, the center to which all these many leaves connect. Running up to the fork we might think the same of it –an independent thing from which all these twigs sprout. But from the branch we can see that these forks and twigs are aspects of a larger whole, though we may not see the trunk until we reach the end of the branch. From the trunk it is clear that the whole network is a single thing, possessing many subdivisions which lead through stages to the leaves through which the tree thrives.

The same is true for the Soul. When we are considering our nature from the vantage point of our contemporary experiences, we may well think that this Life is all there is, an independent thing from which all these experiences proceed. However when we work with the Higher Self, we become aware of the Soul, from which our Life proceeds, but also many other lives and variations on lives which – from that vantage point- we can describe as 'ours'. From this level we might well think that the Soul is an independent thing, just as we first thought this individual Life was an independent thing, because it is the focus of our attention. However, if we continue to work with our Higher Self we will see that the Soul is not an independent thing, but is itself a fork on a branch which is the Monad, which some term "Soul Group" or "Soul Family". However terms like "Soul Group" are misleading, because they fail to grasp the inherent and inseparable connection of the Soul to the Monad, from which it arises in the same way that the Life arises from the Soul, or the experience from the Life. And of course in the end we see that the Monad itself arises in this same way from God/dess, which is the single core of all existence, just as the trunk is the single core of the tree.

A leaf of course is a thing of its own. But a leaf is also inherently part of a tree. A twig too is its own thing, but is also ultimately part of a tree. Just as the leaf and the twig and the fork and the branch can be considered as things in their own right, still they are ultimately by their nature part and parcel of the tree. Both things are true –they are things in their own right from one vantage, but all parts of a tree from another. It all depends upon where the squirrel is sitting.

So too our Life is an independent thing, and our Soul is an independent thing, and our Monad is an independent thing, and all can be considered as separate things in their own right, yet each is also part and parcel of God/dess. It all depends upon the level at which we are looking at it.

This is part of what we mean when we say "You are God".

"But" you say, "a twig may be part of a tree, but the twig is not THE tree."

This is true at one level. But consider that while the twig is only a part of the tree, the life that is in the twig is the life force of the tree and is not separable from it. The twig itself may be separable, but the life force within comes directly from the tree, and does not arise from the twig.

Remove the twig from the tree and this will become immediately obvious, because the twig will no longer be alive. Although the leaf and the twig and the fork and the branch can all be seen as separate if you look at them from a certain angle, still it is just one life force that moves through them all. They are separate in a way, but also inseparable. Remove the twig from the tree and only a dead husk remains —but the life force of the tree is still as it was, and continues forward as it has. The part of the Tree's life force that was in the twig when it was part of the tree is no longer in it once it has been snapped off, but that life force has not ceased to be, and will manifest as new twigs in time. Moreover the twig that has been snapped off leaves a mark upon the branch that remains after it is gone.

So too when this individual Life ends what remains is an empty husk, but the life force that had been in it -being ultimately the life force of God/dess despite the many forks and branchings- remains and will be again expressed through new Lives. That life force is the Eternal Flame, the Spark of Life that is never extinguished. And just as the twig that falls leaves a mark upon the branch, so too past Lives leave their mark within the Soul, even as we go on to new Lives. Every Life leaves its mark upon the Soul, and shapes it – giving each Soul its own distinct quality within the Monad, just as each Life is distinct within the Soul.

"But," you say, "Which one are we? Are we this Life which we are currently living? Are we our Soul, and each Life a secondary feature? Or are we truly the Monad? Are we in fact God/dess? Which is our true essence?"

Well, what is the true essence of the tree? Is the true essence of the tree its leaves? Is the true essence of the tree its twigs? Is the true essence of the tree the forks? Is the true essence of the tree perhaps the branches? Is the true essence of the tree in fact the trunk? Or are all of these part of the true essence of the tree? I would say that the true essence of the tree is in all these things, and which one is preeminent depends entirely from the angle from which the tree is being considered. Granted, the trunk is the origin and the core of the tree, but is a trunk really a tree without branches? Is a tree really a tree without the constant coming and going of leaves?

So too, we are this Life we are leading, but we are also the Soul. We are also the Monad. And we are ultimately also God/dess.

God/dess is the origin and core of our being, the source of the life force that gives us existence, and ultimately we are God/dess —but we are also all the parts between our present point of consciousness and God/dess.

When I was a child I was told that our Soul would ultimately unite with God/dess, and at first I did not understand this idea. I thought that this meant that the Soul would be absorbed into God/dess and lose its individuality. I did not realize that the Soul was already united with God/dess and when we speak of ultimate reunion with Deity we are merely speaking of realizing what has always been true, and embodying it more fully. It is a matter of changing perspective and within the Soul, not an actual change in the relationship between the Soul and God/dess.

The Soul unites with God/dess —through the connection through which it arose from God/dess and from which it is already united to God/dess. The branch connects to the tree —through the spot where it grew from the trunk, and where it has always been connected. However the squirrel running up the branch may not realize that the branch is connected to the trunk until it has reached the spot where the branch has always been connected. So too the Higher Self does not realize that it is connected to God/dess until it reaches that point in its being where it is connected. When we say that the Soul will reunite with Deity, what we really mean is that it will realize that it had never been separate, and rather than losing any part of its being will rather come into the fullness of its being, which is and has always been God/dess.

When we work with the Higher Self we are the squirrel running up the branch. And as we run up that branch what we find is not greater separation but ever-increasing connection. Many Lives connect within one Soul, many Souls connect within one Monad, and ultimately all connects at the core, which is God/dess. It is a journey from the leaf to the trunk -from our momentary experiences in the floating world to the unity of all being in God/dess.

CHOOSING A SPIRITUAL PATH

by **Abby Willowroot**

Healing the heart and mind is often a challenge. For those who have been deeply wounded by traditional religion and the false guilt associated with simply being human, it is often a long journey to finding true peace of mind and happiness. Those who have been raised without any religion sometimes seek one, and choosing a spiritual path may be confusing. It is not necessary to choose a religion, many people are ethical, content and well balanced without any belief in the divine, others seek a spiritual path. If you feel a call to choose a spiritual path we hope this page will help you on your journey toward a belief system that will serve you well.

For many, the journey is worth the effort, at the other end is self-acceptance, a joy in living and a powerful spiritual connection with all life and yourself. Many who have been bludgeoned with religious dogma, need to take time to examine what is truly in their own hearts and replace old judging symbols with new life affirming symbols and a willingness to accept others choices as right for them, before you can make a free choice of a spiritual path that is truly right for you and travel that path happily and securely. There is no hurry, relax.

Your spiritual connection with the Divine is the most intimate, personal relationship you will ever have. No one knows what path best expresses your own unique connection with a Higher Power, not ministers, not priests, not psychics, not your family, not your soul-mate, and not me either. This is journey that can only be walked and explored in fullness by you alone.

Your life is a miracle for YOU to explore. Many people express their spirituality through the honoring of the Great Goddess. I am one who has found that personally, Goddess energy speaks clearly and lovingly to me, I am a Pagan. This is right for me, and has been my path for many, many years, it works well for me, but, that does not mean it is the right path for you, it may be, it may not be.

The many voices of the past that told me of a jealous and punishing God, have no power in my life today. They have been replaced with a deeper knowing. I am only saddened that some would choose to seek out a negative, judgmental deity to express their spiritual selves and their view of the world. Such fear based religions do little to create a true sense of unconditional love and acceptance. Still, they seem to meet some peoples spiritual needs. There are those who see this same God as more loving, balanced and not judgmental or punishing. And that Path seems to works for them and meets their spiritual needs. Your spiritual path need not be what others want, what fits you and your spirit is what is right.

All religions contain grains of truth, all contain flaws. The Path you choose must be one which allows you to fully express your spiritual essence. One which honors and celebrates your values, ethics, beliefs and inner knowings. Whether you choose the Goddess Path, Buddhism, Christianity, Judaism, Catholicism, Islam, Atheism, Paganism, Hinduism, Shinto, Taoism, a Heathen Path, a Solitary path, Indigenous religion, Native American beliefs, or another spiritual path is not nearly as important as the act of freely choosing and practicing of a Faith that fits your beliefs.

All faiths work for some people. The trick is to find the Path that is right for you. Do not be discouraged or coerced into following anyone else's belief system. You have the right to choose your own way of spiritually expressing your connection with the Divine. If you do not believe in a divine being, that is fine too, and is also part of a legitimate spiritual path. Deity is not necessary for a strong spiritual connection with life or being a truly spiritual person. Many Atheists are also deeply spiritual and compassionate people. Belief in a Deity is not the only Path to morality, kindness, compassion, and humanity, it is just a popular one.

I wish you well on your journey of discovery.
May your right and true Spiritual Path find you.
May you always respect the Spiritual Paths of others.
Openness and respect comes before Peace

http://spiralgoddess.com/SpiritPath.html

FIRE CHANT

Fire burn high and bright
In our sacred circle
On this holy night

Fire help us manifest
These goals with which
We would be blessed

MOON LORE AND MAGICK

by **A.C. Fisher Aldag**

The phases of the moon:

Dark:

Not visible at all, fully blocked by the shadow of the Earth.

The three nights that the moon is not visible at all is called the Dark of the moon.

Magickal rites center on mysteries, banishings, divination. This is an optimal time for banishing unwanted situations or negative energies.

New:

Thin sliver or crescent, nearly blocked by the shadow of the Earth. Rises and sets with the sun.

May be seen in early morning or late at night.

In January through March in the Northern Hemisphere, the crescent moon appears as a smile. The rest of the year it appears as an archer's bow, open end facing left.)

Magickal rites include beginning projects, the inception of events, cleansing and purifying.

Waxing Moon:

Half moon shaped like a D or), left half blocked by the shadow of the Earth. The points aim away from the sunset.

Rises at noon, sets at midnight; most visible in the evening sky.

Magickal rites include working on projects, invoking, continuing events that have already been started.

Full:

Round, not blocked by the Earth's shadow.

Rises at sundown, sets at sunrise.

Magickal rites include bringing events to fruition, completion of projects. Full moon rites may honor the Goddess. A time to make requests and give thanks for granted boons. Divination is easiest to perform under a full moon.

Considered the most powerful time for spell workings and rituals.

The night before the moon is completely full is called the daughter moon, the night of the moon being totally full is called the mother moon, and the night following is called the crone or elder moon.

Waning Moon:

Half moon shaped like a (or C, right half blocked by the shadow of the Earth

Rises at midnight, sets at noon; most visible in the morning sky.

Magickal rites include banishing undesirable conditions, ending projects or events.

The average age of the Lunar month is 29.53 days. The word "month" derives from the word moon.

The moon is also called Luna, Chandra or Mona.

The day of the week representing or corresponding to the moon is Monday. Other correspondences with the moon include white, silver, the sephiroth of Yesod on the Cabalistic tree of life, and the Moon card of the Tarot deck which is number 18. Astrological sign is Cancer. The moon is associated with Water and watery elements or signs of the Zodiac. Trees corresponding with the moon are willow, hazel and yew. Plants include moon flowers, night-blooming jasmine, monk's hood, lady's mantle, mugwort, iris, lily of the valley.

Scattering moonstones under the full moon captures the Gods' attention and brings about an answer to prayers.

A blue moon is the second full moon is a calendar month. A black moon is the second new moon in a calendar month.

A ring around the moon can mean rain. In the autumn, if the crescent moon is sharply defined, expect frost. The moon riding unnaturally high in the sky often precludes strange weather

Goddesses associated with the moon include Diana, Artemis, Isis, Danu, Nakomis, Aradia, Hecate, Luna, Chandra, Selena, and Cerridwen. Moon gods include Marama, Aku, Nana, Sin, Mani and Tsukuyomi,

The moon's place in the Zodiac helps to determine the appropriate times for planting and harvest. The best time for planting are during the moon's alignment with Zodiac signs which are associated with Water, including Cancer, Scorpio and Pisces. Above ground crops should be planted during the waxing moon, below-ground crops planted when the moon is on the wane.

133

Some cultures see various shapes in the craters and valleys on the moon. The image may be of a man, woman, hare, toad or frog, or a grove or trees.

A full moon affects tides, women's menstrual cycles and can influence emotions.

The best days for fishing are when the moon is between new and full.

Native American names for the full moons:

JAN	*Wolf, Old, Snow*
FEB	*Snow, Hunger*
MAR	*Sap, Worm*
APR	*Pink, Egg, Fish, Sprouting Grass*
MAY	*Flower, Corn Planting, Milk*
JUN	*Strawberry, Rose, Hot*
JUL	*Buck, Thunder*
AUG	*Corn, Sturgeon, Grain*
SEP	*Harvest* *(Barley in Europe, Corn in America)* *Nearest Equinox*
OCT	*Hunter's, Travel*
NOV	*Beaver, Frost*
DEC	*Cold, Long nights*

THE BLACK MOON

by A.C. Fisher Aldag

The second full moon during one calendar month is often called a Blue Moon, as in the saying "Once in a blue moon". This occurs approximately every two to three years. The second new moon in a month is an even rarer event, and is sometimes called the "Black Moon" by astrologers. Under this definition, the last black moon was on August 30th, 2008. The next black moon is this month, on July 30th, 2011. After that, we must wait until March 30th, 2014 to experience another black moon.

Other definitions for a black moon is a month that has no full moon or new moon, which can only occur during the calendar month of February. This event only happens four or five times every century. The third new moon of a season that has four new moons is also sometimes called the black moon. For magickal purposes, we will stick with the second new moon in a month as the time of the Black Moon.

The new moon is when the moon has orbited directly between the Earth and the Sun, and is therefore hidden from view. It also rises and sets with the Sun, further obscuring its reflected light. The black moon is often even more difficult to see, as it may appear lower on the horizon. Some other names for this phenomenon are the Secret Moon, the Spinner's Moon, and the Finder's Moon. It is sometimes called the Dark Moon, not to be confused with "dark of the moon", which is the day prior to the crescent moon's appearance. The thin sliver of white may be visible low on the horizon at dawn and dusk, eastern or western respectively, if not blocked by trees or buildings. Or the night of the black moon may appear to have no moon at all.

The New Moon Esbat is often celebrated by Wiccans as a time of initiation, change, beginning projects and emerging refreshed from a period of rest. It is an optimal time for casting spells. The new moon often represents the youth or maiden phase of the Goddess. Some Witches use the time right before the new moon, called the dark moon, for invoking the crone aspect of the Goddess. This is a fine occasion for removing negative or harmful conditions, such as illness, addiction, or destructive habits, and ending unsuitable relationships. Hermetic orders suggest performing workings on the new moon that require a long-term magickal commitment, or embarking on a course of study. Initiatory orders sometimes perform rites of passage or degrees of mastery on the new moons. Ceremonial magickians likewise start new ventures and also use the power of the new moon for drawing away undesirable situations, bringing about justice, and exposing untruthful statements. The reflected light of the new moon offers the power of contemplation and inward, reflective thinking. It is an optimal time for divination and meditation.

These circumstances are doubly true for the black moon. It is like a super-charged new moon, with twice the power of this moon phase. Scrying (gazing into a bowl of water, dark mirror, or crystal for the purpose of divination or visions) will reward the seeker with important revelations. New projects begun on the second new moon of a month will be much more likely to succeed. Spellwork will be especially potent. Change will be extreme. Endings will be truly final, while initiations will be much more profound. For this reason, carefully consider the nature of the spells performed on the black moon, for whatever magick is done will be much more intense, and endings or beginnings will cause permanent alterations of life conditions. The Black Moon is a significant time for performing magick, including aspecting, using darker energies for banishing or personal transformation, and for involvement with the forces of chaos. We might begin to understand some of our complex emotions of anger, fear, jealousy or passion. Workings for justice are especially astute, so choose the wording of intentional communication very carefully. When using divination tools, be aware that your findings may contain harsh truths.

Other ceremonies appropriate for the black moon are saging and croning, entering into the phase of life that offers maturity, wisdom and an end to physical fertility. We may initiate a period of contemplation before taking action. The Black Moon is an optimal time to consider the cycle of life and death, birth and renewal, as death must occur to support life. We might meditate upon what is decaying within our own lives, what must be cast aside to begin anew. This is an opportunity to mentally and emotionally prepare for an important life transition such as moving house or changing our career. Or we might simply appreciate the quiet darkness of a moonless night as a time for rest, healing, and replenishment.

Plants which correspond with the black moon are those that have seeds on the inside, such as cucumbers, melons, and other cucurbits; nightshade and other soporific herbs, grapes and pale root crops such as turnips, leeks, onions, garlic and parsnips. A focus for plants is a seed underground, sprouting and emerging – also an appropriate metaphor for life situations. Animal totems include burrowing creatures such as the mole, vole, gopher, badger, fox, skunk, prairie dog, ferret, rabbit, underground dwelling snakes, and burrowing owls. Nocturnal predators have totemic value as well, such as the owl, bat, coyote, wolf, cat, nighthawk, whip-poor-will, and tree frog. The "Spinnner's Moon" aspect can be aligned with the spider.

Tools which are appropriate for a black moon ritual include clothing that is black, dark blue, or dark grey, and wall hangings, table cloths and altar coverings in the same hues; black and white candles, a scrying mirror or dark glass, a "dark" crystal which may be smoky quartz, onyx, or a crystal ball on a dark cloth, or a scrying bowl filled with liquid; other divinations tools such as Tarot cards, Runes or a pendulum; a plate for offerings of grapes, root vegetables, dark wheat or rye bread, a chalice or cup filled with deep red wine such as burgundy, or red grape juice, and incenses containing sage, camphor, cedar, or Nag Champa, "Purification" and /or "Queen of Night" incenses sold commercially. You may wish to use a feather for cleansing and smudging the sacred space, or you may wish to aspurge with water, and / or sprinkle with salt. Anoint yourself with oil while mindfully preparing for ritual.

New Moon or Night Goddesses:
Nyx, Diana, Kore, Persephone, Rhiannon, Rigatona, Nephthys, Devi, Ratri, Inanna, Hecate, Cerridwen, Hathor, Morrighu, Artemis, Juna, Sadarnuna, Techzistecatl, Nott.

New Moon or Night Gods:
Mani, Chandra, Sin, Konshu, Men, Erebos, Nox, Anubis.

Aspecting the "darker" forms of God and Goddess, or avataring them, may help us to fully understand those mysteries of chaos and creation. Many legends worldwide tell of the ultimate darkness that existed before the sun or stars were born, the blackness of night, like the inside of the womb. This darkness was formless, without any conception of up or down, material or physical structure. From this primordial darkness arose the stars, as light is birthed from darkness. From chaos came power and material from. The name of the Greek / Hellenic Goddess Nyx literally translates as "Not", or nothingness. Her name is also associated with night, the space between the stars. From her void, from chaos, was formed the heavenly bodies, the Earth, and all material things.

Aspecting the darker Gods and Goddesses can help with physical and mental transformation, with manifesting or bringing force into form, and with a final ending of a phase of life or an entire period of time or epoch. From the ending we may initiate a beginning of a new period of time which is significant to us personally or important to our family, co-workers, or covenors. However, this work can be rather frightening. The magick user may have the sensation of falling, of spinning, of being without anchor. They might experience fearfulness at the ending of a familiar, comfortable situation. Even an adept may feel blinded or emotionally unbalanced. Mysteries might seem overwhelming. It is best to ground and center, and use an image to tie you to the material plane, such as a photograph or statue, or holding a power object in your hand, and gazing at it to remind you of your physical surroundings. You might set an alarm clock for an hour, so that its shrill sound returns you to the material plane. Afterward, you might wish to speak to a trusted friend about your experiences.

The Black Moon is a perfect time to initiate a project, to start something brand new that has never been done before, to create a new invention. You may begin something that is wild innovative, or be gifted with an idea or concept that has never before been contemplated. Call upon the infinite darkness that births all new things, the dark mother of hyper-creation. Envision the night as she gives birth to the sky and earth. Use that energy for transformation, for conception, for bringing force into form.

As mentioned previously, the Black Moon is also an auspicious time for scrying, for divining the future, for learning truths about life situations, for understanding the interplay of relationships. That which is hidden or occluded is likely to be revealed. You may be rewarded with a new comprehension of an event, or enjoy a wonderful surprise. Information may be divulged that is a great relief to the seeker. You may have a brilliant idea, or find a new way to pursue a goal. This might be why the Black Moon is also called the "Finder's Moon". Conversely, those who perform divination on the Black Moon might be in for a "rude awakening", uncovering a painful but necessary truth. Those who discover some difficult life condition may use the energies of the second new moon to make informed decisions, to mourn, to accept, and to begin healing.

Caveat: As most advanced ceremonial magickians and witches understand, darker energies or "negative" powers – "negative" meaning to "negate" or to "nullify" – are not in and of themselves harmful. Those powers that might be considered hidden or dark may be very useful in knowing, in understanding, and thus removing disagreeable circumstances from our lives. We understand that there is death in life, life in death. Fear, anger, pain and other troublesome emotions might need to be faced. We may have to encounter our "shadow" selves, in order to discover sources of problems, conquer our own unpleasant feelings, address difficulties head on, and gain control of our destiny. Performing this type of magick may cause some short-term distress and emotional upheaval. We might need to end an unhealthy relationship, or cease a behavior that might be comfortable for us, but that ultimately causes long-term damage, such as smoking or overeating. We might wish to speak aloud, "This situation is bad for me. This situation is causing me pain and strife", while naming the condition which is troublesome. If it is a person, you might state "(Name) is causing me problems. Without harming (Name) or impairing them, I end my destructive interaction with (Name)."

Once truths have been revealed and decisions made, a ritual might be performed for banishing, cleansing, and creating necessary change in your personal life. The best time to work this type of magick is at true midnight, the exact hour between sundown and sunrise, which may be determined by looking up these times online or in an almanac, and calculating the hours of darkness during the Black Moon night. You might write down things you wish to remove from your life and burn the paper, sending prayers and words of power aloft with the smoke. You could bury something representational of a bad habit, such as a cigarette. Name and release baleful conditions. Spread your arms wide, envision stress and problems leaving you, dissipating in the air. As you perform your ritual, allow yourself to feel negative emotions, to embrace and understand them. Write about your feelings in a journal, draw images that might not be "pretty" but are effective, scream aloud, punch a pillow, name something such as a ceramic vase "anger" or "sorrow" and break it, release your aggression in a way that is ultimately harmless.

After these rites have been completed, we must consciously make the decision to move onward. The Black Moon is also a time of planning, regeneration, growth, resurrection, and renewal. Revisit the image of the seed germinating beneath the ground. Light a single white candle. Meditate on the stars beginning to glow within the darkness. Mindfully speak the changes that you wish to occur. Call upon help from guides, ancestors or personal Deity. After performing a black moon ceremony, you may wish to change the altar cloth or wall hanging to a lighter, brighter color, and ritually cleanse yourself by taking a hot bath with herbs or a long refreshing shower. Envision animals giving birth, or the burrowing creatures emerging from their underground nests. Contemplate what occurs after the changes you have made.

You may not see immediate, overnight changes in your life circumstances. Instead, you might experience a gradual sense of well-being, power, and strength. People who caused you troubles might now avoid you, or gain a wonderful new job 3,000 miles away. Unhealthy emotions or cravings will occur less frequently, then taper off, then cease altogether. The Black Moon is on July 30th, so begin considering and preparing now for this powerful astronomical event. Blessings.

MAGICAL TOOLS

by **Abby Willowroot**

There are lots of folks that will tell you need fancy magical tools, you do not. Everything you need to really practice magic is already within you, except, maybe a bit of knowledge, and that can be learned. If you want to set up an Altar with some magical tools it can be a fun and easy experience, as long as you use your imagination and creativity.

Magical Tools are fun and can help you to focus your energy for magical work. You can buy magical tools from stores, websites, and thrift stores, you can make magical tools from the things around you, a branch makes a fine magic wand, especially if you carve or decorate it yourself.

An Athame (magical knife) can be any knife that seems right to you, it can be as simple as a kitchen knife or letter opener. Many books advocate a double edged knife, but it isn't necessary. My own magical knife is an old kitchen knife from a thrift store, I bought it because it's wood handle was worn from years of use, and the energy was really wonderful, I have used it faithfully for many years and it only cost $1.49.

Altar items can be mainly found objects from Nature, shells, stones, dried grasses, wood pieces you carve. A Goddess or God representation can be a statue, or a symbolic item that feels like a

God or Goddess. Many people use a feminine and masculine feeling rock, others use bundles of twigs bound together with embroidery floss or cord.

Ancient pagans, shaman and witches made all their own ritual objects and magical tools. A pentacle for your Altar can be drawn on paper, carved in wood, painted or embroidered on cloth, made of recycled materials, or bought, all of these will work equally well for you.

A Chalice can be made of pottery, glass, metal, or wood, it's power is in it's consecration by you, not in its materials. Pagan shops online and off offer these quite reasonably, and thrift stores have a wide variety of good choices for a chalice, your kitchen cabinets may also have something that would work well as a Chalice. A bell can be as simple as a jingle bell from Christmas, or an old push bell from a thrift store, or a bell with a handle. Bowls for salt and water are easy, any tiny bowls will work well, you can decorate them with paint and symbols if you like.

Candlesticks are easy, thrift stores have tons of them and they are very inexpensive. Candles can also be purchased locally at many stores, including dollar stores. Incense can be used for smudging and should be put on a surface that won't get hot when it burns down for cones, and a simple wood incense holder works great for sticks, or stick incense can be put in a small bucket of sand.

Your Altar can be a simple wood board, stool, small table, shelf, or wood tray. Your Altar Cloth can be any piece of fabric that feels good to you, it can be new fabric, or a piece cut from an old, favorite, much loved, piece of clothing.

As a fun exercise in creativity and Green consciousness, why not try making a Recycled Altar? make it entirely recycled objects. If you are in a Coven or group, see if others want to make a Recycled Altar too. This Altar will help to make you more mindful of your choices and the Earth's needs.

I hope this has helped you to understand that the Magic is inside of You, not in the objects that you choose to use in your magical practices. True understanding of ritual, magick and spiritual practices takes time and practice. Everyday you use your skills and grow i knowledge brings you closer to connecting with your most magical and powerful self.

Go forth, Be Magical, and Enjoy!!!

http://www.spiralgoddess.com/AboutMagicalTools.html

GRANDMOTHER! GRANDMOTHER!

Grandmother! Grandmother!
Lady of Life and Death!
Mother of Midnight, You are She
Who gives us each our breath!

Grandmother! Grandmother!
Lady of Earth and Sky
Queen of the Witches, You are She
Who welcomes us when we die!

BIOGRAPHIES: PART THREE

by **Don Lewis**

GERALD B. GARDNER

Gerald Brosseau Gardner is widely considered the "Father of Modern Witchcraft" because of his efforts to publicize religious Witchcraft/Wicca in the 1940s and '50s.

Gerald Gardner was born in England on June 13, 1884 to a wealthy middle class family, but spent much of his life in Asia as a rubber planter and later as a civil servant.

In 1927 Gardner married Donna Rosedale. The marriage was a happy one that would last until Donna's death in 1960.

Gardner was an enthusiastic student of archeology, anthropology, and folklore, as well as historic weaponry.

In the 1930s Gardner and his wife returned to Britain and became involved in the British metaphysical community. In 1939 Gardner was initiated into Witchcraft by Dorothy Clutterbuck. Clutterbuck's coven may have been formed in the wake of Leland and Murray's writings, though some hold that it was founded by George Pickingill.

Gardner would later claim that the ritual system used by Clutterbuck was "fragmentary" and he expanded upon it liberally by drawing from other systems.

Gerald Gardner wrote a number of books including *Witchcraft Today* and *The Meaning of Witchcraft* which publicized the Wiccan religion. Gerald Gardner died in 1964 and is buried in Tunis, Tunisia.

GREY CAT

A native of Tennessee, Grey Cat is perhaps best known as the founder of the Northwind Tradition of Wicca.

Born in 1940, Lady Grey Cat was prominent member of the Pagan Press. Lady Grey Cat was the editor of The Crone Papers, a periodical exploring the wisdom and mysteries of the Elders. She is a two-time winner of the Silver Salamander Award for Excellence in pagan Journalism. Lady Grey Cat has served as Members' Advocate for the Ar n'Draiocht Fein Druid Fellowship as well as Second Officer and Publications Officer of the Covenant of the Goddess.

Lady Grey Cat is the Founder of the Northwind Tradition of Wicca. She is the author of *American Indian Ceremonies* (1990, with Medicine Hawk Wilburn) and *Deepening Witchcraft: Advancing Skills and Knowledge* (2002).

Lady Grey Cat died on March 30, 2012.

CAROLINE HIGH CORRELL

Orpheis Caroline High Correll claimed to come from a family of Hereditary Witches, although what her birth family actually believed or practiced will probably never be known with certainty. What is known is that the family followed some sort of unorthodox religious practice and that they maintained a secluded compound near the Indiana/Illinois border where Caroline High was born on September 4, 1860. In 1864 Caroline's family left the compound, but not the family, to live in nearby Danville, Illinois.

In 1876 the High family compound was destroyed by federal authorities in a Waco-style raid that left many of the family members and their supporters dead. In subsequent months many other family members were tried, imprisoned, or executed including some of Caroline's closest relatives. All her life Caroline maintained that the charges that led to the raid were false, and attributed them to racial and religious bigotry.

In 1879 Caroline founded a "new family" which became known as the Correllian Tradition, after her married name: Correll. Caroline claimed that this Tradition was built upon the beliefs of her birth family, but also incorporated new elements throughout her lifetime, as have her successors.

Caroline and her husband John Correll traveled widely and operated a number of businesses over the years. For many years they operated a carnival during the summer, and worked as "Art Lecturers" during the winter using what was then cutting edge technology that was as much an attraction as the art they exhibited.

Caroline worked as a psychic reader, and was an attraction at her own carnival. Caroline's eldest daughter, Dora High Correll, also was also an attraction at the carnival, performing on the high trapeze without a net. Dora's death in 1898 brought the carnival to an end. Her parent's marriage ended not long after.

Whatever the beliefs of Caroline's ancestors may have been, she became involved in European Witchcraft in the early 1900s. Caroline was a close friend of, and may have been related to, the artist Lydia Beckett.

Beckett introduced Caroline to Aradianism – an Americanized form of Italian Stregheria Witchcraft as filtered through Leland's Aradia. Many Aradian ideas have been central to Correllianism ever since.

Caroline continued to work as a psychic reader until her death. She also performed healings, and sold herbal remedies and charms of various kinds. In addition to Correllianism, which was a private familial tradition at the time, Caroline was also prominent in the Spiritualist movement and in the Universalist movement.

Orpheis Caroline High Correll died in 1939, and was succeeded as Head of the High-Correll family by her daughter Mable.

MABLE HIGH CORRRELL

Mable High Correll was born in 1899 AD, the third daughter and seventh child of Caroline High Correll and John Correll. Mable became Caroline's heir in 1928 AD, after both of her two elder sisters had died. Mable High Correll became Head of the Correllian Tradition in 1939 AD and led the Tradition until her death in February of 1966 AD.

Mable married several times, her second husband being the Jazz Age bootlegger Rae Baxter (ne Smart), and her third husband the Swedish nobleman Sixten Sandberg.

Mable was involved in a number of high profile media stories during her lifetime, perhaps most notably the notorious Harry Parker case.

Mable had two children: Ray Baxter who did not follow her in the Tradition, and LaVeda Lewis-Highcorrell (nee Baxter) who succeeded her as Head of Tradition, and who inaugurated the custom of hyphenating the High Correll name to other surnames, which would be followed by a number of her relatives.

In addition to Correllianism, Lady Mable was also prominently involved in the Spiritualist and Universalist movements, and studied other movements such as Theosophy and Rosicrucianism.

Although she left no writings, Lady Mable strongly influenced many Correllian ideas regarding existential matters such as reincarnation and the nature of the soul, the nature of physical existence and the planes, and time theory. Lady Mable also played a formative role in the creation of Correllian psychic development program, which would be further developed later.

IMHOTEP

Imhotep was a High Priest, a physician, and an architect. He is also said to have excelled in the magical arts.

Imhotep is most famous for designing Pharaoh Djoser's Step Pyramid, at Saqqara. Imhotep may also have been the first architect to use columns in building. Even without magic these innovations guarantee Imhotep a place in history.

As well as being the first great Witch in history, Imhotep is also history's first great physician.

After his death Imhotep was widely venerated, and eventually was considered a God in his own right. As a God Imhotep is a patron of architects, physicians, scribes, priests and witches, and civil servants.

SYBIL LEEK

Born on 22 February, 1917, Sybil Leek claimed descent from a family of Hereditary Witches. She was given an extensive metaphysical education by her father and grandmother, and was also much influenced by their wide circle of acquaintances which included Aleister Crowley.

During the 1950s and '60s Sybil Leek became a prominent spokesperson for Witchcraft in the media, giving many interviews in print, on radio and television.

Born in Britain, Sybil Leek lived in several countries during her lifetime, eventually settling in the United States in 1964 where she lived until her death in 1982.

During her lifetime Sybil Leek wrote more than sixty books on Wicca, Witchcraft, and metaphysics, and had a huge influence on the development of modern Wicca.

CHARLES LELAND

Charles Godfrey Leland is among the greatest scholars of the Pagan revival, and his works were seminal to the development of modern Wicca. He was the first author to write about Witchcraft with inside knowledge, being himself an initiate of Italian Stregheria. Leland was also among the first to use the term "Wicca," and the first to publish a version of the "Charge of the Goddess".

A prolific writer, Leland wrote books on everything from arts and crafts to religion and metaphysics. Leland studied and wrote about the beliefs of Gypsies, Native Americans, followers of Voodoo (at the crest of its U.S. popularity in Leland's day), and of course, Witches.

Charles Godfrey Leland was born in Philadelphia, Pennsylvania, on August 15, 1824. The Lelands were an ancient and wealthy family. They had settled in North America in 1636, but had been prominent in England long before this.

Leland was highly educated, graduating from Princeton, and studying at the universities of Munich and Heidelberg in Germany and the Sorbonne in France.

In 1856 Leland married Isabel Fisher. The marriage was very happy, and lasted for 45 years, until Isabel's death.

While in Europe, Leland took part in the Paris Revolution of 1848 AD. Back in the U.S. he later fought in the civil war as a union soldier. He was present at Gettysburg.

Leland worked extensively as a journalist and editor in the U.S. He also had a number of other careers; as a lawyer, as an oil prospector, but most notably as an author.

During his lifetime Leland published over fifty books on various subjects. He was best known to his contemporaries as the author of *Hans Breitmann's Ballads* a book of comic poetry written in the

style of German-American folk songs, published in 1872.
In 1879 Leland opened The Industrial Art School. Leland was an excellent artist and craftsman, with a strong interest in the folk arts which were then fashionable.

After his parents' death Leland had traveled extensively in Europe, living there for periods of time. Until the end of his life he would make frequent trips back and forth across the Atlantic.

In Europe Leland learned Shelta, the secret language of the Celtic tinkers. And in Europe he lived with and studied the Gypsies – the Romany people. Leland wrote extensively about the Gypsies. He learned to speak their language and studied their traditions, publishing a great deal of material on the subject. In 1888 Leland became the first president of the Gypsy-Lore Society, and in 1891 he published the book *Gypsy Sorcery and Folklore*.

During this same period Leland also became acquainted with another magical Tradition – the Witches of Italy. Around 1886 Leland met the Witch Maddalena Taluti, a Hereditary Italian Strega. Maddalena introduced Leland to the world of the Stregheria, sharing her knowledge of Italian Witch-lore and magic.

In the winter of 1888 Leland became initiated into Stregheria, called La Vecchia Religione or "The Old Religion." In subsequent years he would publish a great deal of what he learned in books such as *Etruscan-Roman Remains in Popular Tradition* (1892) and *Aradia, or the Gospel of the Witches* (1899).

Charles Godfrey Leland died on March 20, 1903. His ashes were shipped back to Philadelphia for burial.

M. REV. DONALD LEWIS

M. Rev. Donald Lewis-Highcorrell is First Priest and Paramount High Priest of the Correllian Tradition, and at Mabon of 2000 AD was acclaimed Chancellor of the Tradition as well.

On September 4, 2001 AD Rev. Don joined with Ed Hubbard and Lisa Tuit to found Witch School (http://www.WitchSchool.com), the world's largest school of metaphysics with students in all over the world.

Rev. Don is also the production head for Magick TV (http://www.Youtube.com/MagickTV) and hosted the series *"Living the Wiccan Life"* and *"The Interactive Grimoire"* as well as doing a daily question-and-answer Vlog.

In his role as Chancellor of the Tradition Rev. Don is responsible for the day-to-day running of the Tradition, and all matters affecting it. The Chancellor is empowered to act on behalf of the Tradition's leadership, both severally and as a whole, to ensure the smooth running of the Tradition.

As First Priest of the Tradition Rev. Don is responsible for co-ordination between Correllian Temples, and implementation of the Tradition's policies. The First Priest is also responsible for the Tradition's records and publications, and acts as chair of the Witan Council, which is composed of the chartered Heads of Correllian Temples.

As First Priest Rev. Don is also the Chief Priest of the Correll Mother Temple. Rev. Don is also the founding Temple Head and for many years Chief Priest of Chicago's Holy City Temple, Est. 1991 AD.

Rev. Don is the son of the Blv. LaVeda Lewis-Highcorrell, who headed the Correllian Tradition from 1966 – 1979 AD. Rev. Don is the head of the Mabelline branch of the High-Correll family. He has been an initiated Priest of the Correllian Tradition since 1976 AD, and a Third Degree High Priest since 1579 Pisces 1979 AD.

Rev. Don received his training from M. Rev. Krystel High-Correll. Rev. Don also received training from the Blv. Lady LaVeda, the Blv. Lady Gloria, and Lady Bitterwind, all Elders of the Correllian Tradition. In addition Rev. Don has studied both formally and informally with a variety of teachers from many Traditions.

Rev. Don is a co-founder and officer of the Pagan Interfaith Embassy, serving for several years as Pagan Interfaith Ambassador to the U.S. The Pagan Interfaith Embassy was founded in the wake of the Parliament of World's Religions held in Chicago in 1993 AD, with the intention of fostering greater communication and co-operation between Pagan groups and Traditions. The Pagan Interfaith Embassy has sponsored such events as the Chicago Pagan Leadership Conferences (in 1994 AD), Pagan Unity Night (1994 AD), and Pagan Expo 1997, 2000, and 2001 AD.

Rev. Don has an extensive background in media, and has edited several magazines over the years, including *The Round Table* magazine (1994 – 2003 AD) and the *Wheel Of Hekate* magazine (1987 – 1989 AD) and was art editor of *Psychic Chicago Magazine* (1990 – 1992 AD).

Rev. Don is well known both as an artist and as an author. Don's writing or artwork has appeared in numerous Pagan magazines, including *Circle Network News, Green Egg, ATC's Panegyria, Harvest, Covenant of the Goddess Newsletter,* Gerina Dunwich's *Golden Isis Magazine,* and Silver RavenWolf's *PWPA Newsletter.* In addition Rev. Don has produced several sets of Pagan-themed clip art, and together with MaryAnn Kay produced *Rev. Don's Omnibus of Incantations and Invocations for All Occasions,* a massive compendium of spells, chants, invocations and artwork.

However as an author Rev. Don is probably best known for the *Witch School* series of books, based upon the classes at Witch School, available from Llewellyn Press (http://www.Llewellyn.com)

Rev. Don is also well-known for having illustrated the beloved pamphlet "*The Other People*" available from Pathfinder Press.

Rev. Don's first published booklet was *The Five Mystic Secrets,* which he edited for his mother the Blv. LaVeda who published it under her pseudonym, Elizabeth Greenwood.

Rev. Don has made numerous TV and radio appearances, was co-host of Chicago's "*The Witching Hour*" radio program in the early '90s, and was a regular guest on the "*Telepathic Radio*" program.

Rev. Don is well known as a professional psychic. He has been a professional clairvoyant since 1984 AD, and is a well-known astrologer. But Rev. Don is best known as a Tarologist, and the designer of the *Tarot of Hekate (1982 AD)*.

Rev. Don was introduced to the Tarot by his mother, who gave him his first deck (T*he Tarot of the Hoi Polloi*) at age 11. The Blv. LaVeda acted as her son's booking agent during the early part of his psychic career.

In 1987 AD, Rev. Don was awarded the Silver Salamander Award for excellence in Pagan journalism, and is listed in the *Who's Who of the Magickal and Pagan Community*, published around the same time.

A prominent member of the Fellowship of Isis, Rev. Don has been involved Chicago's Isian Mystery Conferences since the first one in 1994 AD, and moderates an Isian email list: Fellowship-of-Isis@yahoogroups.com.

In the Fellowship of Isis Rev. Don holds the ranks of Priest of Isis (Sept. 2002 AD), Knight Commander in the Noble Order of Tara (Sept. 2001 AD), Adeptus (2000 AD), Druidic Companion in the Druid Clan of Dana (1999 AD) and heads the Iseum of *Isis Lady Of Lake Michigan*.

LUCIUS APULEIUS

Lucius Apuleius is the author of the *Metamorphoses of Lucius, or the Golden Ass* – a classic novel about magic and the only ancient Roman novel to survive intact to modern times. The novel is the story of a man, Lucius, who experiments with magic and is transformed into a donkey, ultimately regaining his own form by praying to the Goddess Isis.

Apuleius was a Berber, born in Madauros, North Africa, around 125 AD. His father was a wealthy magistrate. Apuleius studied oratory in Rome, and served as a lawyer in his youth. Later he enjoyed a career in politics in his native North Africa.

Apuleius was a Priestly initiate of several mystery religions, including the Mysteries of Isis and the Mysteries of Dionysus, as well as being a Temple Priest of Aesculapius.

Apuleius was considered to be an expert in magic. His reputation in magic was so great that when he married the wealthy widow Pudentilla, the mother of a friend from his school days, he was accused of using black magic to bewitch her. Put on trial, Apuleius made a passionate defense that is preserved today as *Apologia: A Discourse on Magic*. He was acquitted.

In addition to *The Golden Ass* Apuleius also wrote *On Plato and His Doctrine*, *The God of Socrates*, *On The Universe*, as well as many other works that have not survived. Lucius Apuleius died around 180 AD.

DOROTHY MORRISON

Dorothy Morrison is a Third Degree High Priestess of the Georgian Tradition of Wicca, and an award-winning author with thirteen books on magic and Witchcraft. Lady Dorothy also wrote the text for the Whimsical Tarot, illustrated by Mary Hanson-Roberts.

Born in Texas on May 6, 1955, Lady Dorothy currently lives in Virginia with her husband Mark. Through her mother Lady Dorothy is descended from both William the Conqueror of England and Robert the Bruce of Scotland.

Lady Dorothy was introduced to Witchcraft in 1973, becoming a member and later a High Priestess in the Georgian tradition. Lady Dorothy founded the Crystal Garden Coven in 1986. Today Lady Dorothy is studying with the RavenMyst Tradition and is currently a member of the Coven of the Raven.

Lady Dorothy's work has been published in many Pagan journals and magazines, including Circle Network News, SageWoman, and The Crone Chronicles. Lady Dorothy is also a member of the Pagan Poets Society.

Some of Dorothy Morrison's many books include: *Bud, Blossom & Leaf: The Magical Herb Gardener's Handbook* (2001): *Everyday Magic: Spells & Rituals for Modern Living* (2002): *In Praise of the Crone* (1999)

THE AROUSAL

She arose from the darkness
She arose from the night
She arose without form
She arose without sight
She arose at the first
She remains till the last
She arose, mighty Goddess
She arose!

She divided from the darkness
The Lord Who was the light
He arose from the Goddess
As the day rises from night
He appeared in fire and glory
He appeared in fire in might
He arose, mighty God
He arose!

She was as His mother
And He was as Her son
They were brother and sister
She was Moon, He was Sun
She was night, He was morning
As the dawn brought forth the light
They arose in the beginning
They arose!

Light revealed what dark concealed
What was unknown now became known
What was formless now took form
What had been unseen was shown
The world we are familiar with
Unfolded from them both
In seven planes that arose
That arose!

The lord of light fled from the darkness
For He knew that He was free
The dark mother sought the light out
For She created it to see
Light fled into every corner
She pursued in every space
Light and shadow showed the world that arose
That arose!

'To Rise You Must Fall' she learned
For if you want the light
You must too complete the journey
You must travel through the night
Only then can you achieve it
The Union which You seek
And the Great Work arose
It arose!

To reunite Spirit and Matter
Was not an easy task
'Twas a path of many lifetimes
'Twas a great deal to ask
A hundred billion Sparks of Life
She sent from Herself to Him
And our Souls they arose
They arose!

The One became the Nine
And the Nine became us all
Living many lifetimes
In many ports of call

Learning all the lessons
That the world of light can teach
In the pattern of existence that arose
That arose!

From the smallest to the largest
From sub-molecules to suns
All arise from the great Goddess
And to Her all return
As we struggle through the seven planes
Back to the place where we were born
We continually arise
We arise!

Now the blade is in the chalice
And the sun shines at midnight
And the light is one with darkness
And the day is one with night
For all things come together
In the heart of the wise
And the children of the Goddess now arise
We now arise!

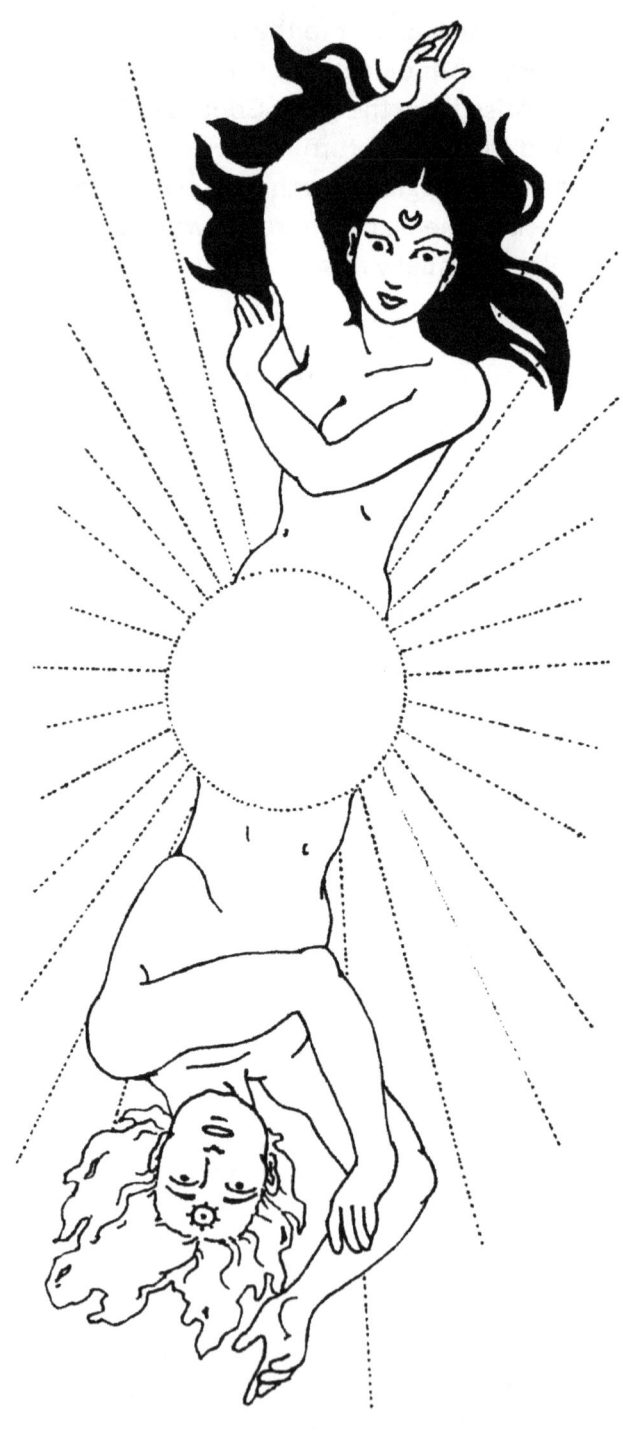

RITUAL AND RENEWAL

by **Abby Willowroot**

East, South, West, North

The Universe of the Goddess is infinite. The four main directions, East, South, West, & North are blessed and honored whenever Goddess folk begin a celebration, group ritual, or a small personal ritual of prayer or meditation. In honoring and greeting the directions, you are acknowledging and blessing your connection with all life, all time, and life everywhere.

Nature's passage through the yearly cycle is celebrated in connection with the four directions.

Each direction is represented by an element.

East ~ Spring ~ Air,
South ~ Summer ~ Fire,
West ~ Autumn ~ Water,
and North ~ Winter ~ Earth.

This cycle is called the "Wheel of the Year", or "Sacred Wheel".

Full Moon is a time for gathering together to celebrate the Goddess and move with the rhythms of the Earth and the Heavens. Each Full Moon for thousands of years Goddess folk have gathered to celebrate the passage of another Moon cycle.

In ancient times, sacred MoonTrees called Asheras were erected at the site of Moon rituals to mark them as sacred places dedicated to the Goddess. There were many Moon-dancers then, it was a time when the Goddess was widely honored. Later, Her sacred Temples were torn down and the Goddess was reviled as wicked by new religions that worshiped a single male god. A jealous God, whose religion did not tolerate other religions at all.

For many years, the number of people dancing the Goddess rituals were sometimes few. Today the numbers increase with each Full Moon. The Culture of the Goddess is re-awakening like a New Moon waxing. New Moon is another special time for gathering to celebrate and honor the powers of the Goddess. Dancers in the moonlight beat out the rhythm of Nature's pulse their feet. As they dance the Moon, they remember the traditions of the Goddess.

*You already know how to celebrate the cycles of the Moon.
Look within yourself and remember.*

The only people left on Earth today are the Winners.
If you are alive, it is because of your ancestors
who were winners in the battle for survival.
For hundreds of thousands of years, your ancestors won,
they battled challenges and adversity to survive, and Win.
You ... are a Winner,
the product of thousands of winners, never doubt that simple fact.
The losers' families are gone now ... they are extinct.

http://spiralgoddess.com/Page3.html

DUAL SABBAT RITUAL CYCLE

by **Don Lewis**

This ritual cycle was originally created for the Pagans Tonight Radio Network, and aired on the Pagan Pundit show. Because they were created to be done on-air as audio rituals that people joined via meditation/visualization, they do not include any physical directions, but they can easily be adapted to real-time performance.

The rituals have been edited somewhat from their original form, to make them more suitable for inclusion in the Common Book. Notably each ritual originally included a section opening and working with the Crystal Web which has been removed because it would have been excessively repetitive. The Crystal Web section is included as an independent ritual at the end of the cycle. Neither as originally broadcast or as they appear in this edited version have these rituals ever appeared in print before -although some passages may have, and of course certain ritual elements are universal.

Because the seasons are reversed in the Northern Vs the Southern Hemisphere, when the North is celebrating one Sabbat the South will be celebrating its polar opposite Sabbat. Thus when the Northern Hemisphere is celebrating Samhain the Southern Hemisphere will be celebrating Beltane. The Pagan Pundit had a global audience, and so these rituals were designed to celebrate both the Sabbat current in the Northern Hemisphere and the Sabbat current in the Southern Hemisphere in the same ritual. This was originally undertaken solely out of respect for the geographic diversity of the audience, but it quickly became apparent that approaching the Sabbats in this joint manner added an extra dimension to the understanding of both Sabbats as well as to the Wheel of the Year, whose equal but opposite nature was thrown into high relief.

I hope that you enjoy using these rituals as much I enjoyed composing them and the Pagans Tonight Ritual Team enjoyed enacting them!

The original rituals as they appeared live on air can be heard in the archives at http://www.PagansTonight.com

IMBOLC / LAMMAS RITUAL
OSTARA / MABPON RITUAL
BELTANE / SAMHAIN RITUAL
MIDSUMMER / YULE RITUAL
CRYSTAL WEB RITUAL

* * * * *

IMBOLC / LAMMAS RITUAL

PRIEST
PRIESTESS
PURSUIVANT
EAST
SOUTH
WEST
NORTH

PRIEST
Let us begin by clearing and releasing all excess energy. Find a comfortable position and release all of the tensions and anxieties of your day – let them flow out of you, like water flowing down through your arms, down through your legs, down and out through your hands and feet, returning to the universe to be re-used in other in ways. Now, let us begin!

PRIESTESS
Imagine with me a strong yellow white light sweeping counter-clockwise through this sacred space. A strong and cleansing light that sweeps out all negativity -imagine any negative or unfocused energy being carried away by this light. Behold – we do cleanse and purify this sacred space that nothing harmful may remain here and good alone may abide!

PRIEST
Imagine with me a strong blue white light sweeping clockwise through this sacred space. A strong and vibrant light that raises the vibration of all it comes in contact with. Imagine the vibration of the sacred space rising, becoming more spiritually charged. Behold, we do Bless and Charge this sacred space, directing its energy to the highest and strongest good!

PRIESTESS
Turn with me now to the East, where the Sun rises. Imagine with me a column of white light arising in the direction of the East, as we invoke the Quarter!

EAST
Hail unto you, O Beautiful Ones of the East!
Golden Powers of Air and Inspiration!
With Love and with respect I call you forth!
With Love and with respect I call forth your children
of Gemini, Libra, and Aquarius!
May we stand together in the Gate of the East!
We bid you Hail and Welcome!

PRIESTESS
Turn with me now to the South, where the noon Sun shines. Imagine with me a column of white light arising in the direction of the South, as we invoke the Quarter!

SOUTH
Hail unto you, O Beautiful Ones of the South!
Crimson Powers of Fire and Manifestation!
With Love and with respect I call you forth!
With Love and with respect I call forth your children
of Aries, Leo, and Sagittarius!
May we stand together in the Gate of the South!
We bid you Hail and Welcome!

PRIESTESS
Turn with me now to the West, where the Sun sets. Imagine with me a column of white light arising in the direction of the West, as we invoke the Quarter!

WEST
Hail unto you, O Beautiful Ones of the West!
Azure Powers of Water and of Emotion!
With Love and with respect I call you forth!
With Love and with respect I call forth your children
of Cancer, Scorpio, and Pisces!
May we stand together in the Gate of the West!
We bid you Hail and Welcome!

PRIESTESS
Turn with me now to the North, where the Night rules. Imagine with me a column of white light arising in the direction of the North, as we invoke the Quarter!

NORTH
Hail unto you, O Beautiful Ones of the North!
Verdant Powers of Earth and Integration!
With Love and with respect I call you forth!
With Love and with respect I call forth your children
of Taurus, Virgo, and Capricorn!
May we stand together in the Gate of the North!
We bid you Hail and Welcome!

PRIESTESS
Behold! The four powers dance and by their dance a circle is formed!

A circle of art to focus and to contain the powers we shall raise herein!

EAST
I am the Air!

SOUTH
I am the Fire!

WEST
I am the Water!

NORTH
I am the Earth!

ALL
I am the Air! I am the Fire! I am the Water! I am the Earth!
I am the Dawn! I am the Day! I am the Evening! I am the Night!
I am the Thought! I am the Act! I am Reaction! I am Integration!
We are the World! We are the Earth! We are Us All! We are the Circle!

PRIEST
Imagine now a circle of light surrounding you – circles of light surrounding us all – clear, bright white light forming a wall around us, moving upwards and downwards, over and under and all around us, a ball of light around each of us, around all of us – many balls of light and one ball of light, many circles and one circle – May our circle now be cast!

EAST
The circle is cast!

SOUTH
The circle is cast!

WEST
The circle is cast!

NORTH
The circle is cast!

ALL
The circle is cast!

PRIESTESS
We invoke you O Great Goddess! We invoke You as the Mother of the Bountiful Earth in the North, Who brings the rich harvests that we might live and thrive! We invoke You as the Lady of the Dawn in the South, Who promises an end to Winter and a return to verdant greenery to come! Holy Lady – Creator and Sustainer of all things – We bid You Hail and Welcome!

PRIEST
We invoke you O Great God! We invoke You as the Spirit of the Fields in the North, John Barleycorn, Who lays down His life that all may live! We invoke you as the Spirit of all green things in the South, Jack in the Green, awakening from Winter sleep to renew the Earth! Holy Lord -Master of the Wheel and of the Dance -We bid You hail and welcome!

PURSUIVANT
O Ancestors, Beloved Ones who have gone before – we invoke you and invite you to be with us this night! You who have prepared the way –walk with us and led us forward! Join with us in our circle tonight, the living and the spirits together – hand in hand! One Circle! One Family! One People! Beloved Ones, we bid you Hail and Welcome!

PRIEST
And behold – we come together this night to celebrate Lammas, the Festival of the First Fruits, the beginning of the harvest. Now the spirit of the grain sacrifices itself, that all may life. John Barleycorn shall die, his body baked in breads and cakes and brewed in beers. Likewise the vegetables and fruits shall fall, giving their lives that all might live. In this moment let us be mindful of their sacrifice, and let us remember that life and death are not opposites, but are part of one wheel – for both are equal, and neither can exist without the other!

PRIESTESS
And behold – we come together this night to celebrate Candlemas, the Festival of Light, the first stirring of spring. Now the Sun grows stronger and the spirit of life begins to move. Green Jack returns, his body in a hundred thousand buds and leaves and new shoots of grass. Likewise the Earth shall soon teem with baby birds and animals. In this moment let us be mindful that the future is fed upon the past, new life growing up in soil composed of the bodies of old life. Let us remember that life and death are not opposites, but are part of one wheel – for both are equal, and neither can exist without the other!

PURSUIVANT
The return of the light and the return of the harvest. Life waxes and is good. The mystery of opposites is resolved as we in the North celebrate the sacrifice which sustains us, and we in the South celebrate the promise of life to come!

PRIEST
Now, let us find ourselves a comfortable position and close our eyes.

PRIESTESS
Imagine with me that you are outside. Where do you find yourself? In a forest? In a meadow? In a desert? In a field? Is it day or night? Or dawn? Or twilight? Do the things that surround you make you feel good? Do they seem healthy? Take careful note of your surroundings, for they speak to the nature of your current spiritual state.

PURSUIVANT
Before you see a ball of white light – just a ball of white light floating in the air. See the light as clear and bright as you can. Reach out and take the ball. As you grasp it, the light will dissipate, and you will be left with a seed in your hands. What does the seed look like? Is it large or small? Smooth or wrinkled? How does it make you feel?

PRIESTESS
What do you want in your life at this time? Think about what you would like to see come into your life, or grow stronger within it. See this as clearly as you can, and focus it into the seed. See the seed glowing with white light again -but this time it is the light of your wish that is within it.

PURSUIVANT
Plant the seed in the ground before you. Is it easy to make a little hole for it? Or is it hard to dig that hole? Cover the seed over.

PRIEST
Divine Mother Goddess, Divine Father God, Beloved Ancestors, we pray that you will lend your aid to our undertaking – that you will help this seed and all that it contains to grow and flourish. Beloved ones – may it be so!

PRIESTESS
Now see a little shoot of green come up out of the ground where you planted your seed. This is your wish beginning to grow! See the shoot grow taller, rising up rapidly to become a sapling. Growing taller and thicker, becoming a fine young tree.

PRIEST
See the tree grow taller and thicker, becoming so wide you cannot embrace it, so tall you cannot see the top. Above you a thick canopy of branches covers all. And in those branches – In the branches of the tree are birds. And squirrels. And cats. And dogs. And horses. And bison. And whales. And people. Everything that exists is in the branches of the tree. Every kind of animal imaginable. Plants too -among the branches of the tree are wheat and rice and flowers and moss. All life is in the tree! Stars too shine among the branches, emitting a gentle yet profound light. Behold the panoply of life in all its majesty, unfolding in the branches of the tree. This is the world tree that stands before us. And our wishes are now within it. See your wish up there among the branches too – see it accomplished and already yours!

PURSUIVANT
Now imagine your heart Chakra. Imagine a ball of clear white light in your Heart Chakra. And from this ball of light, send forth a beam of light to the trunk of the World Tree. And in that beam of light send love and healing energy. Call the divine energy of the universe into yourself and let it flow through you, passing through your heart where it is focused as love and healing energy, and then through the beam and into the World Tree. See the World Tree absorbing more and more of this light – see it absorbing light until it shines forth in all directions like a sun. See it absorbing light until it can absorb no more.

PRIESTESS
Now see that light radiating out in all directions, even as you send in more. See the light suffusing everything that surrounds you, healing all it touches. Any aspect of your surroundings that was not happy and healthy when you started -it is healed now. Allow

the light to come into you as well. Let the light sweep over you, let it suffuse you. Feel its power. Feel the love of Goddess within it! Let it fill every part of you. See the light growing brighter and stronger and stronger and brighter!

PRIEST
Behold! May the world tree be whole and healed!
Behold! May we be whole and healed!
Behold! May the Light of Spirit heal all things!
Behold! So mote it be!

ALL
So Mote It Be!

PRIESTESS
Now release the light! And let the image fade. Return to our sacred space -renewed and healed.

PRIEST
And it is done. So Mote It Be!

ALL
So Mote It Be!

PRIESTESS
Now, let us give thanks!

PURSUIVANT
Beloved Ancestors, you who have gone before, we thank you for your presence and your aid this night and at all times – for we know that you are always with us! Beloved Ones, may the Blessing Be upon you now and always! So Mote It Be!

PRIEST
Beloved Father God, Lord of the Harvests of the North, Lord of the Reborn Sun of the South, Master of Life and its bounty in all forms, Lord of the Wheel of Life and Death and Life! We thank you for your presence and your aid this night and at all times! We know that you are always with us, for we dwell in one another's hearts!

Beloved Father God, may the Blessing Be upon you now and always! So Mote It Be!

PRIESTESS
Beloved Mother Goddess, Lady of the Earth's Bounty in the North, Lady of Earth's Promise in the South, Mistress of the Earth in all its cycles, Mother and Creator of all things! We thank you for your presence and your aid this night and at all times! We know that you are always with us, for we dwell in one another's hearts! Beloved Mother Goddess, may the Blessing Be upon you now and always! So Mote It Be!

PRIEST
Now turn with me to the North. See again the column of white light we erected there when we called the Quarter. As we give thanks, imagine that pillar of light sinking back down into the earth.

NORTH
Beloved Ones of the North, Verdant Powers of Earth and Integration, we thank you for your presence and your aid this night and at all times! Beloved Ones of the North, may the Blessing Be upon you now and always! So Mote It Be!

PRIEST
Now turn with me to the West. See again the column of white light we erected there when we called the Quarter. As we give thanks, imagine that pillar of light sinking back down into the earth.

WEST
Beautiful Ones of the West, Azure Powers of Water and of Emotion, we thank you for your presence and your aid this night and at all times! Beloved Ones of the West, may the Blessing Be upon you now and always! So Mote It Be!

PRIEST
Now turn with me to the South. See again the column of white light we erected there when we called the Quarter. As we give

thanks, imagine that pillar of light sinking back down into the earth.

SOUTH
Beautiful Ones of the South, Crimson Powers of Fire and Manifestation, we thank you for your presence and your aid this night and at all times! Beloved Ones of the South, may the Blessing Be upon you now and always! So Mote It Be!

PRIEST
Now turn with me to the East. See again the column of white light we erected there when we called the Quarter. As we give thanks, imagine that pillar of light sinking back down into the earth.

EAST
Beautiful Ones of the East, Golden Powers of Air and Inspiration, we thank you for your presence and your aid this night and at all times! Beloved Ones of the East, may the Blessing Be upon you now and always! So Mote It Be!

PRIESTESS
Imagine now again that circle of light we created when we began this ritual – a circle of clear bright white light all around us, and above us, and below us. See that circle as clearly and as brightly as you can. And now, allow that image to dissipate as we release the energy of the Circle – see it fade and grow smaller and fall away.

PURSUIVANT
As above – so below!
As the Universe – So the soul!
As without – so within!
May the Circle now be open!

PRIESTESS
May the circle now be open!

PRIESTESS
Let us come back to ourselves now. Settling back into our bodies.

Back into the here and now. On the count of three we are we began. One. Two. Three. Now let us take a moment to clear and release all excess energy.

OSTARA / MABON RITUAL

PRIEST
PRIESTESS
PURSUIVANT
EAST
SOUTH
WEST
NORTH
OSTARA
MABON

PRIEST
Let us begin by clearing and releasing all excess energy. Find a comfortable position and release all of the tensions and anxieties of your day – let them flow out of you, like water flowing down through your arms, down through your legs, down and out through your hands and feet, returning to the universe to be re-used in other in ways. Now, let us begin!

PRIESTESS
Imagine with me a strong yellow white light sweeping counter-clockwise through this sacred space. A strong and cleansing light that sweeps out all negativity – imagine any negative or unfocused energy being carried away by this light. Behold – we do cleanse and purify this sacred space that nothing harmful may remain here and good alone may abide!

PRIEST
Imagine with me a strong blue white light sweeping clockwise through this sacred space. A strong and vibrant light that raises the vibration of all it comes in contact with. Imagine the vibration of the sacred space rising, becoming more spiritually charged. Behold, we do Bless and Charge this sacred space, directing its energy to the highest and strongest good!

PRIESTESS
Now – Let us turn to the direction of the East. Imagine with me a column of white light arising in the direction of the East, as we invoke the Quarter!

EAST
Hail unto you, O Guardians of the Watchtowers of the East!
Powers of Air and Inspiration!
With Love and with respect I call you forth!
With Love and with respect I call you forth!
May we stand together in the Gate of the East!
May the Red Lady of the East Rejoice!
May the Golden Lord of the East open the way!
We bid you Hail and Welcome!

PRIESTESS
Now – Let us turn to the direction of the South. Imagine with me a column of white light arising in the direction of the South, as we invoke the Quarter!

SOUTH
Hail unto you, O Guardians of the Watchtowers of the South!
Powers of Fire and Manifestation!
With Love and with respect I call you forth!
May we stand together in the Gate of the South!
May the White Lady of the South Rejoice!
May the Red Lord of the South open the way!
We bid you Hail and Welcome!

PRIESTESS
Now – Let us turn to the direction of the West. Imagine with me a column of white light arising in the direction of the West, as we invoke the Quarter!

WEST
Hail unto you, O Guardians of the Watchtowers of the West!
Powers of Water and of Emotion!
With Love and with respect I call you forth!

May we stand together in the Gate of the West!
May the Grey Lady of the West Rejoice!
May the Blue Lord of the West open the way!
We bid you Hail and Welcome!

PRIESTESS
Now – Let us turn to the direction of the North. Imagine with me a column of white light arising in the direction of the North, as we invoke the Quarter!

NORTH
Hail unto you, O Guardians of the Watchtowers of the North!
Powers of Earth and Integration!
With Love and with respect I call you forth!
With Love and with respect I call you forth!
May we stand together in the Gate of the North!
May the Black Lady of the North Rejoice!
May the Green Lord of the North open the way!
We bid you Hail and Welcome!

EAST
I am Air! I arise!

SOUTH
I am Fire! I arise!

WEST
I am Water! I arise!

NORTH
I am Earth! I arise!

ALL
Air! Fire! Water! Earth! Arise and Rejoice!
Air! Fire! Water! Earth! Arise and Rejoice!
Air! Fire! Water! Earth! Arise and Rejoice!

PRIESTESS
Arise and Rejoice! The four powers dance and by their dance a circle is formed!
A circle of art to focus and to contain the powers we shall raise herein!

PRIEST
Imagine now a circle of light surrounding you – circles of light surrounding us all – clear, bright white light forming a wall around us, moving upwards and downwards, over and under and all around us, a ball of light around each of us, around all of us – many balls of light and one ball of light, many circles and one circle c May our circle now be cast!

EAST
The circle is cast!

SOUTH
The circle is cast!

WEST
The circle is cast!

NORTH
The circle is cast!

ALL
The circle is cast!

PRIESTESS
We invoke you O Goddess, in your name of Ostara – Lady of the Spring! Mistress of the Dawn! Your many colors herald the return of the Sun and you share them generously with the many flowers that shall emerge with Spring. Mistress of the Rainbow, and of all arts and forms of creation and self-expression – we bid you Hail and Welcome!

PRIEST
We invoke you O God, in your name of Mabon! Maponos, son of Modren! Gentle Lord of the Rising Sun, of Spring and New Beginnings! Lord of Love and Beauty, Passion and Creativity! Your Fire, reborn, only just begins to burn in this Holy Season, Yet we welcome the flame! We bid you Hail and Welcome!

PURSUIVANT
O Ancestors, Beloved Ones who have gone before – we invoke you and invite you to be with us this night! You who have prepared the way –walk with us and led us forward! Join with us in our circle tonight, the living and the spirits together – hand in hand! One Circle! One Family! One People! Beloved Ones, we bid you Hail and Welcome!

PRIEST
And behold -we come together tonight to celebrate in love the twin feasts of Ostara and Mabon! The time of equal day and night, when all is in balance and perfect alignment. So too are the two Sabbats in perfect alignment. In the Northern Hemisphere we gather to celebrate Ostara! In the Southern Hemisphere we gather to celebrate Mabon! One Sabbat celebrates Spring, the other Autumn, but each is an equinox. Thus they beautifully illustrate the unity of opposites which is at the center of existence.

Tonight we shall call upon the Goddess Ostara and the God Mabon, and ask their blessing upon us!

PURSUIVANT
Close your eyes and find a comfortable position. Imagine yourself watching the dawn. Be aware of your surroundings and remember them, for they represent your inner state at this time. The Sun is rising and a woman comes up next to you. This is Ostara, Goddess of the dawn. Have no preconceptions of what the Goddess looks like, but allow her to take whatever form is best for you at this moment.

OSTARA

I am Ostara, Lady of the East, Goddess of the Dawn and New Beginnings, Mistress of creativity and inspiration. With my coming the day awakes. All things begin with inspiration, just as the day begins with the dawn. What things do you desire to open in your life as you go forward? What do you desire the light of dawn to awaken for you?

I give you now a gift – a seed. Receive this seed from me. See the seed as clearly and strongly as you can. Is it a large seed? A small seed? Whatever its nature it is the perfect seed for you at this moment. See the seed glowing with beautiful golden white light. The light shines out in all directions, bright and clear and beautiful. Place the seed into your heart. Allow the light from the seed to expand throughout your chest, out into your arms and legs, until it fills you completely. This is the light of the dawn, the light of new beginnings and inspiration. Allow the light to move through you, opening all potential. And at the center of your chest where the seed is, see the seed begin to sprout and grow. Does it grow quickly? Slowly? Is the growth more prominent on one side than the other? Do you recognize the plant and if so, does it have meaning for you? As you go forward from this place the seed shall continue to grow within you, unlocking new potentials and opening new paths in your life.

PURSUIVANT

Now let the image of Ostara fade. See the sun climb higher in the sky, until it is directly overhead, and then begins to decline. Imagine yourself standing in a field at harvest time. There are workers in the field bringing in the harvest. Do the plants look healthy? Does the harvest look plentiful? The field represents the results of your own actions, so take note of and remember its condition. One of the harvest workers comes up to you. This is Mabon, lord of the harvest. Have no preconceptions of what the God looks like, but allow him to take whatever form is best for you at this moment.

MABON

I am Mabon son of Modren, lord of the harvests that feed and sustain the people, lord of justice and honor. lord of equal night and day. I live in the plants and lay down my own life that all may eat. Thus I make my sacrifice as we all in turn must do, that life may go forward. All actions have a consequence. Some lead to a rich harvest. Others lead to famine. Consider your own actions and whether they have led you to the place you wish to be.

I offer you a gift. This gift may take any form -— have no preconceptions about what it might be but allow it to take whatever form is best for you at this moment. Accept the gift from me. See the gift as clearly as you can. What is it? Is it large? Is it small? Does it seem familiar? Is the gift anything you recognize? This gift represents the harvest of your good acts -the good things you have done that now return to you through the miracle of the harvest. It will bring you luck and success in your undertakings. See the gift shining bright with blue white light. The blue white light shines out in all directions, strong and clear and beautiful. Place the gift into your heart. See the blue white light from the gift expanding to fill your heart. Allow the blue white light from the gift to expand throughout your chest, out into your arms and legs, until it fills you completely. This is the light of harvest, of creation and manifestation. Allow the light to move through you, helping bring your hopes and dreams to fruition and manifestation.

PURSUIVANT

Let the golden white light of Ostara and the blue white light of Mabon move within you. Thing about the new things you wish to create in your life as the year goes forward. Think about your actions in the last year and their results. Think about the things you wish to manifest through your actions as you go forward. Feel the energy of Ostara and the energy of Mabon suffusing you in every part. Now – feel the light of inspiration and the light of manifestation come into perfect balance within you!

Divine Mother Goddess, Divine Father God, Beloved Ancestors, help us to come into perfect balance in this moment! Open the way for us and help us to enjoy the reward of the good we do!

PRIESTESS
Now, let us give thanks!

PURSUIVANT
Beloved Ancestors, you who have gone before, we thank you for your presence and your aid this night and at all times – for we know that you are always with us! Beloved Ones, may the Blessing Be upon you now and always! So Mote It Be!

PRIEST
Beloved God, in your name of Mabon son of Modron, we thank you for your presence and your aid this night and at all times! We know that you are always with us, for we dwell in one another's hearts! Beloved Father God, may the Blessing Be upon you now and always! So Mote It Be!

PRIESTESS
Beloved Goddess, in your name of Ostara, we thank you for your presence and your aid this night and at all times! We know that you are always with us, for we dwell in one another's hearts! Beloved Mother Goddess, may the Blessing Be upon you now and always! So Mote It Be!

PRIESTESS
Now turn with me to the North. See again the column of white light we erected there when we called the Quarter. As we give thanks, imagine that pillar of light sinking back down into the earth.

NORTH
Beloved Ones of the North, Powers of Earth and Integration, we thank you for your presence and your aid this night and at all times! Black Lady of the North, Green Lord of the North, may the Blessing Be upon you now and always! So Mote It Be!

PRIESTESS
Now turn with me to the West. See again the column of white light we erected there when we called the Quarter. As we give thanks, imagine that pillar of light sinking back down into the earth.

WEST
Beloved Ones of the West, Powers of Water and of Emotion, we thank you for your presence and your aid this night and at all times! Grey Lady of the West, Blue Lord of the West, may the Blessing Be upon you now and always! So Mote It Be!

PRIESTESS
Now turn with me to the South. See again the column of white light we erected there when we called the Quarter. As we give thanks, imagine that pillar of light sinking back down into the earth.

SOUTH
Beloved Ones of the South, Powers of Fire and Manifestation, we thank you for your presence and your aid this night and at all times! White Lady of the South, Red Lord the South, may the Blessing Be upon you now and always! So Mote It Be!

PRIESTESS
Now turn with me to the East. See again the column of white light we erected there when we called the Quarter. As we give thanks, imagine that pillar of light sinking back down into the earth.

EAST
Beloved Ones of the East, Powers of Air and Inspiration, we thank you for your presence and your aid this night and at all times! Red Lady of the East , Golden Lord of the East, may the Blessing Be upon you now and always! So Mote It Be!

PRIESTESS
Imagine now again that circle of light we created when we began this ritual – a circle of clear bright white light all around us, and above us, and below us. See that circle as clearly and as brightly as

you can. And now, allow that image to dissipate as we release the energy of the Circle – see it fade and grow smaller and fall away.

NORTH
As above -so below!

WEST
As the Universe – So the soul!

SOUTH
As without – so within!

EAST
May the Circle now be open!

PRIESTESS
May the circle now be open!

PRIEST
Let us come back to ourselves now. Settling back into our bodies. Back into the here and now. On the count of three we are we began. One. Two. Three. Now let us take a moment to clear and release all excess energy.

BELTANE / SAMHAIN RITUAL

PRIEST
PRIESTESS
PURSUIVANT
EAST
SOUTH
WEST
NORTH

PRIEST
Let us begin by clearing and releasing all excess energy. Find a comfortable position and release all of the tensions and anxieties of your day – let them flow out of you, like water flowing down through your arms, down through your legs, down and out through your hands and feet, returning to the universe to be re-used in other in ways. Now, let us begin!

PRIESTESS
Imagine with me a strong yellow white light sweeping counter-clockwise through this sacred space. A strong and cleansing light that sweeps out all negativity -imagine any negative or unfocused energy being carried away by this light. Behold – we do cleanse and purify this sacred space that nothing harmful may remain here and good alone may abide!

PRIEST
Imagine with me a strong blue white light sweeping clockwise through this sacred space. A strong and vibrant light that raises the vibration of all it comes in contact with. Imagine the vibration of the sacred space rising, becoming more spiritually charged. Behold, we do Bless and Charge this sacred space, directing its energy to the highest and strongest good!

PRIESTESS
Imagine now a circle of light surrounding you – circles of light surrounding us all – clear, bright white light forming a wall around us, moving upwards and downwards, over and under and all around us, a ball of light around each of us, around all of us – many balls of light and one ball of light, many circles and one circle – May our circle now be cast!

PRIEST
Behold! I do cut apart a place between the realms of humankind and of the Mighty Ones! A Circle of Art, to focus and to contain the powers we shall raise herein!

ALL
The circle is cast!

PRIESTESS
Now – Let us turn to the direction of the East, lair of birds and butterflies and all that traverse the skies! Imagine with me a column of white light arising in the direction of the East, as we invoke the Quarter!

EAST
We call to You, Dawn-Red Phoenix of the East! Power of Air!
Swift Spirit of the Winds! Arise and join us!
Share with us Your powers of inspiration and delineation
That we may have clarity of mind and thought.
As we enact our holy ritual!
We bid You Hail and Welcome!

ALL
Hail and welcome!

PRIESTESS
Let us turn to the direction of the South, lair of snakes and dragons and salamanders! Imagine with me a column of white light arising in the direction of the South, as we invoke the Quarter!

SOUTH
We call to You, Noon-White Serpent of the South! Power of Fire!
Fierce Spirit of the Flames! Arise and join us!
Share with us Your powers of creativity and courage
That our actions may be confident and effective!
As we enact our holy ritual!
We bid You Hail and welcome!

ALL
Hail and welcome!

PRIESTESS
Let us turn to the direction of the West, lair of fish and water mammals and all who swim in the deep! Imagine with me a column of white light arising in the direction of the West, as we invoke the Quarter!

WEST
We call to You, Dusk-Gray Whale of the West! Power of Water!
Sweet Spirit of the Oceans! Arise and join us!
Share with us Your powers of love and empathy
That our emotions may be open and free-flowing!
As we enact our holy ritual!
We bid You Hail and Welcome!

ALL
Hail and welcome!

PRIESTESS
Let us turn to the direction of the North, lair of creatures great and small who live upon the land! Imagine with me a column of white light arising in the direction of the North, as we invoke the Quarter!

NORTH
We call to You, Midnight-Black Stag of the North! Power of Earth!
Wise Spirit of the Forests! Arise and join us!
Share with us Your powers of focus and integration

That we may be steady and well grounded
As we enact our holy ritual!
We bid You Hail and Welcome!

ALL
Hail and welcome!

PRIESTESS
We invoke you O Great Goddess! We invoke You in the South as the Lady of Life, arrayed with flowers and with light, Who makes the Earth to bring forth life and abundance of all kinds! We invoke You in the North as the Lady of Death, arrayed with the black night and the silver stars, Who transforms all things that new life may come when old life has faded! Holy Lady of Life and Death – With love and with respect, we do invoke You!

ALL
Hail and welcome!

PRIEST
We invoke you O Great God! We invoke You in the South as the Lord of Life, crowned with golden rays, the smiling Sun that warms the Earth and causes field and forest to thrive! We invoke You in the North as the Lord of Death, crowned with branching antlers, Lord of the gate between the Worlds and of all the cycles of Life! Holy Lord of Life and Death – With love and with respect, we do invoke You!

ALL
Hail and welcome!

PURSUIVANT
O Ancestors, Beloved Ones who have gone before – we invoke you and invite you to be with us this night! You who have prepared the way – walk with us and led us forward! Join with us in our circle tonight, the living and the spirits together – hand in hand! One Circle! One Family! One People! Beloved Ones, with love and with respect, we do invoke you!

ALL
Hail and welcome!

PRIEST
Behold, we come together this night to celebrate the Sabbat of Samhain.

PRIESTESS
Behold, we come together this night to celebrate the Sabbat of Beltane.

PRIEST
In the North, Samhain brings the end of the harvest, as the days grow shorter and world slips on toward Winter. Now the mirror of life turns inward, and we open our hearts to dreams and visions!

PRIESTESS
In the South Beltane brings the onset of the growing season, as the Sun's warm moves the Earth to ever greater expression of life and love! Now the mirror of life turns outward and we, like the Earth, blossom and grow!

PRIEST
Samhain is the Feast of Death. Beltane is the Feast of Life. Each is a gate of the year – One Yin, that carries us inward. One Yang, carrying us outward. These are the cycles of life!

PRIESTESS
It is even so in all things! That which goes out must come in. That which goes up must come down. That which lives must die. And that which dies must live again!

PRIEST
For all that rises at Beltane, dies at Samhain – but all that dies at Samhain, rises again at Beltane. Thus at Beltane we celebrate the union of the God with the Lady of Life, and their union brings fertility to the Earth. Yet at Samhain we celebrate the union of the

same God with the Lady of Death, and their union brings rejuvenation and eventual rebirth to the soul!

PRIESTESS
We too unite for a time with Life, and then must unite with Death, only in time to return to Life again. As the cycle of incarnation goes forward, we bring more and more of our Spiritual nature into this world, and in time there shall seem no more separation between the worlds, when this life can fully encapsulate the whole nature of our Spirit.

PRIEST
Find now a comfortable position. Relax, and allow all of the stresses and anxieties of your day pour away, running out of you like water, returning to the universe. Imagine yourself at the mouth of a cave. See the scene as clearly and vividly as you can. Feel the air, the ground beneath your feet. See the cave before you. Is the mouth of the cave large, or small? Does it seem inviting, or fearsome? As you look into the cave, is it night or day? Summer or winter? Step into the cave -walk into its darkness. At first you can see only the light entering through the mouth of the cave, beyond that all is blackness. Enter the blackness, and walk forward. In the distance, you can see a bit of light – firelight, it would seem. Walk toward the light.

As you near the light, your path becomes brighter. You enter a chamber within the cave, lit by a fire at its center. Hanging over the fire is a cauldron. How does this chamber seem to you? It is large or small? Cheerful or eerie? Is it a large fire that burns so brightly, or a small one? What does the cauldron look like? Is it a simple iron pot? Or is it intricately worked like the Gundestrop cauldron? How does it make you feel to look at it?

This is the womb of the Goddess, the cauldron of Life ... and Death.

You become aware of a woman now – the Goddess. She is near the cauldron, though you had not seen Her previously. What is she like? Is She the lovely Mother Goddess of Life? Or the Wizened

Crone Goddess of Death? Is She beautiful? Is She frightening? Does She seem welcoming? Or stern? Or indifferent?

Whatever the case, give Her greeting, and thank Her for the many blessings in Your life -for no matter what your condition, you have many blessings if you take the time to see them.

Now think about your life. Samhain and Beltane are gateways – one to increasing and one to releasing. They are different – yet they are the same in that each ushers in change. What is it in your life that you would like to see change? Either to increase or to release? Think about this and see it as clearly as you can. When you are very clear on what it is you desire, imagine a ball of light between your two hands, and place your desire for increase or release within it. Then throw this ball of light into the cauldron!

How does the cauldron react? Does it splash? Does it boil? Does it smoke? Does it spill over? Imagine your goal inside the cauldron, being transformed within it.

Now the Goddess will offer you a gift. It may appear as an object, or it may be a message, it may even be a knowing – or in some cases the gift may not become apparent to you until later. Whatever the gift is, accept it – whether it first appears to be or not, it is directly tied to your goal.

The Goddess now takes up a cup of some sort, and fills it with liquid from the cauldron. She hands you this cup. Imagine the cup suffused with bright white light, shining out in all directions.

O Holy Goddess – may this cup be blessed! May it be a token of the bond of love between us now and always!

Drink the liquid from the cup. How does it feel? Can you taste it? Is it warm or cold? Sweet, savory, or bitter? Drink it all, and feel its energy going into every part of your body.

How does the Goddess seem now? Has She changed or is She the same? Is the chamber the same as it was when you entered? Are you yourself the same?

Give thanks to the Goddess. Leave the chamber as you entered, and walk through the darkness back to the mouth of the cave. Step out of the cave into the open air. Is it day or night now? What do you see outside of the cave? Take a moment to savor the experience.

Now, return to yourself, and this -our ritual space. Again, release any excess energy.

PURSUIVANT
What are these things, and who do they serve? The initial scene outside of the cave represents how you feel about your life. The nature of the cave mouth represents how easy or hard it is for you to access your higher self. How you felt entering the cave represents how you feel about your own spiritual state, which is represented by the chamber within. The fire represents your connection to Deity, the Eternal Flame. The cauldron represents your own ability to manifest, or to receive from Deity. The way in which the Goddess presented Herself represents your interaction with Deity at this moment in your life. And any changes in these things during the visualization represent the affects of the working itself.

PRIESTESS
And was this the Goddess of Life or the Goddess of Death?

PURSUIVANT
The Goddess of Life is the Goddess of Death. The Goddess of Death is the Goddess of Life. When Yang has gone as far forward as it can, it must turn back and become Yin. When Yin has gone as far inward as it can, it must turn back and become Yang. Obverse and Reverse are they: Life and Death, God and Goddess, Light and Darkness -all is One.

PRIESTESS
So mote it be!

ALL
So mote it be!

PRIEST
Now, let us give thanks!

PURSUIVANT
Beloved Ancestors, You Who have gone before, Your wisdom and Your example guide us. We pray that You will be with us and aid us as we go forward, that we may call upon the strength and knowledge of the past, even as we build the future. We thank You for Your presence and Your aid this night, and at all times. May You Blessed be in all things. We offer You our love and our respect! May the Blessing Be upon you now and always! So Mote It Be!

ALL
So mote it be!

PRIESTESS
O Mighty Goddess, Lady of Life and Death, You Who are the Creator and Sustainer of the Universe, the very Soul of Existence – O Lady we do thank You for Your presence here tonight – Though we know that you are always with us, for we dwell in one another's hearts! Beloved Mother Goddess, may the Blessing Be upon you now and always! So Mote It Be!

ALL
So mote it be!

PRIEST
O Mighty God, Lord of Life and Death, You Who are the Lord of Cycles, of Time and Space, the very Vehicle of All Things – O Lady we do thank You for Your presence here tonight – Though we know that you are always with us, for we dwell in one another's hearts! Beloved Father God, may the Blessing Be upon you now and always! So Mote It Be!

ALL
So mote it be!

PRIESTESS
Now turn with me to the North. See again the column of white light we erected there when we called the Quarter. As we give thanks, imagine that pillar of light sinking back down into the earth.

NORTH
We thank You, Midnight-Black Stag of the North! Power of Earth!
We rejoice in the guidance and the aid You give us!
May the Blessing Be upon You now and always!
With love and with respect we bid You Hail and Farewell!

ALL
Hail and farewell!

PRIESTESS
Now turn with me to the West. See again the column of white light we erected there when we called the Quarter. As we give thanks, imagine that pillar of light sinking back down into the earth.

WEST
We thank You, Dusk-Gray Whale of the West! Power of Water!
We rejoice in the guidance and the aid You give us!
May the Blessing Be upon You now and always!
With love and with respect we bid You Hail and Farewell!

ALL
Hail and farewell!

PRIESTESS
Now turn with me to the South. See again the column of white light we erected there when we called the Quarter. As we give thanks, imagine that pillar of light sinking back down into the earth.

SOUTH
We thank You, Noon-White Serpent of the South! Power of Fire!
We rejoice in the guidance and the aid You give us!
May the Blessing Be upon You now and always!
With love and with respect we bid You Hail and Farewell!

ALL
Hail and farewell!

PRIESTESS
And finally turn with me to the East. See again the column of white light we erected there when we called the Quarter. As we give thanks, imagine that pillar of light sinking back down into the earth.

EAST
We thank You, Dawn-Red Phoenix of the East! Power of Air!
We rejoice in the guidance and the aid You give us!
May the Blessing Be upon You now and always!
With love and with respect we bid You Hail and Farewell!

ALL
Hail and farewell!

PRIESTESS
Imagine now again that circle of light we created when we began this ritual – a circle of clear bright white light all around us, and above us, and below us. See that circle as clearly and as brightly as you can. And now, allow that image to dissipate as we release the energy of the Circle – see it fade and grow smaller and fall away.

PURSUIVANT
As above – so below!
As the Universe – So the soul!
As without – so within!
May the Circle now be open!

PRIESTESS

May the circle now be open!

PRIEST

Let us come back to ourselves now. Settling back into our bodies. Back into the here and now. On the count of three we are we began. One. Two. Three. Now let us take a moment to clear and release all excess energy.

* * * * *

MIDSUMMER / YULE RITUAL

PRIEST
PRIESTESS
PURSUIVANT
EAST
SOUTH
WEST
NORTH
GAIA
OAK KING
HOLLY KING

PRIEST
Let us begin by clearing and releasing all excess energy. Find a comfortable position and release all of the tensions and anxieties of your day – let them flow out of you, like water flowing down through your arms, down through your legs, down and out through your hands and feet, returning to the universe to be re-used in other in ways. Now, let us begin!

PRIESTESS
Imagine with me a strong yellow white light sweeping counter-clockwise through this sacred space. A strong and cleansing light that sweeps out all negativity – imagine any negative or unfocused energy being carried away by this light. Behold – we do cleanse and purify this sacred space that nothing harmful may remain here and good alone may abide!

PRIEST
Imagine with me a strong blue white light sweeping clockwise through this sacred space. A strong and vibrant light that raises the vibration of all it comes in contact with. Imagine the vibration of the sacred space rising, becoming more spiritually charged. Behold, we do Bless and Charge this sacred space, directing its energy to the highest and strongest good!

PRIESTESS
Turn with me now to the direction of the East. Imagine with me a column of white light arising in the direction of the East, as we invoke the Eastern Guardian!

EAST
As inspiration is the beginning of all things, we call You first, O East!
For You are the power of Inspiration!
Yours is the Air! Yours is the Dawn! Yours is the Spring of the Year!
You begin the dance, and with Love we call you forth!
Dance with us O Beautiful One!
Power of Air and Imagination - We bid you Welcome!

ALL
Hail and Welcome!

PRIESTESS
Turn with me now to the direction of the South. Imagine with me a column of white light arising in the direction of the South, as we invoke the Southern Guardian!

SOUTH
As action is the manifestation of all things, we call You now, O South!
For You are the power of Action!
Yours is the Fire! Yours is the Day! Yours is the Summer of the Year!
You manifest the dance, and with Love we call you forth!
Dance with us O Beautiful One!
Power of Fire and Creation - We bid you Welcome!

ALL
Hail and Welcome!

PRIESTESS
Turn with me now to the direction of the West. Imagine with me a column of white light arising in the direction of the West, as we invoke the Western Guardian!

WEST
As emotion is experience of all things, we call You now, O West!
For You are the power of Emotion!
Yours is the Water! Yours is the Sunset! Yours is the Autumn of the Year!
You experience the dance, and with Love we call you forth!
Dance with us O Beautiful One!
Power of Water and Compassion - We bid you Welcome!

ALL
Hail and Welcome!

PRIESTESS
Turn with me now to the direction of the North. Imagine with me a column of white light arising in the direction of the North, as we invoke the Northern Guardian!

NORTH
As integration is the understanding of all things, we call You now, O North!
For You are the power of Integration!
Yours is the Earth! Yours is the Night! Yours is the Winter of the Year!
You understand the dance, and with Love we call you forth!
Dance with us O Beautiful One!
Power of Earth and Wisdom - We bid you Welcome!

ALL
Hail and Welcome!

PURSUIVANT
Behold! The four powers dance and by their dance a circle is formed!
A circle of art to focus and to contain the powers we shall raise herein!

PRIEST
Imagine now a circle of light surrounding you —circles of light surrounding us all —clear, bright white light forming a wall around us, moving upwards and downwards, over and under and all around us, a ball of light around each of us, around all of us —many balls of light and one ball of light, many circles and one circle —May our circle now be cast!

EAST
The circle is cast!

SOUTH
The circle is cast!

WEST
The circle is cast!

NORTH
The circle is cast!

ALL
The circle is cast!

PRIEST
We invoke you O Father God, Son, Brother, and Consort of the Goddess, you are the vehicle of creation! Lord of Light and Darkness, Lord of Time and Space, Lord of Life and Death, we call to You now! In all Your names and all Your forms, O God -we bid you Hail and Welcome!

ALL
Hail and Welcome!

HIGH PRIESTESS
We invoke you O Mother Goddess, You who are the source and sustenance of all creation! You who were before the first beginning and shall endure eternally, the Eternal Flame and Divine Spark of Life, we call to You now! In all Your names and all Your forms, O God -we bid you Hail and Welcome!

ALL
Hail and Welcome!

PURSUIVANT
O Ancestors, Beloved Ones who have gone before – we invoke you and invite you to be with us this night! You who have prepared the way –walk with us and led us forward! Join with us in our circle tonight, the living and the spirits together – hand in hand! One Circle! One Family! One People! Beloved Ones, we bid you Hail and Welcome!

ALL
Hail and Welcome!

PRIEST
We come together tonight to celebrate the blessed Solstice. For those of us in the North it is the Summer Solstice, while for those of us in the South it is the Winter Solstice. But while these two are opposites, one the longest day and one the longest night, yet they have this in common – each marks the furthest extent of their respective energy. The Summer Solstice marks the height of the Yang energy – the energy of action and movement. The Winter Solstice marks the height of the Yin energy –the energy of stillness and introspection. The former is ruled by the Oak King, Lord of Light and Life. The latter is ruled by the Holly King, Lord of Death and Dreams.

PRIESTESS
At Solstice the Oak and Holly Kings do battle, to see which of them shall reign as the Lady's consort. Light and Darkness meet in pitched combat, as the wheel of the year turns anew!

GAIA
I am Gaia, the Mother of all life. The green earth is my body and the stars of the sky are my adornments. All things come from me, and all things shall return to me, as surely as a river returns to the ocean. From my abundant love I created the universe and all

things in it. I am the Maiden, and in time I shall also be the Crone – for I resolve within myself the Oneness of all things.

OAK KING
I am the Oak King – Lord of the Sun! I am the warmth that gently dries the rain from the Earth: the Light that gilds the forest leaves with gold. I am the great Poet, the Lover, and from my magic harp comes the music of the heart. Young love belongs to me. I am the son of the Goddess, her brother and her lover. Born at Yule, I grow in strength until I wed the Goddess at Belteine, and reach the height of my power at Midsummer.

Thereafter I decline and die, only to be reborn again when Yule returns. I am the Lord of Light and Life. The Lord of love and beauty. Dance the dance of life with me.

HOLLY KING
I am the Holly King – Lord of Winter! I am the ancient Greenwood Lord. I rule the forest and all the creatures that dwell within it. I am crowned and bearded with verdant, twining greenery – and I sing with the voice of the stag! I am Pan! I am Cernunnos! I hold the Cauldron of Plenty and wield the Staff of Life and Death. I am the Lord of the Dance and – birth or death – none may refuse to dance with me! I am at the height of my power at Midwinter, when the night is longest and dreams of the Otherworld are deepest.

Thereafter I shall decline and die as the Oak King rises to displace me, and the Light returns to the world.

OAK KING
Lord of Midwinter – I challenge You!

HOLLY KING
Lord of Midsummer, I challenge You!

OAK KING
Let us contest! Let us fight for pride of place! One shall rule, and one decline! You or I – which will it be?

PRIESTESS

At Solstice the Oak and Holly Kings do battle, to see which of them shall reign as the Lady's consort. Light and Darkness meet in pitched combat, as the wheel of the year turns anew! Who shall win? Each in his turn. In the north the Holly King displaces the Oak King as the Longest day gives way to waning light. In the South the Oak King displaces the Holly King as the Longest Night gives way to the waxing light. The only constant between them is change ...

GAIA

I am the Crone, Lady of Winter, Mistress of Death and Regeneration. Once I wore the red dress of the Maiden, red as the Maiden's Moon-blood. Then I wore the white cloak of the Queen – white as the holy Moon. But now I wear the black veil of the Crone. The flowers have withered, for the King has died.

I am the Mother of Knowledge, the Poser of Riddles. I offer you now this paradox, upon which all life is based: When the fruit reaches perfection it falls from the tree: when power is at its height, then change must come ... Thus it ever is on the Solstice, when one King overcomes the other. Light gives way to darkness: darkness gives way to light: Light gives way to darkness again. Even as day follows night and night follows day, so the wheel of the year turns ever onward. For my wheel is never still, and the bright stars spin on forever.

PRIEST

All things must change. For we in the north the Longest Day marks the decline of the Light toward inevitable winter. Though the warmest days are yet to come – still the dye is cast. For we in the South the Longest Night marks the return of the Light, as the winter inevitable gives way to the Spring – even though the coldest days are yet to come. It is even so in life – whenever we think we have reached perfection, then we must change – we must move and grow, for nothing can be stagnant.

Consider now your own life. What in your life is ready for change? Consider those things that you desire to see change – that are outgrown and outmoded in your life. See them clearly in your mind — and release them Now!

ALL
So mote it be!

PRIESTESS
We will now bless the chalice.

Behold, in the name of the Goddess and the God, may this cup of love be Blessed. As we share it, may it be as a bond between us, a token of the love we bear for Them, and They for us, and we all for each other! So Mote it Be!"

ALL
So mote it be!

PRIESTESS
Imagine with me the chalice filling with light — with beautiful white light shining forth in all directions. See the light as clearly and as strongly as you can. Feel the energy in the light — feel the power of the blessing, the love of Goddess and God filling the cup.

Now bring the cup to your lips and drink from it. Imagine the liquid entering your body, and with it the clear, shining white light. Let the light come into you. Let it go to every part of you, filling you completely. Imagine the white light shining out from every part of you, and filling you with divine blessing. Whatever you need: love, strength, healing — let the blessing give this to you now, as it brings you into perfect alignment with your highest self.

ALL
So mote it be!

PRIESTESS
Let us now give thanks!

PURSUIVANT
Beloved Ancestors, you who have gone before, we thank you for your presence and your aid this night and at all times – for we know that you are always with us! Beloved Ones, may the Blessing Be upon you now and always! So Mote It Be!

PRIEST
Beloved Father God, in all Your names and all Your forms we thank you for your presence and your aid this night and at all times! We know that you are always with us, for we dwell in one another's hearts! Beloved Father God, may the Blessing Be upon you now and always! So Mote It Be!

PRIESTESS
Beloved Mother Goddess, in all Your names and all Your forms we thank you for your presence and your aid this night and at all times! We know that you are always with us, for we dwell in one another's hearts! Beloved Mother Goddess, may the Blessing Be upon you now and always! So Mote It Be!

PRIEST
Now turn with me to the North. See again the column of white light we erected there when we called the Quarter. As we give thanks, imagine that pillar of light sinking back down into the earth.

NORTH
Beloved Ones of the North, Powers of Earth and Integration, we thank you for your presence and your aid this night and at all times! Beloved Ones of the North, may the Blessing Be upon you now and always! So Mote It Be!

PRIEST
Now turn with me to the West. See again the column of white light we erected there when we called the Quarter. As we give thanks, imagine that pillar of light sinking back down into the earth.

WEST
Beloved Ones of the West, Powers of Water and of Emotion, we thank you for your presence and your aid this night and at all times! Beloved Ones of the West, may the Blessing Be upon you now and always! So Mote It Be!

PRIEST
Now turn with me to the South. See again the column of white light we erected there when we called the Quarter. As we give thanks, imagine that pillar of light sinking back down into the earth.

SOUTH
Beloved Ones of the South, Powers of Fire and Manifestation, we thank you for your presence and your aid this night and at all times! Beloved Ones of the South, may the Blessing Be upon you now and always! So Mote It Be!

PRIEST
Now turn with me to the East. See again the column of white light we erected there when we called the Quarter. As we give thanks, imagine that pillar of light sinking back down into the earth.

EAST
Beloved Ones of the East, Powers of Air and Inspiration, we thank you for your presence and your aid this night and at all times! Beloved Ones of the East, may the Blessing Be upon you now and always! So Mote It Be!

PRIESTESS
Imagine now again that circle of light we created when we began this ritual – a circle of clear bright white light all around us, and above us, and below us. See that circle as clearly and as brightly as you can. And now, allow that image to dissipate as we release the energy of the Circle – see it fade and grow smaller and fall away.

PRIEST
As above – so below!
As the Universe – So the soul!
As without – so within!
May the Circle now be open!

PRIESTESS
May the circle now be open!

PRIEST
Let us come back to ourselves now. Settling back into our bodies. Back into the here and now. On the count of three we are we began. One. Two. Three. Now let us take a moment to clear and release all excess energy.

CRYSTAL WEB RITUAL

PRIEST
PRIESTESS
PURSUIVANT
EAST
SOUTH
WEST
NORTH

PRIEST
Let us begin by clearing and releasing all excess energy. Find a comfortable position and release all of the tensions and anxieties of your day – let them flow out of you, like water flowing down through your arms, down through your legs, down and out through your hands and feet, returning to the universe to be re-used in other in ways. Now, let us begin!

PRIESTESS
Imagine with me a strong yellow white light sweeping counter-clockwise through this sacred space. A strong and cleansing light that sweeps out all negativity – imagine any negative or unfocused energy being carried away by this light. Behold – we do cleanse and purify this sacred space that nothing harmful may remain here and good alone may abide!

PRIEST
Imagine with me a strong blue white light sweeping clockwise through this sacred space. A strong and vibrant light that raises the vibration of all it comes in contact with. Imagine the vibration of the sacred space rising, becoming more spiritually charged. Behold, we do Bless and Charge this sacred space, directing its energy to the highest and strongest good!

PRIESTESS
Turn with me now to the Eastern Quadrant. Here all things begin! Imagine with me a column of white light arising in the direction of the East, as we invoke the Eastern Guardian!

EAST
We call to You, Golden Guardian of the East!
Adorned with Amber and Citrine and Topaz!
Power of Air and Imagination
Join us now and Bless us with Inspiration
As we go forward in this rite!
Beloved One! – We bid you Welcome!

ALL
Hail and Welcome!

PRIESTESS
Turn with me now to the Southern Quadrant. Here all things unfold! Imagine with me a column of white light arising in the direction of the South, as we invoke the Southern Guardian!

SOUTH
We call to You, Scarlet Guardian of the South!
Adorned with Carnelian and Garnet and Ruby!
Power of Fire and Manifestation
Join us now and Bless us with Passion
As we go forward in this rite!
Beloved One! – We bid you Welcome!

ALL
Hail and Welcome!

PRIESTESS
Turn with me now to the Western Quadrant. Here all things are experienced! Imagine with me a column of white light arising in the direction of the West, as we invoke the Western Guardian!

WEST
We call to You, Azure Guardian of the West!
Adorned with Turquoise and Lapis Lazuli and Sapphire!
Power of Water and Reaction
Join us now and Bless us with Compassion
As we go forward in this rite!
Beloved One! – We bid you Welcome!

ALL
Hail and Welcome!

PRIESTESS
Turn with me now to the Northern Quadrant. Here all things are reconciled! Imagine with me a column of white light arising in the direction of the North, as we invoke the Northern Guardian!

NORTH
We call to You, Vernal Guardian of the North!
Adorned with Peridot and Malachite and Emerald!
Power of Earth and Integration
Join us now and Bless us with Wisdom
As we go forward in this rite!
Beloved One! – We bid you Welcome!

ALL
Hail and Welcome!

EAST
I am the Golden One of the East! I am the Air!

SOUTH
I am the Red One of the South! I am the Fire!

WEST
I am the Red One of the West! I am the Water!

NORTH
I am the Green One of the North! I am the Earth!

ALL
We are the circle – who form the Circle
We are All – and All is One
We are a river – that flows forever
We dance the dance – that's never done!

PURSUIVANT
Behold! The four powers dance and by their dance a circle is formed!
A circle of art to focus and to contain the powers we shall raise herein!

PRIEST
Imagine now a circle of light surrounding you – circles of light surrounding us all – clear, bright white light forming a wall around us, moving upwards and downwards, over and under and all around us, a ball of light around each of us, around all of us – many balls of light and one ball of light, many circles and one circle – May our circle now be cast!

EAST
The circle is cast!

SOUTH
The circle is cast!

WEST
The circle is cast!

NORTH
The circle is cast!

ALL
The circle is cast!

HIGH PRIESTESS
We invoke you O Goddess, Spider Mother Who wove the web of creation! The stars light Your way as You traverse eternity! Ancient

and Eternal One, Queen of Witches all! Inspire us with love, even as You love all creation! Inspire us with wisdom, even as You wisely balance all existence! Guide and Aid us, O Mother! With love and with respect we bid you Hail and Welcome!

ALL
Hail and Welcome!

PRIEST
We invoke you O God, Lord of the Four Quarters of Being! You are the Rainbow Lord of the Seven Planes, the Vehicle of Existence! Ancient and Eternal One, Lord of Magic! Inspire us with courage, as You had the courage to fall into matter! Inspire us with joy, even as you delight in all existence! Guide us and Aid us, O Father! With love and with respect we bid you Hail and Welcome!

ALL
Hail and Welcome!

PURSUIVANT
We invoke You, O Ancestors, Beloved Ones in Spirit! You set the example and prepared the way! Ancient and Eternal Ones, Who have gone before! Inspire us with strength that we may continue the great work, even as You began it! Inspire us with persistence, that we may continue to tread the path You laid! Guide us and Aid us, O Father! With love and with respect we bid you Hail and Welcome!

ALL
Hail and Welcome!

PRIEST
We will now open the Crystal Web.

PRIESTESS
Let us find a comfortable position. Imagine with me the sleeping crystals in the Web. All over the world, hundreds, thousands of crystals buried in the Earth or otherwise linked into the Web, all

sleeping in their cubes of white light. Cubes of light which slowly spin clockwise around the crystals they encase.

Let us call into ourselves the energies of the universe. Imagine the energy of the universe coming into you – a beautiful, clear white light coming down into you through the crown of your head. A beautiful, clear white light, full of strength and joy and love; The light of Spirit; The Light of Being; The Light from which all things are made. Let that beautiful,

clear white light enter you and fill you. Let it go into every part of your body. Let it suffuse you. Let it move within you. Be one with the Light. Feel its power. Feel its strength. Feel its love.

Now imagine that light most strongly in your Heart Chakra. Feel the light growing stronger and brighter in your heart – stronger and brighter, brighter and stronger! See it shining out from your heart like a white sun within you!

PURSUIVANT
Now, from your heart send out a beam of white light to your Crystal Access Point. See that beam of light go out to your Access Point, no matter how close or far your Access Point may be – see the beam of light from your heart connect to the Access Point. See the light flow from your heart through the beam and into the cube of light surrounding your crystal. See the cube of light begin to glow with the white light from your heart – see the cube grow brighter, see it spin faster! Send more and more light into the cube! See it spin faster and faster! See the cube transform into a tetrahedron – a triangle of light spinning clockwise around your Access Crystal! The Access Point is now open!

Continue to send light from your heart into your Access Point. And in that light let us set our intent: it is our intent in this to aid and strengthen the Spirit of the Earth and all those who live upon the Earth, to send positive and healing energy to aid them to their highest good and best outcomes whatever these may be, to aid their highest selves in manifesting their highest purposes!

PRIESTESS
Divine Mother Goddess, Divine Father God, Beloved Ancestors, we pray that you will help us to send this energy in love and trust to aid and strengthen the Spirit of Earth. We pray that the Earth may have the healing it needs; that the changes which are unfolding shall take the most positive and peaceful form possible; if it be in accordance with the free will and highest purpose of all! Beloved Ones, may it be so!

PURSUIVANT
Now see the light spread out from your crystal, traveling along the lines of the Web to join with other crystals – see the light spreading through the whole of the Web, illuminating it across the globe – continue to send light from your heart into your Access Point, and from your Access Point throughout the Web! And may the Guardians of the Web anchor and direct this energy for the highest good of the Earth and all her people! By our will – So Mote It Be!

ALL
So Mote It Be!

PURSUIVANT
Now let the image fade from your mind – it will continue forward without our further attention.

PRIESTESS
Let us now give thanks!

PURSUIVANT
Beloved Ones in Spirit! You Who have gone before! We thank You for Your presence here this night! Ancient and Eternal Ones, Who have prepared the way for us! – we know that you are always with us, for we dwell in one another's hearts! Beloved Ancestors, may the Blessing Be upon you now and always! So Mote It Be!

PRIEST
Rainbow Lord of the Seven Planes! Vehicle of Existence! We thank You for Your presence here this night! Ancient and Eternal One,

Lord of Magic — we know that you are always with us, for we dwell in one another's hearts! Beloved Father God, may the Blessing Be upon you now and always! So Mote It Be!

PRIESTESS
Spider Mother! Weaver of the web of creation! We thank You for Your presence here this night! Ancient and Eternal One, Queen of Witches all — we know that you are always with us, for we dwell in one another's hearts! Beloved Mother Goddess, may the Blessing Be upon you now and always! So Mote It Be!

PRIEST
Now turn with me to the Northern Quadrant. See again the column of white light we erected there when we called the Quarter. As we give thanks, imagine that pillar of light sinking back down into the earth.

NORTH
Vernal One, Green and Glorious One one North, we thank you for your presence and your aid this night and at all times! Beloved Ones of the North, may the Blessing Be upon you now and always! So Mote It Be!

PRIEST
Now turn with me to the Western Quadrant. See again the column of white light we erected there when we called the Quarter. As we give thanks, imagine that pillar of light sinking back down into the earth.

WEST
Azure One, Blue and Beautiful One of the West, we thank you for your presence and your aid this night and at all times! Beloved Ones of the West, may the Blessing Be upon you now and always! So Mote It Be!

PRIEST
Now turn with me to the Southern Quadrant. See again the column of white light we erected there when we called the Quarter.

As we give thanks, imagine that pillar of light sinking back down into the earth.

SOUTH
Scarlet One, Red and Radiant One of the South, we thank you for your presence and your aid this night and at all times! Beloved Ones of the South, may the Blessing Be upon you now and always! So Mote It Be!

PRIEST
Now turn with me to the Eastern Quadrant. See again the column of white light we erected there when we called the Quarter. As we give thanks, imagine that pillar of light sinking back down into the earth.

EAST
Golden One, Yellow and illustrious One of the East, we thank you for your presence and your aid this night and at all times! Beloved Ones of the East, may the Blessing Be upon you now and always! So Mote It Be!

PRIESTESS
Imagine now again that circle of light we created when we began this ritual – a circle of clear bright white light all around us, and above us, and below us. See that circle as clearly and as brightly as you can. And now, allow that image to dissipate as we release the energy of the Circle -see it fade and grow smaller and fall away.

PRIEST
As above -so below!
As the Universe – So the soul!
As without – so within!
May the Circle now be open!

EAST
The circle is open!

SOUTH
The circle is open!

WEST
The circle is open!

NORTH
The circle is open!

ALL
The circle is open!

PRIESTESS
Let us come back to ourselves now. Settling back into our bodies. Back into the here and now. On the count of three we are we began. One. Two. Three. Now let us take a moment to clear and release all excess energy.

SAMHAIN IS NOT OVER YET!

by **A.C. Fisher Aldag**

More Harvest Holidays, Ancestor Rites, and New Year Celebrations

"Some Pagans celebrate Samhain on different days than October 31st to November first."

Many Wiccans, Pagans, Witches and other Earth Religious people celebrated Samhain or Halloween on Monday, October 31st. This is the midpoint between the Autumn Equinox and Winter Solstice. As most of us know, the word "Hallowe'en" is a contraction of "Hallowed Evening", and refers to the night before the new year as observed in many cultures. Witches sometimes call it Hallows, Hollantide or Hallowmas. Gerald Gardner simply called the holy day "November Eve". Nearly all of these sacred days honor the dead, mark the new year, and rejoice in the harvest. Catholics observe All Saints' Day as a way to pay homage to people who were beatified and All Souls' Day to pray for the souls of the departed. Welsh and Cornish people hold Nos Galan Gwaef (spelled various ways) which means the night before the first day of the new year, sometimes called "Merry Night" in English. People from the Baltic countries of Europe observed Velu Laiks which means "Time of Spirits". Voudoun adherents hosted the Fete Gede, Hindus celebrated the festival of lights called Diwali or Deepavali, Finnish people enjoyed Kekri. Others had their harvest holiday earlier: Jewish people celebrated Rosh Hashanah near the end of September and Yom Kippur in late October, while Asatrur observed the beginning of Winter Nights, called the Winter Finding, on October 14th. Yet other harvest and new year's holidays are still to come.

Some Pagans celebrate Samhain on different days than October 31st to November first. Like the neo-Pagan or Wiccan observance of the sabbat, these holy days are viewed as dividing the year into two halves, and mark the beginning of the "dark" portion of the year or beginning of the winter season. The holiday often begins at sunset. In some traditions, the festivities last for three days. Ancient people in the British Isles usually counted the day as beginning at sunset, and the number three was magickally important. Many modern Druids or Celtic Reconstructionists will hold their rites on Nov. 7th, which is the astrological date of Samhain. Some Pagans observe Samhain or New Year's Day on the first full moon of November, which this year falls on Nov. 10th. These dates reflect modern interpretations of ancient time-keeping systems as depicted on the Coligny Calendar, which aligns moon phases with the agricultural seasons, or as marked by the positioning of monuments such as Stonehenge (corrected for present times, after shifts in the Earth's orbit affected patterns of the stars), or as determined by present-day astronomy or astrology.

In some Witchcraft traditions, the Sabbats fall upon a date during which the Sun is in a certain degree of a specific astrological house. These astrological dates are more technical, calculated by an astrologer, and have the planetary layout and subsequent astrological influences to one's advantage.

Here is the astrological date chart for all the Sabbats:

> Samhain: Sun is at 15° Scorpio
>
> Yule: Sun is at 1° Capricorn
>
> Imbolc: Sun is at 15° Aquarius

Ostara: Sun is at 1° Aries

Beltaine: Sun is at 15° Taurus

Litha: Sun is at 1° Cancer

Lammas: Sun is at 15° Leo

Mabon: Sun is at 1° Libra

In the Celtic lands, Samhain is also called Samhein, La Fheille Samhuinn, La Samhne, Sauin, Oíche Shamhna, or Gam, most of which connote summer ending and the beginning of winter. These alternate spellings reflect various Celtic languages from place where the holiday was originally celebrated. In ancient Ireland the year was divided into "Raitheanna", quarters and cross quarters, headed by "Raithe", the beginning day of the quarter. These quarter days were used in the British Isles to divide the year for the purpose of paying rents, taxes and wages. The term Samhain may derive from the Irish language word Sámh, meaning peaceful or at ease, the implication being that nature was quieting down, agricultural activities were ending for the season, and that winter was coming. The word is also used in modern Irish as the word for November, the Irish word for Halloween being 'Oíche Shamhana', or 'November Night'. Perhaps Samhain means "the peaceful time is over"?

Historians have traced some Samhain lore to the 5th century B.C.E. Samhain is referred to several times in older Irish literature, including the stories of CuChullain and Fionn mac Cumhaill. Julius Caesar documented Celtic bonfire rites, including one held in late autumn. Pope Gregory the third set the date of the Roman Catholic festival of All Saints' Day as November 1st sometime between 731–741, but the Venerable Bede wrote that Nov. first had previously been used for this holy day since the beginning of the 700s. Originally held in May, it is believed that All Saints' Day might have been moved to coincide with the celebration of the Pagan's holiday, Samhain. In 835 Louis the Pious made the custom of celebrating All Saints' Day on November 1st official. A writer called James Bonewick journaled about Irish customs of the mid-1800s which had survived from ancient times, including bonfires, divination and feasting. Sir James George Frazer wrote about Samhain lore and traditions in *The Golden Bough*. He and Sir John Rhys may be responsible for some revivals of Halloween in Europe. Sir Walter Scott wrote about Hallowmas legends, including the ride of the "Night Hag" and alluding to the Wild Hunt, as well as performing a spell in her name, although the poem contains some Christian references:

> *On Hallowmas Eve, ere ye boune to rest,*
> *Ever beware that your couch be blest;*
> *Sign it with cross and sain it with bread,*
> *Sing the Ave and the Creed.*
> *For on Hallowmas Eve, the Night Hag shall ride*
> *And all her nine-fold sweeping on by Her side,*
> *Whether the wind sing lowly or loud,*
> *Stealing through moonshine or swathed in cloud.*
> *He that dare sit in St. Swithin's Chair,*
> *When the Night Hag wings the troubled air,*
> *Questions three, when he speaks the spell,*
> *He must ask and She must tell.*

On the various nights of Samhain, Druids, Witches and Pagans may participate in rituals, honor their ancestors, worship the Gods and partake of a feast to commemorate the harvest. These activities can also take place on Nov. 7th or the full moon. Samhain was considered to be outside of the calendar, a time when the boundaries between the material world and the unseen realms were able to be crossed. Several Halloween rites involve contacting the spirits or protecting oneself from their wrath. Pagan ceremonies may include divination to learn about the events of the coming year. Ritualized fortune-telling of old included "scrying" or "kenning" using the flames of a bonfire or candle, or gazing into a bowl of water or a dark mirror, and such natural forms of divination as observing the flights of birds and seeing images in the patterns of branches. Ancient methods of divination such as casting stones or bones, or using the peel of an apple to form letters or shapes, were performed, and sometimes, those with "the second sight" were invited to attend gatherings and offer their talents. Other rites of forseeing the future on Samhain include eating an apple while gazing into a mirror, roasting hazel nuts to see which way they move, or allowing an egg white to drip into water. These methods are included in this article from the "Order of Bards, Ovates and Druids" website, about the sacred day from a Druid perspective: http://goo.gl/msTQc6 ... this article also contains rituals, legends, lore and a couple of delightful ghost stories.

In *The Golden Bough*, Sir Frazer lists several older Samhain ceremonies, including, divination and offering food to ancestors or spirits. The "dumb supper" may be one such ritual, or it could be attributed to spiritualism, which enjoyed a revival during the Victorian era. The dumb supper was practiced in Appalachia by Scots-Irish immigrants as a rite of prognostication or communion with the departed, recorded by a folklorist in 1954. The table was to be set backward, with forks on the right. A plate of food was prepared for the dead loved one, or empty plates left to represent future marriage prospects. Both ceremonies required all participants to eat silently. Some scholars believe this rite was not originally part of the Celtic holiday. Others think it was equated with offerings left out of doors for ancestor spirits.

Numerous legends of Samhain center on ghosts, frightening old hags, monsters and the Gods of death, including the Wild Hunt riding to collect departed souls. The Cailleach Bheur is a fearsome blue-faced crone representing winter in Ireland, while the Mailte y Nos is the night-hag of Wales, who rides along with the wild hunters. Both of these incarnations may be associated with the Morrighan. (More information about these possible models for modern witches appear in this issue of Magickal Media.) Fairies and mystical beings were given offerings to appease them, lest they make mischief. Perhaps the legends of darkness, death, and fierce supernatural beings of Samhain can be traced to actual events common in Western Europe during ancient times in late autumn. This was typically the season to slaughter animals to provide enough food to last throughout the entire winter. It was also the deadline to harvest the crops, bring in the hay and straw, and gather wood from the forests before harsh rainy or snowy weather made it difficult to find sources of food or fuel. Other concerns included hunting and gathering enough medicinal herbs. Many of the older ceremonies focused on preserving and maintaining the food supply. In several cultures, Death is personified as a specter or fearful entity, and with good reason. Ill preparation for the season could have meant starvation or hypothermia. This may be why so many older rituals focus on placating spirits and appeasing the gods.

The custom of guising or guizing, wearing costumes, may have arisen as a way to disguise the wearer from spirits, or to mimic or honor the dead. Masks were worn, or faces blackened by fireplace ashes. Animal skins were worn in the rite of hoodening, which is described further in the articles about Cernunnos here on Magickal Media. These magio-religious traditions may be the precursor of our modern Halloween costume. Of course, costumes may also have been worn to disguise pranksters who soaped windows, upset outhouses, took carriages apart and engaged in other acts of "hooliganism". Modern Pagans may wear special costumes for the reason of personal transformation or to commune with other entities.

Many modern Druids host rituals to honor the Gods on the astronomical Samhain or the full moon of November. Some act out the union of the Dagda, the good God of Ireland, whose cauldron can heal wounded soldiers and provide a never-ending supply of victuals, and the Morrighan, the Goddess in her dark aspect of Crone. The Morrighan is also the Goddess of war, sexual pleasure, and death, and is sometimes viewed as the Lady of Witchcraft. Some Druids re-enact the story of the Goddess of springtime and love, Rhiannon, and her marriage to Arawn, the God of Death, which causes the surface worlds to experience winter. This legend is much like the Greek tale of Persephone and Hades, or the Roman legend of Kore and Pluto. Sometimes, an apple and pomegranate are used to represent life and death and ritually consumed. Others revere Cernunnos, the horned God of animals, the woodlands, sexuality and the Underworld. Hazel nuts symbolize the Stag Lord, and are ritually eaten to commune with him. Pagans may journey to the Otherworlds, meditate on the nature of life and death, and perform vision quests for personal enlightenment.

Hellenic or Roman Reconstructionists may act out the legends of ancient Greece or Rome, including the relationship of Persephone and Hades or Kore and Pluto, using the pomegranate fruit's seeds as a symbol of wisdom and mystery. Deities are thanked for their gifts of the harvest. Goddesses include Demeter, Pomona, Annona, and Ceres, and Gods include Dionysus, Vertumnus, Ammon,

Priappus, Sylvanus and Mars, who is a God of agriculture as well as war. Hecate is honored as the Goddess of Witchcraft and divination. The ancient Greeks and Romans did not experience such a profound change of season as did the Celtic lands; hence, Greek and Roman rites are more about gratitude for the harvest, honoring ancestors, and the acquisition of wisdom. Libations are given to deities, patrons and patronesses, and ancestors. Liber Pater, the God who grants his name to both "libation" and "patron", is the deity who represents fertility and wine in the Roman pantheon. His consort is Libera, the Goddess who also represents fecundity and alcoholic spirits. Their feast in ancient times was the occasion for wearing masks, singing funny songs, merrymaking, sexuality and sometimes mischief. A cornucopia may be used in these rites as a symbol of abundance. Some Roman reconstructionists celebrate a festival to honor the dead in mid-May, called "Lemuria".

Samhain was a traditional "fire festival", documented by various writers from the time of Julius Caesar. Bonfires were a common sight in the British Isles and America well into modern days. In the 1860s, one Scots Protestant clergyman despaired, "The practice of lighting bonfires prevails in this and the neighboring Highland Parishes." Mr. James Bonwick wrote, "In the Western Islands (of Ireland) the old superstition is dying very hard, and tradition is still well alive." In some locations, all of the hearth fires were extinguished and re-kindled from a common village bonfire. In other places, this ritual was performed on Yule, Beltain, or all of these holidays. Fire was used as a fertility symbol, to protect animals, to scare away harmful entities, and in some cases to light the way for friendly spirits. Burning rushes or torches were often paraded through town, or taken around the perimeters, or carried along the boundaries of a homestead. Turnips, or beets were hollowed out and filled with oil, or carved into skull-like faces and placed over a candle, to create a light to scare off baneful specters or welcome ancestors to the home. They may have been used to fetch a coal from the communal "need fire". This custom later evolved into the legend about "Jack of the lantern", or "Stingy Jack" a dead man forced to wander earth searching for an honest person. Irish immigrants brought the tradition to America, and soon found that pumpkins were much easier to carve into Jack O'Lanterns. The familiar orange gourd may have taken its name from "punkies", the gourds or turnips used as containers for fire in Somerset, England at Samhain. This tradition was observed in the Isle of Man and continued to the present day, as outlined in this article, below. Other Samhain rituals, customs and history can be found here: http://goo.gl/kWPdBL

In Britain, some Halloween and Samhain traditions were transferred to Guy Fawkes Night. Puritan colonists in the 17th and 18th centuries also celebrated this secular festival. In 1605, a man called Guido Fawkes plotted with other dissatisfied Catholics to blow up Protestant King James in London. They rented the cellars below the British Parliament and filled the area with barrels of gunpowder. Someone told authorities, and Fawkes was arrested on Nov. 5, tried and hanged. This act of terrorism was commemorated for many years by parading in the streets, singing, lighting fireworks, and burning straw effigies of Guy Fawkes, or possibly the Pope, depending on if revelers were Catholic or Protestant. These processions and ceremonial fires may harken back to Pagan rites were scarecrows and representations of a harvest God were carried through the streets of a village, then ritually burned. Guy Fawkes Night also included begging for coins and treats, which may be another precursor of trick-or-treating. Although largely forgotten in America, Guy Fawkes Night is still celebrated in some parts of Britain.

The modern Halloween holiday is celebrated nearly worldwide, including many of the same traditions as Americans enjoy, such as dressing in costume, wearing masks, partying, trick-or-treating and feasting. In many places, ancestors are honored, ghost stories are told, paranormal investigations ensue, divination is performed, and parades and dances are held. In the Magickal Media news feed many Halloween news stories from around the world can be found, from Russia, Argentina, India, Japan, Western Europe, the Philippines, Canada and America. Some ancient traditions have survived to the present day. Several are included, below:

Halloween / Samhain festivities in Edinburgh, Scotland in 2010 featured a huge parade and bonfires. A report with many photos can be seen here: http://goo.gl/JAahji ... a quote from this website:

> "It's the time of the year again where people around the world decorate their houses with jack o'lanterns (scary pumpkin face cut out), kids don scary masks and costumes 'trick-or-treating', and people having ghostly parties, visiting haunted attractions and watching horror films.
>
> "Halloween has its origins derived from the Gaelic harvest festival of Samhuin (pronounced "sow-en"). For Pagans, it is a time to honor their ancestors and loved ones who are deceased, a time to celebrate the cycle of life and also the end of the harvest season where Summer meets Winter.
>
> "In Edinburgh, the locals celebrate this festival by

> holding a parade every year. People would turn up in colorful costumes playing flutes, drums, carry torches and parade down the Royal Mile from Edinburgh Castle to the West Parliament Square near the St. Giles Cathedral. It is here that the festival takes on a more fiery approach with impressive fire displays while captivating the spectators with a theatric play of Summer versus Winter."

In China, the ethnic Qiang people celebrate New Year's Day in late autumn. This year's festival occurred on Oct. 27th in Beichuan County. A parade is held, and participants wear beautiful embroidered finery decorated with furs. A Shaman drums to lead holy rites, and the Qiang people dance in a sacred circle, singing traditional folk songs, while sacrifices are burned on an altar. More photos and the full article can be viewed here: http://goo.gl/kVfSHI ... a quote from this site:

> "The Qiang Ethnic Group is one of China's 55 ethnic minority groups. According to the Chinese lunar calendar, the first day of October represents New Year for the Qiang nationality (the date falls on October 27 this year). On this special day, the Qiang people often hold a sacrificial ceremony to celebrate the occasion.
>
> "Qiang people dance around the altar and yell, setting light to the branches of cypress trees which creates a thick plume of smoke which rises into the air. It is said that through the smoke, God can hear the voices of the Qiang People."

On the Isle of Man, traditional Celtic culture is still very much alive, having survived or been reconsturcted. This includes the celebration of the original new year's eve, or Hop-tu-Naa, which likely derives from Shogh ta'n Oie, meaning "this is the night" in Manx Gaelic. It is also called Sauin, which is pronounced pretty much the same as Samhain. The holiday, which takes place on Oct. 31st, pre-dated the modern Halloween, yet contains many similar customs, including a harvest fair or Mhelliah, costumed trick-or-treating and processions, carving turnip lanterns, and a witch figure whose name has been Anglicized to Jinny.

According to an article in the "Manx Independent" newspaper in October 2007, Jinny's real name was Joney Lowney. She was tried at Bishop's Court for witchcraft in 1715 and 1716. Her offense was hexing a grist mill. Joney was sentenced to 14 days' imprisonment, fined £3 and made to stand at the crossroads dressed in sackcloth.

Like other Celtic-based Samhain or Halloween holidays, on Hop-tu-Naa feasting is enjoyed and divination is practiced. In olden times, cakes called Soddag Valloo, which means "dumb cakes", were made from flour, eggs, salt and fireplace ashes by all female members of a family, and eaten in total silence by the unmarried women. They were expected to walk backward to their beds. While they slept, they would dream of a future spouse. This is reminiscent of the Dumb Supper practiced in the Appalachians. On the night of Hop-tu-Naa, ashes were smoothed out on the hearth before bedtime. If a footprint was found the next morning, it had special significance. A track pointing toward the door indicated that someone in the household would die, but if the footprint pointed inward, it indicated a birth.

While Manx children are trick-or-treating, they often carry the lit turnip lanterns and sing a traditional song, which contains lyrics about "Jinny the Witch" and proclaims, *"I met a witch cat, it grinned at me, and I ran away."* At the end of the song, the kids announce:

> *"If you are going to give us anything, give it us soon,*
> *Or we'll be away by the light of the moon.*
> *Hop-tu-naa, Trol-la-laa."*

Another version of the song goes:

> *"Shoh shenn oie Houiney, Hop-tu-naa,*
> *T'an eayst soilshean, Trol-la-laa"*
> In English:
> *"This is old Hollantide night, the moon shines bright".*

You can view an article about the modern-day Hop-tu-Naa festivities here: http://goo.gl/9xCOIX ... which includes a calendar of events that coincided with Halloween activities on the Isle of Man, including "a competition for the best home-made turnip lanterns". One commentator added: "Mhelliah fairs are held traditionally at the end of summer or harvest time at which all produce grownmade is sold to the highest bidder in auction fashion. Dating back over a century, a mhelliah is thought to have originated in Celtic countries and is still a popular social occasion on the Isle of Man where they are held traditionally in the September / October of each year."

The BBC website, which has many photos, offers a more detailed explanation of the Hop-tu-Naa celebration's history and customs ... http://goo.gl/8ilNuQ

We hope you enjoyed reading about these various Samhain customs, history and traditions, and that you continue to celebrate a very blessed Holy Day and happy New Year... at least until November 7th!

OUROBOUROS

Winged Lord of the Sky
Scaled Lord of the Flame
Swimming Lord of the Deep
Horned Lord of the Wood

> Sun above our heads we call
> Earth below our feet as well
> Ourobouros encircles all
> The Dragon of the Universe

Hero fighting the good fight
Lover loving loyal and true
King who leads us wisely forward
Sorcerer who shapes and changes

> Sun above our heads we call
> Earth below our feet as well
> Ourobouros encircles all
> The Dragon of the Universe

FLOWER WATER

by Don Lewis

Begin with one gallon of water.

Cleanse and bless the water. Use your hand to make three counter-clockwise circles over the water, and imagine the water filling with a beautiful yellow white light. Say something like "I exorcise you, sending out from you any impurity that may lie within!" and imagine any negative energy rushing out of the water, like little bits of darkness or some similar image.

Now charge the water. Use your hand to make three clockwise circles over the water, and imagine the water filling with a beautiful blue white light. Say something like "I do bless and charge you to my purpose" and focus on the vibration of the water raising - imagine it glowing brighter and brighter with the blue white light, and concentrate on attuning it to your purpose (that is, the creation of water for blessing and cleansing).

Now, to the gallon of water add once fluid ounce each of the following oils. You can add more or less than one ounce if you wish, according to taste, so that your mixture becomes unique.

> Bergamot
> Orange or Neroli (which is a kind of orange)
> Lemon
> Rose
> Lavender
> Jasmine
> Cinnamon
> Clove
> Rosemary

Mix the oils gently into the water.

You can also, if you like, use the actual plants rather than or together with the essential oils -for example a sprig of rosemary, dried rose petals, grated lemon or orange rind. But if you do this then instead of a gallon of water you should use equal parts of water and vodka, or distilled alcohol, so that the plant material will not go bad as quickly as it will otherwise.

Now charge your Flower Water. Place your hands above or around the container and flood it with white light. Focus as much light into the bowl as you can, while concentrating on what you want the water to do -that is, to cleanse and purify. Make an incantation to seal your intent. You might say something like:

"I charge you, O water, to be an agent of purification, cleansing all you come into contact with of any negativity it may contain," or words to this effect.

Now place your water into one or more bottles and seal tightly until use.

To use as a liquid: Prepare a bowl of plain water and cleanse and bless as above. Pour as much Flower Water as desired into the bowl of plain water. Add floater candles. As you light the floaters, repeat the incantation you used to charge the Flower Water, or something similar to it, and visualize the water filled with light. Asperse each person as they enter the ritual space, or allow them to asperse themselves.

One can also place the water in spray bottles to be used as a spray.

WASSAILING THE TREES

by A.C. Fisher Aldag

An older tradition, enacted around the British Isles during the days between the Winter Solstice and mid-January, is Wassailing the Trees. This entails a procession into the apple orchards with a bucket of cider and some toasted bread, soaking the bread with the cider, and leaving it in the branches or at the bases of the trees. Participants propose toasts to the health of the trees and offer blessings. A King and Queen may be selected to make the libations. Songs are sung, dances are enjoyed and prayers or incantations are recited as this ritual is performed. Mummer's plays and games may be included in the ritual, as well as firing guns into the air and/or banging on pots and pans to frighten away evil spirits. And of course, a bowl of hot apple cider, or Wassail, is enjoyed.

While Wassailing the Trees may have originally been performed at the Winter Solstice, it is now primarily associated with Christmas, New Year's Eve, or "Twelfth Night", also called the Epiphany on the Christian calendar. This is the day that Christmas festivities come to an end. Some celebrate the holiday around January 17th, which was Twelfth Night on the old Julian calendar. The earliest known reference to Wassailing in literature dates to the sixteenth century, although some scholars can trace it to the 1400s, and others believe it may hearken back to Anglo-Saxon Pagan times. Most participants agree that the custom's purpose is to honor the trees and to increase their fertility, leading to a healthy, abundant apple crop in the fall.

The word "Wassail" likely comes from the Middle English "Waes Hail" which means "To your health", which probably comes from the old Norse "Wes Hale", literally to be "hale" or healthy. The Wassail songs we enjoy at Christmas or Yule, including "Here We

Come a-Wassailing" and "Wassail all over the Town" are now associated with singing carols from door to door, yet may derive from the tree blessing rites. The "Twelve Lords a-Leaping" in the "Twelve Days of Christmas" song may refer to the Morris dancing that often accompanies the Wassail rituals. Another custom includes going from door to door either carrying a bowl of hot cider mixed with spices and wine, or singing at each home and being invited indoors for a cup of the drink. Feasting is often held after the ceremony.

The Wassail Song:

Wassail! Wassail! All over the town,
Our toast it is white and our ale it is brown;
Our bowl it is made of the white maple tree;
With the wassailing bowl, we'll drink to thee.

This song dates back to the Middle Ages in Gloucestershire, England.

Historian A. H. Bullen writes:

> "This custom was kept up till the end of the last century. Brand relates that in 1790 a Cornish man informed him it was the custom for the Devonshire people on the eve of Twelfth Day to go after supper into the orchard with a large milk-pan full of cyder with roasted apples in it. Each person took what was called a clayen cup, i.e. an earthenware cup full of cyder, and standing under each of the more fruitful trees, sung —
>
>> *"Health to thee, good apple-tree,*
>> *Well to bear, pocket-fulls, hat-fulls,*
>> *Peck-fulls, bushel-bag-fulls."*
>
> "After drinking part of the contents of the cup, he threw the rest, with the fragments of the roasted apples, at the trees, amid the shouting of the company. Another song sung on such occasions was:

> "Here's to thee, old apple-tree,
> Whence thou may'st bud, and whence thou may'st blow,
> And whence thou may'st bear apples enow
> Hats full! caps full!
> Bushel-bushel-sacks full,
> And my pockets full, too, huzza!"

"It is supposed that the custom was a relic of the sacrifice to Pomona [the Roman Goddess of Fruits]."

Henry David Thoreau also cited Brand's *Popular Antiquities* in his essay *Wild Apples: The History of the Apple Tree* in 1862. He wrote that young men engaged in the practice of "Apple Howling" on New Year's Eve in some English counties, which included blowing horns, rapping the tree trunks with sticks, and chanting:

> "Stand fast, root! Bear well, top!
> Pray God send us a good howling crop:
> Every twig, apples big;
> Every bough, apples enow!
> "WASSAIL the trees, that they may bear
> You many a plum and many a pear:
> For more or less fruits they will bring,
> As you do give them wassailing."

The tradition of wassailing is offered on this blog, with a video ...
http://goo.gl/XWHZDk

A wassail celebration with a photo – this one includes lanterns ...
http://goo.gl/QhBqP8

Wassail Recipe:

Alcoholic—

- One gallon cider. Twist open the cap 1 turn, allow to set for a week to get "hardened".
- One standard bottle of a sweet red wine
- One "tea bag" of muslin, filled with a pinch of whole cloves, ½ teaspoon of ground nutmeg, and One tablespoon of whole cinnamon, crushed

- One teaspoon ginger
- Three cider apples, cored, cut into slices
- One orange and one lemon, cut in half, skin left on.
- Mix in an enamel or Teflon pot – no ferrous metals.
- Heat until steaming but not boiling, slowly, stirring often
- Ladle into a ceramic bowl
- Serve with lightly toasted wheat or rye bread

Non-alcohol –
- Do not allow the cider to harden; substitute red grape juice for wine

CORRELLIAN SOUL CREED

by **Rt. Rev. Stephanie Neal**

Introduction

The following creed holds the main tenants of the Correllian Tradition in part. Whereby M. Rev. Don Lewis Highcorrell expresses many tenant in his books, thus this creed is meant to give a snap shot of our beliefs within the Correllian Tradition.

> We believe that everyone and everything are a perfect reflection of Deity. Everything is a timeless, ageless soul. Our soul is ours to explore and expand. Leaning on our own, Source-given understanding.
>
> Our soul travels to every place, every time, every being for every reason. It can be found in the smallest atom and the most distant galaxy.
>
> Our Deity is female, male and everything, all in an equal union; Goddess, God, and Universal Soul.
>
> We believe that you have the wisdom of the ages, thus you know how to instinctively walk your path to the radiant light.
>
> We believe everyone is home with Deity. That every human is equal, holding all races, genders, and sexual preferences in high esteem. We are souls expressing ourselves in many forms, within this eternal moment.
>
> We believe that Deity has many names some of their names are Mother, Father, Sister and Brother.
>
> We believe in peace and that love will eventually overrule greed and fear in every form.
>
> We believe Deity is multi-faceted which leads to and is the One Holy Source, which all things are part. Every living thing is eternal and loved by Deity. The soul returns again and

again, becoming more evolved and compassionate to all, for all.

We believe in unity and harmony.

We believe in harming none. Our souls pray that all be found with an open mind and open heart for everyone's perspective.

Correllianism is a life-affirming way to live. Not the only way, a way to learn about our soul family and our many lives. Deity is bigger than any single doctrine and cannot be contained inside one perspective, nor described fully by any one person, book, or one experience. Yet Source is fully capable of reaching and teaching every living thing.

We believe everything lives and is part of our Universal soul. We believe that every human being is equal and should be given every protection, opportunity, and privilege under the stars.

We believe that every human has the right to live a bright, expressive life.

We believe we have lived forever. With no beginning or end. Only our earthly bodies, transition.

We embrace the notion that all beings have the capacity for many purposes, an aware consciousness, and a fully developed soul.

We believe in blessing others, while fully expressing our own sacred voice. Free will belongs to us; with every decision we make, we move closer to our own soul path, and that our peace and joy are found within. We learn and evolve through life's storms and sunny days equally.

All humans have the right to live in happiness, freedom, and love; suffering no harm at the hands of anyone.

We believe that animals are to be respected and protected from isolation and pain.

We encourage harmony among all nations; all have the right to live a free, peaceful existence.

We believe in protecting and sustaining water, air, the Earth and plant life.

All of nature and science is a perfect reflection and condition of our soul.

All things are one thing. A single thing consists of everything. All things and us are the One.

We are part of Source. We are inside Source and Source is inside us.

Mother Goddess and Father God are one with us.

It took millions of years to form us and millions more for our continued evolution. Every soul is lovingly fashioned by Deity as we create our future. We are in complete partnership with Deity while ever becoming and learning as we live these lives together. We believe together we can change our world.

And so it is.

THE SUN SHALL RISE

The Sun shall rise, the Sun shall set
The Moon shall wax and wane
For even as the Tide goes out
It must come in again

The Sun shall rise, the Sun shall set
The Moon shall wax and wane
Though Winter is upon us now
Summer shall come again!*

The Sun shall rise, the Sun shall set
The Moon shall wax and wane
Though all things die you can be sure
They'll be reborn again!

(For the opposite season replace this line with:
Though Summer is upon us now
Winter shall come again!")

A COMMENTARY ON "A CORRELLIAN CREED"

by **Rev. Terry Power, HP**

We will start this commentary with a presentation of a core set of statements about what Correllians believe:

A Correllian Creed

We believe that Inner Truth is universal in Nature. It is expressed through many outward forms. Deity comes to each person in the way that is best for that person, and which is unique to him or her.

We believe that "the Gods" are human's ways of understanding and interacting with Deity. These many faces are equally true and equally valid. They are all attempts to understand the ultimate transcendent nature of Deity.

We believe in the providence of Deity; that all things happen according to the will of Deity, which is ultimately to the good.

We believe that as humans we have many levels to our being. These include the physical, emotional, and mental levels as well as the astral and soul levels.

We believe in reincarnation; that the soul is created from Deity and is never separate from Deity. The soul shares, on an inner level, the attributes of Deity, which include immortality, magic, and powers of the soul.

We believe in a living, spiritually sentient Universe, of which all galaxies, stars and planets are components. The Earth as one of these components is equally living and spiritually sentient and as such all systems and creatures on Earth are components.

> We believe that everything is in a state of constant and ultimately beneficial growth and evolution. This growth and evolution occurs to all of existence, be it the soul, the planet, or the Universe, all being a mirror of Divinity, which evolves and grows as well.
>
> We believe that the Wiccan Rede, "Do As You Will, But Harm None" is the highest moral statement. It is an effective pattern for a moral life.
>
> We believe that ultimate truth is beyond the understanding of humans. Therefore, it is natural for a person's belief and Deity should develop to reflect the individual's personal relationship with the Divine.
>
> We believe that all Pagan religions should acknowledge one another as kindred and stand together as equals. Our similarities as Pagans far outweigh our differences.

This creed is intended to serve as a basic statement of Correllian belief. It is open enough to allow for individual expression as described in the Rede.

It should serve as a good starting place for what we believe. Let's examine each statement in a bit more detail and discuss how they apply to our lives and in our ministries.

> We believe that Inner Truth is universal in Nature. It is expressed through many outward forms. Deity comes to each person in the way that is best for that person, and which is unique to him or her.
>
> We believe that "the Gods" are human's ways of understanding and interacting with Deity. These many faces are equally true and equally valid. They are all attempts to understand the ultimate transcendent nature of Deity.

The first two statements express the Universalist approach with which Correllians deal with all forms of Deity. To my mind, and in my ministry, these two statements call us to lay aside ideas of differences and to focus on the commonalities. This is true, not just among fellow Wiccans or Pagans, but among ALL religions.

If we truly believe these first two statements, we cannot continue the Christian-bashing, or the Muslim-bashing, or the any other kind of "-bashing." If we truly accept that all forms of Deity are equally valid, then we MUST set aside our prejudices and face all religions with equal respect. Only then, can we expect others to respect us. We should lead by example.

> *We believe in the providence of Deity; that all*
> *things happen according to the will of Deity,*
> *which is ultimately to the good.*

This statement, I admit, sounds a lot like the presumably mindless response to bad things happening as being "God's will ..." and all other similar platitudes. But when you take into account our Cosmology that expresses that we are here to experience and to learn, the whole idea of Divine Providence takes on an entirely new meaning.

Since we believe in reincarnation, another statement in this creed, we also believe that we must experience all aspects of existence in the material plane that we have. Bad things happen as a way to allow us to experience EVERYTHING about being human – yes, even the bad things. It is part of the learning process we will take to higher levels of existence.

When we consider that we each carry a spark of the Divine within us – that we are each a microcosm of Deity – we can see that we ARE following the will of the Divine in our very life. And we believe that it IS ultimately for the good.

This statement of Divine Providence also points us to a discussion of "Harm None ..." that will come later in this commentary.

> *We believe that as humans we have many levels*
> *to our being. These include the physical,*

> emotional, and mental levels as well as
> the astral and soul levels.
>
> We believe in reincarnation; that the soul is
> created from Deity and is never separate from
> Deity. The soul shares, on an inner level, the
> attributes of Deity, which include immortality,
> magic, and powers of the soul.

These two statements reflect our Correllian concepts of our place within the Universe. They are powerful statements, when we look at them closely. As discussed above, we carry a piece of the Divine within us. Because of this Spark, we share that Divine nature. We say all the time that we are witches; we are empowered; we create our own reality. These statements go straight to that concept. We really do create our own reality.

As we talk about the powers of the soul and how we create our own reality, we must realize that we are also the canvas on which we create. True magick is accomplished by living as if what we want to achieve and the energy that we are putting out is occurring right now and has already occurred.

Another point to remember in these statements is that the soul is created from Deity and is never separate from Deity. We spend so much time in our lives seeking to reconnect with something from which that we were never separated. It is amazing the number of people that feel this illusion of separateness, and yet the Divine is with us always. Whatever we do, we can never get away from the Divine and the Divine will never leave us. We may choose to ignore. We can choose to hide. But we are only hiding from ourselves. We are ALWAYS connected to the Divine. The illusion of separation is just that, an illusion.

> We believe in a living, spiritually sentient
> Universe, of which all galaxies, stars and planets
> are components. The Earth as one of these
> components is equally living and spiritually
> sentient and as such all systems and creatures on
> Earth are components.

> *We believe that everything is in a state of constant and ultimately beneficial growth and evolution. This growth and evolution occurs to all of existence, be it the soul, the planet, or the Universe, all being a mirror of Divinity, which evolves and grows as well.*

These statements define our basic cosmology that ALL things are sentient and worthy of respect. They also reinforce the concept that we are each a microcosm of Earth; which is a microcosm of the Milky Way; which is a microcosm of the Universe; which is ultimately a microcosm of Deity. In a holographic Universe, even the smallest piece of the whole contains the true image of the whole. Each Galaxy contains the true nature of the Universe. Each planet carries the true nature of the Galaxy. Each one of us possesses the true nature of Earth. So ... you can now see that each of us reflects the True Nature of the Divine, in whole, within us.

> *We believe that the Wiccan Rede,*
> *"Do As You Will, But Harm None"*
> *is the highest moral statement.*
> *It is an effective pattern for a moral life.*

"Harm None ..." is discussed in greater detail in other works. Here, I will only point out that "Harm None ..." should be taken as one normally uses the word "harm." Any extreme view should be avoided. It doesn't include hurt feelings or healthy competition. "Harm None ..." calls us to have a conscious approach to our actions. It calls us to consider the full ramifications of our actions beyond our personal goals.

> *We believe that ultimate truth is beyond the understanding of humans. Therefore, it is natural for a person's belief and Deity should develop to reflect the individual's personal relationship with the Divine.*

This statement is about growth and change. It goes to the idea that what I thought, as a person of 35 years, when I first came into

Wicca, is very different than what I feel and how my relationship works with the Divine now, 15 years later. So, as a person who has been through 15 more years of life experience, and all the initiations that go with this – all the official ones and all of the unofficial ones that the Holy Ones give us – my understanding is different. Therefore it is acceptable and expected that my relationship with the Divine will change also.

We should not expect that our relationship with the Divine is going to remain stagnant. We should not even expect necessarily that spirit guides will stay with us for our entire incarnation. People will come and go in our lives and so will manifestations of the Divine. What we needed at one time in our life may not be what we need at this stage, and it may be different again in another 15 years.

So, this statement is just trying to say that we expect relationships will evolve and change and shift. This is a good thing. It shows we are growing and learning and experiencing life.

> *We believe that all Pagan religions should acknowledge one another as kindred and stand together as equals. Our similarities as Pagans far outweigh our differences.*

The final two statements return us to the beginning. We again state concepts of peace tolerance, and unity. The final statement uses the words "We believe that all Pagan religions should acknowledge one another as kindred and stand together as equals. Our similarities as Pagans far outweigh our differences." We will take this a step further and suggest that ALL RELIGIONS should be seen as equal. And we should treat them ALL with respect.

As we say in the first statement … "Inner Truth is universal in nature." It is incumbent upon us to make that one simple statement a mantra for peace and unity in the entire world.

This commentary on A Correllian Creed is only intended to introduce the concepts. I am sure you will have questions. Believe me when I say that I still have questions. It is in the questioning itself that we grow. Take some time to meditate on these statements. Read them again in a week – in two weeks – in a month – and so on.

I know you will see something new in it each time. As your connection with Deity deepens, so will your understanding of the basic beliefs set out in these simple lines of text.

SING A SONG OF SAFETY

Be secret they say, be silent they say
Be quiet and crafty and coy
Stay in the basement and hide away
In fear of the neighbors and of light of day!
Never come out and never speak up
Safety in shadows and hiding!

But if magic is power then why would you hide?
And what help is silence from those who are wise?
For wisdom unspoken is wisdom unknown
And who shivers in shadows shivers alone!
Be loud, I say, and stand up for yourself!
Safety's in numbers and courage!

For who's secret in life will be secret in death
And who even knows when they're taken?
No one will step forward for one who's unknown
And the secret martyr's forsaken!
But they who are known go not quietly
And they who have friends will have help!

Wiccan Morality
by **Don Lewis**

Many non-Wiccans have the impression that Wicca is a religion with no moral teachings. This is not true – though Wicca, like other religions, does have some members who pay less attention to its moral teachings than others.

Many years ago when I was a teenaged Wiccan I saw an episode of the Phil Donahue Show (which will tell you how long ago this was) on which a number of Wiccan leaders of the day appeared, notably Selena Fox. A member of the audience made the comment that it sounded to them as if Wiccans had no moral concepts. I found this rather appalling.

My response to this was and is that Wicca is very concerned with moral ideas, though our ideas of morality differ in some points than from of Christians. Where Christians and some other religions focus much of their moral teachings on sexual issues, namely sexual prohibitions, Wicca has a very open attitude toward sex. Sexuality between consenting adults is not of itself an issue in Wiccan morality – unless someone is being harmed, as by the breaking of vows, intentional deception, or cruelty, in which case it is the harm rather than the sexuality that is the moral issue.

Other than our more open attitude toward sexuality, which we regard as a sacred gift of the Gods, Wicca's view of morality is not strikingly different from most other religion's view of morality. Things like stealing, rape, and murder are as morally wrong in the Wiccan religion as they are in all other religions. WHY these things are wrong in the Wiccan moral view is however different from the reasons which might be attributed by some other religions.

Many religions attribute their moral teachings directly to their Deity, as channeled through a prophet, and equate them with Divine Law. In Wicca, moral teachings and Divine Law are different things. The Wiccan Rede, which teaches "Do As You Will But Harm None" is a moral teaching: the Threefold Law, which shows how our actions return to us multiple times ("Three" being understood as "multiple", not as literally "three") through the Karmic attachments those actions create, is Divine Law. The former is created by humans out of their advancing moral understandings and reflects human needs independent of cosmic principles (For example the Wiccan Rede is not the principle governing nature): the latter is a cosmic principle whose origins and operation is not dependent upon human understandings.

Karma, the Threefold Law, Destiny, Fate, - whatever you might choose to call it- is a universal principle that acts regardless of our teachings. This universal principle has been discovered over time, and understanding of it deepens constantly – but while our understanding of it may change, its nature does not.

On the other hand, Wiccan moral teachings such as the Wiccan Rede or the Nine Virtues are created by people as a kind of social contract: to govern behavior in such a way as to create a better world. Moral teachings are certainly influenced by cosmic principles, and exist in part to help bring us into better balance with cosmic principles, but are themselves uniquely human and subject to change and evolution as human understandings grow.

Our actions create karmic attachments that pull us back to them until the lessons they offer are learned, however many incarnations that may take – this is the Threefold Law. The "three" in the Threefold Law of course must be understood as representing plurality rather than literally "three" – we repeat our Karmic lessons as many times as necessary, often many more than three times.

The Wiccan Rede, "Do As You Will But Harm None" exists to help us avoid forming such Karmic attachments in the first place, an aspect of the Rede which is directly connected to cosmic principles: but it also exists to illustrate contemporary Wiccan ideas of how to act morally, an aspect of the Rede which is connected to social contract rather than cosmic principle.

Social Contract is the idea that we agree to certain behaviors in return for certain behaviors: we agree not to steal in return for society protecting us from theft: we agree not to murder in return for society protecting us from murder: in the Wiccan Rede as a social contract we agree not to harm in the expectation that we will be protected from harm by others who follow the Rede. Of course religiously there is the added expectation of being protected from harm on a cosmic level by not having created karmic attachment to harm.

Here again we have a difference from some other religions. If the Wiccan Rede is not a Divine Command, why do we follow it? I have heard members of some other religions say that if they were not afraid of Divine retribution they would not be moral people. As Wiccans we do not fear Deity in the first place – why then should we be moral people at all?

The answer is that moral behavior, as derived from the Wiccan Rede, is good for its own sake: the results of moral behavior, which are a better world in the present and better karma for the future, are far better than the results of immoral behavior, which are short term gain but future degeneration. The satisfaction derived from following the Rede— which shares happiness with others and magnifies it- are far greater than the temporary selfish happiness of creating harm.

Wrong vs Evil

In Wicca we do not believe in "sin" or "evil". This causes some people to think that we have no sense of Right and Wrong. This is due to sloppy use of language.

Because in certain religions "sin" and "wrong" are used in very much the same way, members of those religions sometimes think they mean the same thing – though this is not what they themselves formally teach. "Sin" according to Judeo-Christian religion, is anything that separates a person from God. Many things in Judeo-Christianity are considered "sins" which would not ordinarily be considered "wrong" – and some things that would ordinarily be considered "wrong" are not considered "sins". "Sin" is a very different concept from "wrong".

In Wicca we believe that Deity is within the person –that all people, and all things, are ultimately manifestations of Deity through the Monad, the Soul, and the Incarnation. Because Deity is within you, you can NEVER be separate from Deity. You can forget Deity is in there, but Deity is no less there because you may not be aware of it. Consequently we can have no idea of "sin" because nothing can ever separate us from Deity.

The same is true for "evil". Although many people of other religions use the word "Evil" as if were exactly the same word as "bad" they are in fact very different terms. The idea of "Evil" is the idea of a cosmic force that inspires harm or bad behavior in opposition to Deity. This is completely contrary to Wiccan teaching in several ways: as Wiccans we believe that Deity is within all things, therefore nothing can ever be in opposition to Deity, because all things ultimately come from and are motivated by Deity: and because we believe that all things have a reason and a place in the Divine Plan, attributing unpleasant occurrences to "Evil" is not acceptable.

Does the non-existence of "Evil" mean that as Wiccans we do not believe that anything is "bad"? Not at all. Many things are "bad" – but not because of a cosmic "Evil" force inspiring them. They are "bad" because they produce bad effects, both socially and karmicly speaking.

It is bad to murder for any number of social reasons, including the effect on the victim and their family as well as society itself – not to mention creating a karmic attachment that will bind the murderer until the lessons of the situation are learned. In Wicca however the responsibility for murder belongs to the murderer, and not to a putative "Evil" force in the Universe.

Wicca also rejects the pairing of "Good and Bad" as polar opposites, which is found in some other religions. Rather we agree with the Aristotelian view that "Good and Bad' represent a continuum in which Good lies at the center and Bad lies at either extreme. Thus "Bad" will be seen to be either too much of a Good thing or too little, rather than the opposite of a Good thing.

Learning is a Good Thing. However when we think of learning as a continuum and look to either extreme end, we will see how this same Good thing can be a bad Thing. At one end too little education is ignorance, a Bad Thing. But at the other end of the continuum too much education can become pedantry, fossilizing ideas into the forms already learned and making new learning and intellectual growth impossible – also a Bad Thing.

Thus not only we do we reject the idea of an external force of "Evil" operating to do bad for its own sake, we also have a different understanding of the relationship between Good and Bad and how a quality or situation can move from one to the other. This creates a very different way of thinking.

The Wiccan Rede

The pre-eminent Wiccan moral teaching is the Wiccan Rede: "Do As You Will, But Harm None" or "An It Harm None, Do As You Will". This is the one moral teaching most all Wiccan Traditions agree on, though there are a few who don't and even among the majority who do agree the meaning of "Harm" is a subject of great disagreement.

In the Correllian Tradition our understanding of the Wiccan Rede is simple and easily stated: the Rede should not be "interpreted" and as a result can only be understood in light of the ordinary meaning of the word "Harm". By this understanding you must consider whether a thing would normally be considered "harm" by common definition – not by broad extrapolation. This understanding of the Rede is both practical and livable.

Some Wiccans interpret the Wiccan Rede in a very Jainist manner, feeling that "Harm None" means avoiding anything that might cause any sort of physical or emotional pain to any creature. Some people interpret the Wiccan Rede so broadly that it cannot be lived by, bringing the Rede into disrepute in many circles – because after all, by the extreme interpretation of "harm" you cannot eat (because everything eaten must first die), you cannot breath (lest you accidentally harm tiny microbes or bacteria) you cannot speak (lest you hurt someone's feeling) in short, you cannot live at all. Clearly, this cannot POSSIBLY be what is actually meant by the Rede.

Another interpretation of the Rede holds that you must never, ever, interfere with another person's free will in any way. And yet, the mother whose young child wants to put their hand directly upon the red hot stove burner MUST interfere with the child's free will and prevent the injury. Similarly, if someone is trying to rape or murder you or a loved one (or anyone, for that matter), do you NOT interfere with the rapist/murderers free will by resisting and if possible escaping? As a society do we NOT interfere with the rapist/murderer's free will by imposing and enforcing laws against rape and murder? This too cannot POSSIBLY be what the Rede really means.

Stopping the young child from putting their hand on the burner may interfere with the child's free will and may even (probably) momentarily hurt their feelings – but NO ONE would ever define it as "harm". Prosecuting and imprisoning the rapist/murderer definitely impinges upon their free will to rape or murder, and the process may hurt their feelings – but NO ONE would ever define laws against rape and murder as harm. Indeed, in the ordinary sense of the word, most people would say that you do "harm" by not restraining people from such actions.

Where Does the Wiccan Rede Come From?

The origins of the Wiccan Rede are shrouded in mystery, and more than this in controversy.

It is said that a little knowledge is a dangerous thing, and those with a little knowledge would no doubt insist that Gerald Gardner must have made the Wiccan Rede up out of whole cloth.

However despite the strident insistence of some, the story is nowhere near that simple.

The Wiccan Rede reads: "An You Harm None, Do As You Will" or "Do As You Will But Harm None". "Rede" by the way has nothing to do with the word "read" but is an old word meaning "advice" or "counsel".

The phrasing of the Wiccan Rede leaves little doubt but that it is a corollary to the Law of Thelema, a point which I think would be rather hard to argue for the Law of Thelema is "Do As You Will".

Adding "But Harm None" to "Do As You Will" is a pretty obvious modification that could have been made by any sensible person.

The Law of Thelema is quite old – it comes from the novel "Gargantua" or "Gargantua and Pantagruel", written by the great French satirist Francois Rabelais (1494–1553). Gargantua is not at all an obscure work: it was and is a staple of European classical writing, known in former years by most well educated persons.

Written in early modern French, "Gargantua" is over 400,000 words long and was published in five volumes between 1532–1562. The title character, Gargantua is a giant, and the King of Utopia. He is the son of the giant Grangousier and his mother is Gargamelle the daughter of the King of Butterflies. Gargantua's son is Pantagruel. The many adventures of Gargantua and Pantagruel satirize many aspects of human life and society in a manner very similar to Jonathon Swift's "Gulliver's Travels" –which also features a macrophiliac theme.

In the novel Gargantua establishes the Abbey of Theleme as a reward for Friar John, in recognition of Friar John's efforts in the war against King Picrochole of Lerne. The abbey of Theleme is presented as a kind of hedonistic Utopia. The Abbey accepts women on an equal status with men, and has only one rule: "Do As You Will".

Because of the general currency of "Gargantua" the Law of Thelema was well known and shows up in a variety of places through the centuries as a maxim of free-thinkers.

In the metaphysical movement the Law of Thelema was given new impetus when restated by Aleister Crowley in his famous Liber Legis, or "Book of the Law". The Liber Legis was supposedly channeled by Rose Crowley from the Spirit Guide Aiwass in 1904. The Liber Legis includes an elaboration of the Law of Thelema, to whit: "Do As You Will shall be the whole of the law, for Love is the Law: Love under Will", generally simply expressed as "Do As You Will".

To Crowley "Do As You Will" did not mean what it first appears. To Crowley it meant not that you should do anything you wanted, but rather that you only ever could do what you actively Willed – and particularly what came from your True Will, a concept comparable to our Higher Self. This very esoteric interpretation was not generally understood, however. Crowley's writings were popular throughout the metaphysical community – the lines between Traditions were not nearly as strong as they are today - but many people misunderstood Crowley's actual teaching and took "Do As You Will" in a very literal way.

Most people agree that Aleister Crowley was involved in the formation of the modern Wicca movement, though how and when is extremely controversial, as is everything about the origins of the modern Wicca movement. The older view holds that Crowley was involved in one of the Temples answering to George Pickingill, but was dissatisfied with the pre-eminent role of the High Priestesses and as a consequence left.

Crowley is supposed to have known a number of early modern Wiccans including Lydia Beckett and Sybil Leek, and certainly many early modern Wiccans were admirers of his work. However Crowley was a bit too extreme for many of these people, and the idea that a corollary of his Law of Thelema amended with "And It Harm None" should trace to one or more of them is no stretch of the imagination.

In recent years other views of Crowley's connections with modern Wicca have become current including the popular Ceremonial view that Crowley "invented" Wicca intending it to be merely an arm of Ceremonialism with Gerald Gardner as his flunky – but died before he could put it in place, leaving Gardner to carry on alone: and the popular Gardnerogenesist view that Crowley acted as an advisor and ghostwriter for Gardner when Gardner "invented" Wicca. In either case the Wiccan Rede would then be presumed to trace not to a third party's corollary of Crowley's Law of Thelema but directly to Crowley himself.

However, the idea that the Wiccan Rede could have taken form as late as these theories suggest is thrown a bit of a curve by the famous "Wiccan Rede" poem. Originally called the "Rede of the Wiccae" –"Wiccae" being the earlier plural of "Wicca"- the poem sets out Wiccan ideas in 26 rhyming couplets, ending with the maxim generally known as the "Wiccan Rede".

This poem is attributed to a Bostonian Priestess named Adrianna Porter, said to have written it around 1939 when she was already quite an old lady —she was in her nineties when she died in 1946. Many of the aspects of the poem are out of step with modern Wiccan practice – which is only to be expected considering how far the modern Wiccan movement has evolved in the years since the Blv. Adrianna wrote the poem. That the Blv. Adrianna could include the Rede in a work of that date suggests that it is a corollary of the Law of Thelema created either in reaction to Crowley's version of the Law or directly in reaction to Rabelais, and not a late creation of Crowley's or a creation of Gardner's.

Gerald Gardner himself was quite explicit in his idea of where the Wiccan Rede might have come from, and his version is different from all of the above. According to Gerald Gardner, who always steadfastly claimed that the Rede predated him, as he claimed most Wiccan teachings did, suggested that it might have been derived from a different French novel: "Les Adventures du Roi Pausole" by Pierre Louys. Much more obscure than Rabelais' Gargantua or Crowley's Liber Legis, "Les Adventures du Roi Pausole" tells the story of the fictional King Pausole and his utopian realm. Among the principle themes of the book is "Free Love". In the book King Pausole attempts to synthesize the ancestral laws of his land into one moral teaching, the result of which is a single two-part law which reads: "I. Do no harm to thy neighbor. II. Observing this, do as thou pleasest".

While this is certainly possible, it seems like a pretty obscure origin and the wording is quite different from the Rede as we know it – unlike the Law of Thelema. That the Rede arose as a response to the popularity and real or perceived misuse of the Law of Thelema seems much more likely.

In any event, the sentiment expressed by the Wiccan Rede is pretty universal. "Do As You Will But Harm None" is very much the same sentiment expressed by Christians as "Do Unto Others As You Would Have Others Do Unto You," and in various other ways by religions around the world: it is a natural human desire.

What does the Wiccan Rede mean?

Obviously our real question is not "Where does the Wiccan Rede originate?" but rather "What does the Wiccan Rede mean to us?"

We have discussed the origins of the Rede in part to show that the idea has been percolating about in society for rather a long time before taking shape as the Rede, and in part to show that there is no definite point of origin. Because there is no definite single point of origin, it is no surprise that there is no single definite understanding of the Rede, but varying definitions according to specific Traditions.

As we have said, the Correllian recension of the Wiccan Rede requires the Rede to be understood according to the ordinary meaning of the word "Harm" and allows no interpretation of this. "Harm" has a pretty clear meaning in ordinary use, and as established by custom: that meaning does not extend to the extremes that some people would like to take the Wiccan Rede to.

Pressed to come up with a simple explanation of "Harm" we some time ago defined it as "Unprovoked or egregious damage."

Killing a virus with antibiotics is not Harm. Killing bacteria when you clean your bathroom is not Harm. Hurting someone's feelings is not Harm, unless it is through intentional cruelty. Serving in the police or the military is not Harm. The term Harm never meant things like this in its ordinary usage. "Harm" can only be extended to include these things through the most extreme interpretation – and as we have said, the Rede is not to be interpreted.

So what DOES Harm mean?

We all know what is normally meant by "Harm", but putting it into words is not so easy for most of us. "Unprovoked or egregious damage" is pretty succinct, and as a definition of "Harm" is pretty helpful – but some examples will perhaps serve better to illustrate what this actually means.

If someone walks up to you and hits you for no reason, they have done harm – that is pretty easy to see. But what of your reaction?

If someone walks up to and hits you for no reason, and you hit them back, have YOU done harm? Certainly not. No ordinary definition of "Harm" would suggest that this is "Harm". In striking you, the other person has declared that THEY consider you an equal opponent, and have willingly incurred your response that they have themselves demonstrated as acceptable to them by initiating the exchange. A fair fight between equals is never Harm, and when a person starts a fight it must be assumed that the fight is fair in their eyes. This too is ultimately a pretty clear answer.

If someone walks up to you and hits you for no reason, and you beat them to a bloody pulp, have you done harm? This is a harder answer: most often the answer is yes, because the response is out of proportion to the situation. But what if this person has beaten other people severely, and given you reason to believe that they will do the same to you? Then beating them to a pulp may be merely self-defense. However in general ones response to such a situation should be in proportion to the threat displayed, and an excessive response would be considered "Harm".

Virtue

As we have said earlier, Good and Bad are not opposites, but rather represent a continuum with Bad at either end and Good in the middle. Thus moderation is always the Good choice. This view is quite ancient, having been beautifully articulated by Aristotle in antiquity.

In Correllian Wicca we have a set of Nine Virtues which we encourage. These are inspired by similar sets of Nine that have come down from various sources in the ancient world, as well as by the idea of the Enneagram and the Nine Monads. The Correllian Virtues encapsulate our ideas of proper morality.

It should be noted that no person can perfectly embody all Virtues, nor should any person be expected to. People, by definition, are human and must be viewed as such. Rather Virtue is the goal we aim for and manifest to the best of our abilities.

The Nine Virtues of Correllian Wicca

Honesty

The First of the Nine Virtues is Honesty. To be Honest is to be straight-forward in one's dealings, to tell the truth and abide by one's word. Honesty allows people to trust one another, and makes it easier to deal with one another.

However like all qualities, Honesty exists in a continuum in which both too little and too much are Bad. The person who has too little Honesty is deceptive, untruthful, and crooked in their dealings. The person who has too much Honesty can be inconsiderate or hurtful to other through extreme candor or through indiscretion, or through repeating what though true should have been confidential.

Generosity

The Second Virtue is Generosity, whether generosity of act, thought, or feeling. Generosity allows movement and encourages growth – both in the world about the generous person, and also within them. Generosity of action makes for generosity of spirit, and so the generous help themselves as well as others through their Generosity. Generosity can be expressed through sharing - whether sharing resources, ideas, or emotions. But Generosity can also be expressed through allowing – allowing freedom of action, thought, etc. Another way to describe Generosity is Freedom.

The person who has too little Generosity is miserly in thought and action, and has too little movement in their heart. The person who has too much Generosity however is profligate, giving everything away and finding themselves with nothing left to share.

Sincerity

The Third Virtue is Sincerity, or being true to yourself and truly embodying what you believe. Sincerity is walking the walk as well as talking the talk, both internally and externally. The sincere person is at pains to make sure that their internal self and their external self are in alignment. Another way to describe Sincerity is Integrity.

The person who has too little Sincerity hides their true self, often even from themselves. They are alienated from their true nature and their true motivations, and may not understand the reasons why they do things. The person who has too much Sincerity however may be so highly aware of their own nature as to be unable to consider other people or external conditions, falling into hubris and placing their own ideas and ideals above all other things.

Courage

The Fourth Virtue is Courage, or the ability to meet and overcome challenges. Courage is what allows us to go forward in the world, even when we are afraid. Courage permits us to grow and to accomplish. Courage allows us to see that perceived barriers can be overcome, perceived limitations transcended.

The person who has too little Courage is cowardly – that is, they are ruled by their fear and imprisoned by it. The person who has too much Courage is foolhardy, disregarding reasonable fears and failing to properly consider or prepare for actual dangers.

Service

The Fifth Virtue is Service, the desire to help others and to create better situations in the world around one. Being of Service is a willingness to pitch in and improve circumstances and better situations. By helping others and improving their world, we often find that we improve our own world as well. If Courage allows the individual to move forward, Service allows the group to move forward.

The person who has too little sense of Service never extends themselves for others or concerns themselves with the wider world, allowing bad situations that they might have been able to improve to instead worsen. The person who has too much sense of Service however may give so much of themselves that they find themselves enslaved to others needs, neglecting their own.

Practicality

The Sixth Virtue is Practicality, or considering the outcome of one's actions and acting accordingly. Practicality allows us to use knowledge or past experience or to judge how best to create favorable outcomes to our actions, as well as to foresee unfortunate consequences and avoid them. Practicality allows us to spare ourselves and others much pain by applying to present or future circumstances the wisdom we have gained from lessons already learned.

The person who has too little Practicality does not consider the consequences of their outcomes and so frequently experiences bad outcomes and often repeats unpleasant situations. The person who has too much Practicality however can be imprisoned by expectation, never being willing to take a chance, make a change, or venture into uncharted territory.

Modesty

The Seventh Virtue is Modesty, which is to allow room for the recognition of other people and their skills and achievements, rather than promoting your own character, skills, and achievements to the detriment of others. Modesty manifests as moderation in self-estimation and self-promotion, an avoidance of egotism and braggadocio. The modest individual, being confident of their knowledge and abilities does not need to brag about themselves, and still less needs to denigrate others, but rather shows their worth through competence.

The person who has too little Modesty is arrogant and focused only upon themselves and their own accomplishments. The person who has too much Modesty is self-negating, not valuing themselves or their actions, and as a result denying the world what they have to offer.

Compassion

The Eighth Virtue is Compassion, or understanding and sympathy for others. Through Compassion we not only help others, but grow emotionally ourselves. Through Compassion we gain understanding of others' needs, and increase our own understanding of others and their situations, allowing us greater insight into our own inner nature and outer situations. Acts motivated by Compassion build a better world both improving the lot of others, and often by stabilizing difficult situations which might otherwise grow worse, affecting all around them.

The person who has too little Compassion has no understanding of others and consequently can be hard-hearted and may be cruel. The person who has too much Compassion, however, may find themselves enabling the bad behavior or abusive actions of others by being too understanding of these.

Piety

The Ninth and final Virtue is Piety, by which we mean Right Relationship. Piety is the respect and consideration appropriate to any relationship. In religious terms Piety is the respect and devotion of the person toward their Patron Deity, or toward the ideals of their faith. Filial Piety is the respect and devotion of children toward parents, and in a wider sense of persons toward their families — whether family by blood or by choice. One can also have a pious attitude toward education, career, law, etc. ... In short, Piety refers toward the social bonds on which society is built.

The person who has too little Piety has respect for nothing, and destroys all they touch through not caring about the consequences to personal and societal relationships. The person who has too much Piety can turn personal and societal relationships into rigid and fossilized forms, ultimately destroying them by preventing any sort of growth, change, or adaptation.

COLORS OF LIFE

Golden clouds, crimson flame,

Azure waves and verdant earth,

These are the colors of our lives,

The colors that give us birth

A COMMENTARY ON THE NINE VIRTUES

by **Rev. Terry Power, HP**

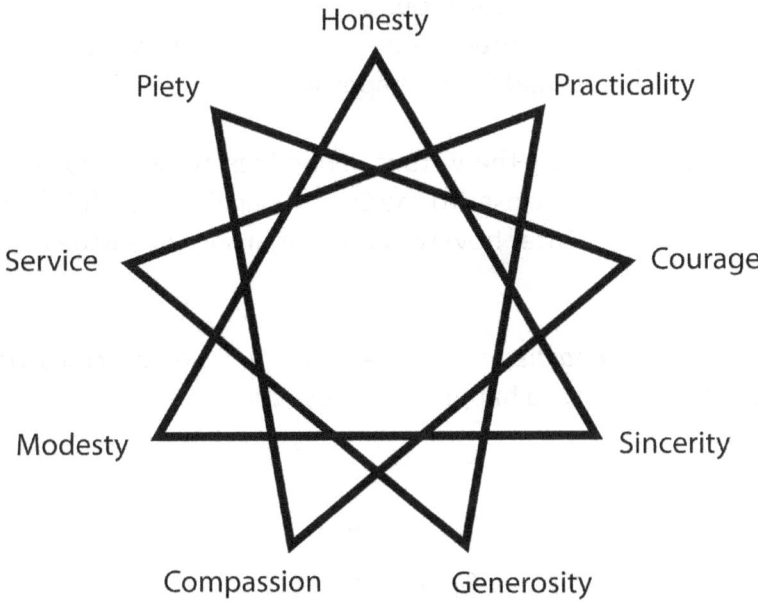

On the surface, virtues appear to be merely an outward expression of our inwardly held beliefs. And to a degree this is true. According to "Collins English Dictionary", virtue is defined as *"any admirable quality, feature, or trait."*[1] On the surface, there is much to consider in that definition. But there is also a deeper level to pursue. In this commentary, we will look at how the Virtues begin within us at a personal level and express themselves outward into our communities and, ultimately, to the Divine.

In a purely philosophical way, Aristotle posited that a virtuous life leads to a happy life. He suggested that through virtue we can find the true happiness that comes from inner peace and a deep connection with the Divine – a happiness that transcends external influences or circumstances.

In a magickal sense, reflecting on the Rule of Threes, the same holds true. A virtuous life is a self-fulfilling proposition. If we believe that we get back what we put out (whether exactly three times or not), we must see that if we express the Nine Virtues in our lives, we will receive virtuous actions returned to us. Basically, if we act well toward others, people will act well toward us. And that will, ultimately make for a happy life.

Further, by expressing the Virtues in our lives, we will find an inner peace and be drawn closer to the Divine – again, a self-fulfilling proposition. No matter how we look at it, living the Virtues leads to happiness.

In his work, *Nicomachean Ethics*, Aristotle gives nine virtues which he feels are the key to happiness. These are:

1) Bravery
2) Temperance
3) Generosity
4) Self-respect
5) Mildness
6) Friendliness
7) Honesty
8) Wit
9) Modesty

Rev. Donald Lewis, in the Lessons for the Correllian Third Degree, adds the following:

> *In each case Aristotle maintains that in order to be a virtue the given quality must be followed with moderation. All extremes are by nature vicious – thus even a virtue taken to excess can become a vice. Thus by Bravery Aristotle does not mean foolhardiness, nor recklessness. Similarly by Generosity he does not mean that one should be a wastrel or a spendthrift.*[2]

The Correllian Tradition of Wicca has developed its own list of virtues over the years. They differ slightly from Aristotle's list and the order is different as well. The Correllian Nine Virtues are:

1) Honesty
2) Generosity
3) Sincerity (Integrity)
4) Courage
5) Service
6) Practicality (which could be said to include Temperance)
7) Modesty
8) Compassion (which could be argued to correspond to Aristotle's Mildness)
9) Piety (Piety being "Respect" for Deity, as well as for oneself and for others)

The Correllian list reflects a contemporary understanding of these concepts and puts them into modern usage. The updated order of the Virtues also seems to correspond more to modern Wiccan thought. How can we live any of the virtues unless we start with honesty – especially with ourselves?

After years of contemplation and meditation on these virtues, I have found a pattern that leads me to a slightly different order. In keeping with magickal thinking and the power of the number nine as three groups of three, the pattern emerges. Using three triangles, nested together to form an enneagram, I created a mandala of sorts to aid in meditation and contemplation of the Virtues.

This does, however, require us to organize the Nine Virtues into a slightly different order to reflect this pattern:

> Honesty
>
> Practicality
>
> Courage
>
> Sincerity
>
> Generosity
>
> Compassion
>
> Modesty
>
> Service
>
> Piety

You will note almost immediately that Honesty and Piety remain as the first and last virtues on the list. They are the anchors, if you will, of the pattern itself – the beginning and the culmination.

The pattern begins with the three Personal Virtues – Honesty, Practicality, and Courage. These are the most inward of the Virtues. It is from these that the others grow and develop.

The Expressive Virtues grow out of the Personal Virtues. Sincerity is an outward expression of Honesty. Generosity is possible to express only when Practicality is handled at the personal level. Compassion expresses Courage into action.

The last group is the Spiritual Virtues. These, by their very nature, draw us to a deeper connection with the Divine. Modesty develops from Honesty and Sincerity, Service from Practicality and Generosity, and Piety from Courage and Compassion.

The Common Book of Witchcraft & Wicca

Triangle 1:

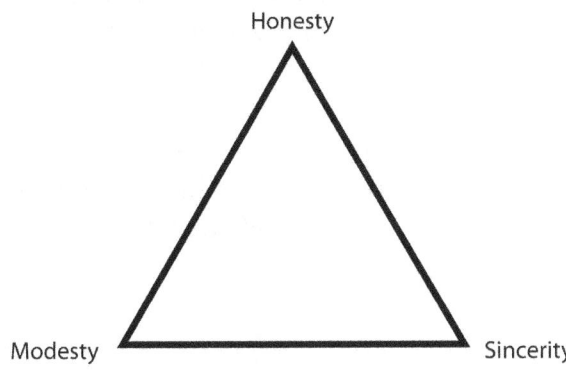

Personal Virtue:
Honesty

Expressive Virtue
Sincerity

Spiritual Virtue
Modesty

Triangle 2:

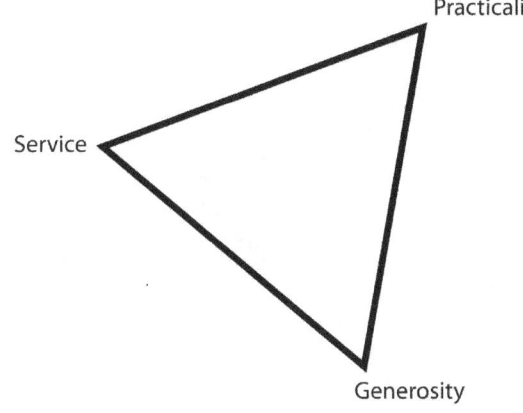

Personal Virtue:
Practicality

Expressive Virtue
Generosity

Spiritual Virtue
Service

Triangle 3:

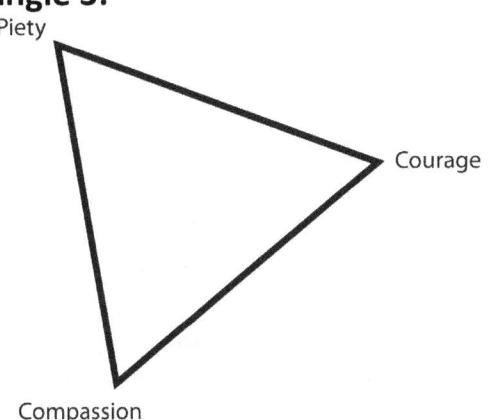

Personal Virtue:
Courage

Expressive Virtue
Compassion

Spiritual Virtue
Piety

By placing the virtues that emanate from Honesty onto Triangle #1, we can contemplate that line of growth and development from the Personal, through the Expressive, to the Divine itself. Triangles #2 and #3 are organized in the same fashion.

When all three triangles are nested together, we have an enneagram and mandala that can be viewed as a whole for contemplation and meditation or each triangle can be used individually.

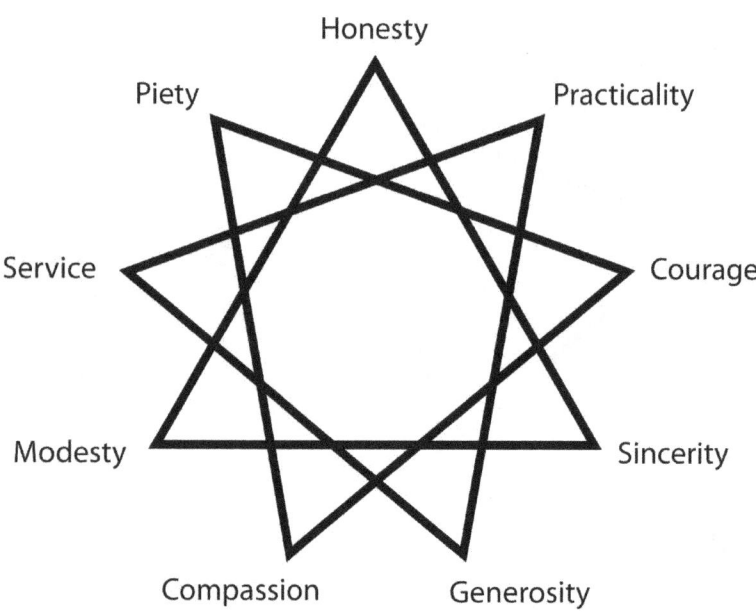

Now, let's return to the overarching theme of the Virtues – that of developing a manner of living that leads one to peace and true happiness. The following few paragraphs will discuss each virtue and put them into the context of a meaningful and happy life. Please understand that the definitions used were chosen to reflect this context.

Honesty

"3. freedom from deceit or fraud..."[3] Honesty is a quality of truthfulness that is the first step in growth and development. The first step in any spiritual program is awareness. That awareness grows from our being honest with ourselves. Until we are honest with ourselves, we cannot make the changes we need. Through Honesty, we begin the process of changing our lives toward a life of Virtue. Further, being free of deceit will allow people to trust our words and believe that we do not lie.

Practicality

"7. mindful of the results, usefulness, advantages or disadvantages, etc., of action or procedure."[4] This is about a level-headed approach to life. Balance is needed in all aspects of being. The ordinary aspects of life must be dealt with so that we are free to express ourselves spiritually. For example, it is very difficult to gain a meditative state when your stomach is grumbling in hunger. It is hard to help others when our own needs are not met first.

Courage

"1. the quality of mind or spirit that enables a person to face difficulty, danger, pain, etc., without fear; 3. to act in accordance to one's beliefs, especially in spite of criticism."[5] Here we need to make a comment about fear. Having the courage of one's convictions does not mean that we do not have fear. Courage is acting on our beliefs in spite of fear. Fear is a natural reaction to a concern for ourselves and others. Courage is overcoming those feelings and facing needed action. Courage is acting out of Love instead of succumbing to Fear.

Sincerity

"1. not hypocritical or deceitful; open; genuine"[6] This is Honesty expressed outward. When we act in an honest manner, we are more believable. When we are open and genuine, we gain the ability to better build and belong to community. If we are invested in that community, we gain an even greater sense of belonging.

Generosity

"1. willingness and liberality in giving away one's money, time, etc.; magnanimity; 2. freedom from pettiness in character and mind"[7] This is relatively straight-forward, but it must grow out of Practicality. Our willingness to give of ourselves tends to make us feel like we are a part of the world at large. Often we gain a sense of belonging by investing ourselves in this way. When we feel invested in our communities, we are more inclined to want to improve it.

Compassion

"... deep concern for the well-being of other..."[8] This virtue speaks for itself. It also goes to our understanding of Perfect Love and Perfect Trust. As we overcome Fear and experience Courage, we are freer to express Compassion. Concern for the well-being of others is a deeper expression of Courage. It actually requires us to seek a greater understanding of the needs of those with whom we interact.

Modesty

"1. the quality of being modest; freedom from vanity, boastfulness, etc.; 2. regard for decency of behavior, speech, and dress, etc."[9] This is the spiritual expression of Honesty. It is the total freedom from ego. If we are overblown in our opinions of ourselves, it will be difficult to interact successfully with the Divine. We may also find it harder to be involved in our communities. Think about vain or boastful people you know. Do you want to be around them? Do you think they can find a state of mind that will allow them to commune with the Gods? Through Modesty – which is Honesty at our deepest core – we are allowed our greatest connection with the Divine.

Service

"1. an act of helpful activity; help; aid 9. The duty or work of public servants."[10] Here is the heart of what leadership is all about. As leaders, we are called to serve our communities. When we are helpful, we are expressing Generosity. But Service takes Generosi-

ty to a higher level. Entering our community's public service – as ritual leaders, teachers, etc. – we have given of ourselves most deeply and have accepted that we will serve others and our faith.

Piety

"1. ... devout fulfillment of religious obligations; 3. dutiful respect or regard for parents, homeland, etc."[11] Clearly, piety is about respect. And while many equate piety solely with devotion to our concepts of Deity, the dictionary points out how that pious respect should also be extended to others.

The definitions used here for Piety include words like "devout" and "dutiful." This indicates that Courage and Compassion have developed to the highest level. Looking also at the Spiritual Virtues, we see that Modesty and Service also go to that highest development of respect.

Piety is an expression of the respect for all things. It is a respect that grows from our understanding of our place, and the place of all things, in the Universe. This virtue is the fullest expression of Perfect Love and Perfect Trust. It is the culmination of all the Virtues.

As we conclude our discussion of the Nine Virtues, it would be remiss to not discuss one other concept mentioned above. That concept is Moderation. In fact, it is perhaps the Tenth Virtue. This should be the over-riding concept that holds the others in check. Without moderation, any of these virtues could be pushed to excess. And through such excess, even virtue could become a vice.

At this point, we refer again to Rev. Don's writings:

> *Like Aristotle we would argue that a virtue taken to an extreme can be a vice. Thus by Service we do not mean being a doormat to others. By Modesty we do not mean self-abasement. Nor by Practicality do we mean materialism or ruthlessness. Rather in each case we are referring to a sensible, temperate practice.*[12]

One might argue that a virtue cannot become a vice. But how many of us have been wounded by the brutal criticism from someone and when confronted, they say, "Well, I'm just being honest!"? Would it not be more virtuous to find a compassionate way to express the same feelings?

We cannot cast one virtue aside for another. Extreme actions and reactions have caused too many rifts in our communities. They have destroyed friendships and broken marriages.

It is sincerely hoped that these concepts will lead to meaningful contemplation of the Nine Virtues. And like Aristotle, with an eye toward moderation, let us look at these virtues – all the virtues – and seek the middle path. Then together, we can all find inner peace, connect with the Divine, and achieve True Happiness.

Blessed Be!

End Notes:

1. "Virtue." *Collins English Dictionary - Complete & Unabridged 10th Edition*. HarperCollins Publishers. 29 Apr. 2014.
2. *Witch School Third Degree: Lessons in the Correllian Tradition*. Witch School. 2005.
3. "Honesty." *Dictionary.com Unabridged*. Random House, Inc. 06 May. 2014.
4. "Practicality." *Dictionary.com Unabridged*. Random House, Inc. 06 May. 2014.
5. "Courage." *Dictionary.com Unabridged*. Random House, Inc. 06 May. 2014.
6. "Sincerity." *Collins English Dictionary - Complete & Unabridged 10th Edition*. HarperCollins Publishers. 06 May. 2014. .
7. "Generosity." *Collins English Dictionary - Complete & Unabridged 10th Edition*. HarperCollins Publishers. 06 May. 2014.
8. Citation unavailable.
9. "Modesty." *Dictionary.com Unabridged*. Random House, Inc. 06 May. 2014.
10. "Service." *Dictionary.com Unabridged*. Random House, Inc. 06 May. 2014.
11. "Piety." *Dictionary.com Unabridged*. Random House, Inc. 06 May. 2014.
12. *Witch School Third Degree: Lessons in the Correllian Tradition*. Witch School. 2005.

FOUR LADIES

Dawn Maiden come!
Dawn Maiden beautiful!
Dawn Maiden golden bright!
Dawn Maiden come tonight!

Noon Warrior come!
Noon Warrior passionate!
Noon Warrior red as flame!
Noon Warrior join the game!

Dusk Mother come!
Dusk Mother nurturing!
Dusk Mother mellow blue!
Dusk Mother we call to You!

Midnight Grandma come!
Midnight Grandma magical!
Midnight Grandma verdant dressed!
Midnight Grandma manifest!

DEEP AT YOUR CORE

by **Abby Willowroot**

There is a knowing and an understanding that goes beyond words, beyond images, beyond logic or reason. Deep at your core there are all the secrets of the Universe. Discovering those secrets is your task.

Like the thousand petaled Lotus, the thousand prismed crystal opens to reveal layer upon layer of wisdom & insight.

The answers you seek are inside you, not in your mind, or your heart, or even your soul, but in the deeply buried place which has no name. Meditation and silent walks in Nature will connect you with your deep, eternal, internal wisdom, and open you to your own "Well of Knowing". It is here that your ancestors will speak to you of their world and wisdom. It is here that you will find the lasting peace of unity with all life.

The Great Goddess lives within you as a genetic memory from ancient generations of your family line, it carries with it, memes & memories of awe & reverence for the natural world.

Memories of Earth's cycles and their celebration in ancient times. Memories of what it means to be truly alive, to be a child of the ever powerful, ever present Great Goddess,

Memories of the Goddess, Mother of All Life, live deep within every cell of your body.

Do you remember? Do you want to remember? Watch the Moon every night, cherish it's luminosity, watch its shape change, as it moves through its cycle. Do this every night for a month, watch a full lunation. As you gaze at the Moon, let your mind & your instincts carry you back to earlier times, to times before time, when humans were new, a time when we began the journey. Gaze at the Moon and remember, who you truly are, at your core.

CHANT FOR WITHIN

Spiraling inward ... Spiraling downward
Deeper than this life ... Deeper than memory
Whirling through .... Dancing in eternity
Fragments come ... Knowings speak in images
Remembering comes ... Wrapped in sounds
Pulse drums, the eternal chant of life

Just as the tiniest crystal retains the blueprints of its fiery birth deep in the Earth, you contain the blueprints of your own origins, the legacy of your most ancient ancestors.

In every cell of your body there are memories, encoded secrets and ancient instincts ...

Scientists seek them by reading DNA codes.
Mystics seek them through the reading of vibrations and energies.

Both are correct, but neither can read them with the depth and clarity of one who is the living compilation of these sacred blueprints. The fullness of your own codes is there, pulsing within every cell of your body, and it is decipherable only by you, seek it out.

You ARE your ancestors.

I have the power to pour out the rainbow inside me to pour it into the Universe, and replenish it again within me. I have the power to share the magic that is always there inside of me, to allow myself to experience my glorious eternal self, in all its strength & beauty.

http://spiralgoddess.com/Core.html

THE PLOW PLAY

by **A.C. Fisher Aldag**

A plow play, or in the old-fashioned way of spelling, Plough Play, was held around Twelfth Night or the Epiphany, or around Imbolc or Candlemas during olden times in the British Isles. A holiday called "Plow Sunday" or "Plow Monday" featured decorating a plow, which was taken from house to house. Participants often sang, danced, played music, performed a dramatization, and begged for "money for the plow" which was used for a charity. In Christian times, this was sometimes a light in a church called a "Plow Light". During years when the economy was poor, it may have been a way for workers to earn money. Young men called "Plow Jacks", "Plow Stotts" or even "Plow Witches", wearing rags or funny clothing and with blackened faces, would threaten to plow up the front yard of anyone who refused to give an offering.

Some scholars believe that the plow play was originally a Pagan ritual, perhaps to ensure the fertility of the fields, a custom that was later adopted by Christians. In much of Great Britian, Ireland, Scotland and Wales, Imbolc was the day to begin plowing the fields, as the climate was warmer during the Bronze and Iron ages. Pliny the Elder noted in the first century C.E. that the Celts had better plows than the Romans, and that they began plowing "early". These tools were also used to cut turf for fuel. However, plowing the fields may have begun even earlier, as evidenced by a poem that signifies the end of the Christmas season, when Jack returns to his plow, and Jenny to her loom, traditionally sung or recited on Twelfth Night.

On Plow Sunday or Monday, plowing games and races were and are enjoyed, dances were held, including the Morris, with attendant feasting and drinking. The Ploughboys are sometimes accompanied by a Molly or Malkin, a man dressed as a woman who performs a lively rustic dance. Sometimes a person dressed in a costume made of straw, called a "Straw Bear", proceeds the dancers. The custom of the Plow Play was first written about in the sixth century, when some plow jacks got into trouble for plowing up the kirkyard in Scotland. The tradition all but died out early last century, except in the most rural areas of Britian and Ireland. Recently, the Plow Play custom has been revived by communities for fun and tourism, as well as by neo-Pagans as a type of sacred ritual to honor the land.

The Magickal Media crew was seen decorating an old-fashioned horse drawn plow for Imbolc, blessing it, then placing it outdoors to protect the home and to bring fertility to the garden. You can try this ritual for yourself, or with your family or coven – if no plow is readily available, you can decorate a garden cultivator, or make your own plow from two broomsticks and cardboard. Adorn it with silk flowers, ribbons, tinsel and streamers. Paper flowers can also be used, if your plow is kept indoors. This tradition has helped to bless our home and make our garden fertile for years.

> Plow Monday held this year in the UK, celebrated by middle schoolers. With photos and a video. ...
> http://goo.gl/2jMcmo
>
> Plow Jacks tow a plow through a town in the UK. ...
> http://goo.gl/iztqgO

BIOGRAPHIES: PART FOUR

by **Don Lewis**

THOMAS MORTON

Thomas Morton was the first prominent European Pagan in North America. Morton was a lawyer, a writer, a prominent royalist, and a devotee of classical Paganism. Morton was also, not surprisingly, a fierce and outspoken opponent of Purtitanism.

Thomas Morton was born in Devonshire around 1578. Morton immigrated to the New World in 1618. By 1624 Morton was a leader of the Mount Wollaston colony, in what is now Massachusetts. By 1626 Morton had fallen out with Wollaston and taken over the colony, which he renamed Merrymount.

Morton's Merrymount was run as a multicultural settlement with both European and Native American residents, featured Pagan rites dedicated to classical Deities including Venus and Bacchus, and notably an annual May Day celebration. Morton encouraged intermarriage between the Europeans and Native Americans, as well as cultural assimilation.

The Puritan settlers were deeply upset by the goings on at Merrymount, which they regarded as expressly Pagan, and their condemnations accuse Morton of worshipping a number of classical Deities and of promoting drinking and sexual license.

In June of 1628 Puritan forces under Miles Standish attacked and captured Merrymount, chopped down it's Maypole, and arrested Morton on the charge of selling guns to Native Americans. Morton was marooned on the Isles of Shoals, off New Hampshire, until he could be deported back to England. Meanwhile the Puritans renamed Merrymount as "Mount Dagan", ultimately burning it to the ground the following year. The area that was once Merrymount is today Quincy, Massachusetts.

Deported to England, Morton began a lawsuit against the Massachusetts Bay Company, and garnered considerable support. The Massachusetts Bay Company held the charter for the Massachusetts Bay colony. In 1635 Morton won his lawsuit and the colony's charter was revoked.

Morton would go on to rebuke the New England Puritans in his three-book series *New English Canaan* in which he compared the behavior of the Puritans to the biblical slaughter of the Canaanites.

With the beginning of the English Civil War in 1642, Morton returned to New England as the agent of the Governor of Maine, Sir Ferdinando Gorges, his longtime friend and patron. After foolishly traveling to Plymouth, Morton was arrested and imprisoned by Puritan forces. After some time Morton was released due to his advancing age and failing health, and fled to Maine where Gorges' supporters gave him shelter. Morton died in Maine in 1647 at the age of 71.

MARGARET A. MURRAY

Margaret Alice Murray was a prominent Egyptologist, Anthropologist, Folklorist, and campaigner for Women's Rights.

Margaret Murray was born in Calcutta, India, on July 13, 1863. For most of her professional career Murray was known as an Egyptologist of high repute. She accompanied leading Egyptologist Sir William Flinders Petrie on several archeological expeditions in Egypt in the late 1800s, and was first Curator of the Egyptian Collection at the Manchester Museum in the University of Manchester, England.

As an Egyptologist Murray is most famous for the unwrapping and autopsy of the "Two Brothers" in 1908, the first interdisciplinary unwrapping of an Egyptian Mummy, which revolutionized how such things were done thereafter.

Margaret Murray published a number of books during her lifetime, the last two of which – *The Genesis of Religion* and her autobiography *My First Hundred Years* – were published when she was 100 years old.

Most of Murray's books dealt with Egyptian or Classical archeology. However it was her three books on Witchcraft that revolutionized modern Paganism. In *The Witch-Cult in Western Europe* (1921), *God of the Witches* (1933), and *The Divine King in England* (1954) Murray popularized the idea that the Witches persecuted during Europe's Witch Hunts were the survivors of ancient Pagan religion.

Together with the work of Charles Leland and Dion Fortune, Murray's books popularized the idea of Witchcraft as the Old Religion, and led to the foundation of many modern covens and groups dedicated to this idea.

Margaret Murray died on November 13, 1963, at the age of one hundred years.

RT. REV. STEPHANIE NEAL

Rt. Rev. Stephanie Neal is a Correllian Arch Priestess and Elder, Head of Sacred Sea Temple, and the current First Elder of the Correllian Tradition.

Lady Stephanie is the Founder and Head of Sacred Sea Temple, established in 2006 AD. Lady Stephanie became an initiated Correllian Priestess in 2004 AD. She went on to be initiated as a High Priestess in 2007 AD.

Lady Stephanie was acclaimed as an Elder of the the Correllian Tradition in 2011 AD. In 2012 AD, Lady Stephanie was acclaimed First Elder of the Tradition.

In 2011 AD Lady Stephanie was made Co-Head of the Order of World Walkers under Her Eminence the Arch Priestess Lady Krystel. In 2012 AD Lady Stephanie was declared sole Head of the Order.

Lady Stephanie is also the Head of the Correllian Order of Shamans.

Lady Stephanie began her spiritual training in 1962 AD under two Root Women in Hawaii. She became an initiated Sea Priestess in 1968 AD at the age of 18.

She has taught Spiritual Counseling since 1978 AD.

In the Fellowship of Isis Lady Stephanie holds the rank of Magi.

Lady Stephanie's career has been varied and distinguished, and has included serving a Teacher, an Outreach Director, and school Principal.

Before coming to Correllianism Lady Stephanie served as the Associate Pastor of two mainstream churches, and also taught in and served as a head of a mainstream Prison Ministry.

Lady Stephanie has also worked as a Designer, Artist, and Spiritual Counselor. In the mid '80s Lady Stephanie was entered into the "Who's Who of American Business Women". In the early '90s She was named "Teacher of the Year".

NOSTRADAMUS

Michelle de Nostre Dame, better known as Nostradamus, is the most famous prophet of modern times. Nostradamus made his famous prophecies using a number of techniques including water-scrying and Horary Astrology.

Nostradamus was born in Provence in 1503, to a wealthy Catholic family of Jewish ancestry. He grew up to be an astrologer and medical doctor -an expected combination in that era.

After losing his young wife and children to the plague in 1534 Nostradamus made plague his specialty and had unusual success in its treatment. For many years he worked as an itinerant doctor, traveling wherever he was needed.

In 1547 Nostradamus married his second wife, Anne Ponsart and settled in Salon.

Beginning in 1550 Nostradamus published an annual Almanac, which included his psychic for the coming year. This proved to be immensely popular, and in 1555 he published the first part of his famous Prophecies.

The success of the Prophecies brought Nostradamus to the attention of the French royal house, and in 1556 he was summoned to Paris to meet King Henri II and Queen Marie de Medicis: the Queen asked Nostradamus to make predictions for the royal house and the royal children. Nostradamus famously and correctly predicted that three of the royal sons would become Kings.

After this Nostradamus received royal patronage from the House of Valois. When King Henri II died in 1559 in circumstances which seemed to confirm Nostradamus prediction with uncanny accuracy, the prophet's reputation was set. The Dowager Queen Marie de Medicis appointed him Physician in Ordinary in 1564, a high honor.

Nostradamus died in 1566, and the definitive edition of his Prophecies was published posthumously in 1568, by his widow and his student Chavigny.

Nostradamus' prophecies are decidedly obscure, but have been held to predict a wide range of events including the English civil war and French revolution, Napoleon and Hitler. Indeed, in WWII both the British and German propaganda departments had special subsections dedicated to interpreting and if need be manufacturing Nostradamus prophecies of their eventual victory.

GEORGE PICKINGILL

George Pickingill was a prominent English Witch born in 1816 at Hockley, Essex.

Pickingill came from a family of farm workers with a long history in the area. The Pickingill family claimed to be descended from "Julia, the Witch of Branden." This woman supposedly lived at the time of the Norman conquest of England (1066 AD). The legend states that a Saxon Lord called Hereford the Wake retained Julia to work magic for him against the invading Normans. She failed and died during the fighting –but her descendants were said to form a line of Hereditary Witches.

During his lifetime Pickingill established a network of Temples spread throughout Essex, Hampshire, Hertfordshire, Norfolk, and Sussex. These were termed the "Nine Covens.

The Nine Covens were made up of both female and male initiates, but were strongly matriarchal and were led by their Priestesses who could only be drawn from Hereditary lines.

Pickingill's own coven was known as the "Seven Witches of Canewdon."

Since Pickingill came from a Tradition which could only be passed from woman to man, or from man to woman, all of his immediate initiates were female, and all of their immediate initiates male.

Two initiates who are said to have come through the Nine Covens would have a far reaching impact on the future of the religion:

Aleister Crowley and Dorothy Clutterbuck.

Crowley would later become the leading exponent of Ceremonial Magic, and his works are often considered seminal to modern English Wicca. Crowley did not remain long in Wicca, though he maintained a long association with several prominent Wiccans: supposedly he resented the power of the High Priestesses.

Dorothy Clutterbuck on the other hand is best known as the High Priestess who initiated the great Wiccan reformer Gerald Gardner. It is interesting to note that Gardner and his followers felt that the materials which Clutterbuck gave them were fragmentary.

Pickingill had wide-ranging connections in the Masonic and Ceremonial movements, both of which were of great importance during the latter years of his life. Pickingill is said to have been involved in the founding of the Rosicrucian Society of England and the Hermetic Order of the Golden Dawn.

Pickingill lived to be 93 years old, dying in 1909.

PLUTARCH

Plutarch was born in the city of Chaeronea around 46 AD. A leading philosopher of his time, Plutarch's ideas are still very important in modern Pagan religion today.

Plutarch was educated at Athens, then the intellectual center of Grecco-Roman civilization, and traveled widely throughout Egypt and Italy. Plutarch lectured in Rome, and also served as a Priest at the Temple of Delphi, the principle Oracle of the Greek world. But eventually returned to settle in Chaeronea, where he had been born.

Plutarch wrote many books on a variety of subjects, but is best known for Parallel Lives, a book of biographies paralleling the lives of famous Greeks and Romans. Plutarch also wrote a number of works on religion and philosophy, including volumes on the nature of Oracles, and the worship of Isis and Osiris.

For the modern Witch Plutarch's most important work is *De Superstitione*, in which he discusses the differences between superstition and true religious feeling. Plutarch defined superstition as being beliefs based on fear of Deity and religion as being beliefs based upon love of Deity.

Plutarch died around 120 AD.

PYTHAGORAS

Pythagoras was a Greek philosopher and mathematician best known for formulating the Pythagorean Theorem. Among the earliest and greatest Greek philosophers, Pythagoras made many important contributions to philosophy and religious teaching in the late Sixth Century BC.

Known as the "Father of Numbers' Pythagoras pioneered the metaphysical art of Numerology and believed that everything could be defined by Number and predicted and measured through rhythmic cycles.

Pythagoras was born around 580 BC, on the island of Samos, off the coast of Asia Minor. He was the son of Mnesarchus, a merchant of Tyrian origin who had trading interests throughout the Mediterranean world, and Parthenis, a Samian noblewoman.

Before Pythagoras' birth the lady Parthenis consulted the Oracle of Delphi. The Oracle, or Pythia, predicted that Parthenis' unborn child would be "of great beauty, great wisdom, and would be of great service to humankind." Parthenis was so moved by this unexpectedly grand prophecy that she change her own name to Pythais in honor of the Pythia, and when her son was born she named him "Pythagoras" or "The Pythia has Spoken".

Young Pythagoras was given an excellent education and is studied under several well-known philosophers of the time including Pherekydes, Thales, and Anaximander. These three teachers are particularly noted for their teaching about the nature and immortality of the Soul, and the relationship between Spirit and Matter. Anaximander is also the first recorded proponent of the idea of physical evolution, though he believed that humans descended from an aquatic ancestor.

Pythagoras is also said to have studied under Aristoclea, a Priestess and Oracle of Delphi who is the first female Greek philosopher recorded. Because of his experiences under Aristoclea's tutelage Pythagoras and later Pythagoreans would always treat women as being equal to men —a rarity in ancient Greece.

Mnesarchus is also said to have arranged for his son to study with the Chaldean priests of his native Tyre, who were famous for their metaphysical teachings, especially dealing with Astrology. The young Pythagoras is also said to have traveled to Marseilles at one point where he met and studied with Celtic Druids.

Around 538 BC Pythagoras traveled to Egypt, which was at the time allied with Polycrates of Samos. Here he studied at the great Temple of An, or Heliopolis, an ancient center of Egyptian religious teaching. Later he studied at the Temple of Wast, or Thebes, where he was initiated as an Egyptian Priest.

In 525 BC Egypt was invaded and conquered by Cambyses II of Persia. This ended Egypt's last native dynasty, Dynasty XXVI. Pythagoras is said to have now gone to Persia, as a prisoner of war according to some sources, and ended up studying under Persia's Magi Priesthood.

Pythagoras eventually returned to his native Samos where he founded his first school of philosophy, called the Hemicycle. Pythagoras did not remain in Samos long however, because the island was torn with political unrest. Instead he moved on to Croton, in Southern Italy, where he settled in 520 BC and opened his famous School of Crotona.

The students at Crotona were divided between casual students or Akousmatikoi (Those who Listen) and full-time students of Mathematikoi (Those who Study). Both grades of students were open to men and women on an equal basis.

It was at Crotona that Pythagoreanism developed and synthesized the knowledge of the many systems that Pythagoras had studied as a young man. The Pythagoreans taught that the Soul was immortal and lived many lifetimes, practiced past-life regression, and placed great importance on the relationship between Spirit and Matter which they understood as Apieron (The Formless) and Pieron (The Form).

Above all the Pythagoreans used Numerology to study the nature of existence through numeric symbolism and mathematics. The Pythagoreans also encouraged vegetarianism, pacifism, and restraint in all things.

As their symbol the Pythagoreans took the Pentagram, an ancient symbol long used in Egypt to symbolize magic and the spirit world, which they are said to have marked on their palms as a sign of recognition.

The Pythagoreans understood the Pentagram also in light of Anaximander's teachings that the universe was composed of Four Elements (Air, Fire, Water, and Earth) plus a Fifth Element: Spirit. The Pythagoreans transformed the Pentagram, creating a new form of the ancient symbol, drawn with a single line to represent the unity of all things.

Pythagoras is said to have lived to around the age of one hundred, and to have died peacefully in his sleep. Pythagoras was succeeded as head of the Pythagorean School by his wife Theano.

RASPUTIN

Russian mystic Grigori Yefimovich Rasputin was arguably the most politically influential psychic of the twentieth century, in that he briefly (and more or less officially) dominated the government of one of the great nations of his time.

Born in 1869 AD, Rasputin was a Starets, or wandering mystic, who rose from humble beginnings to become the confidant of Russian Tsaritsa Alexandra Feodorovna, wife of Tsar Nicholas II. Many witnesses at the time insisted that Rasputin was a highly gifted psychic and spiritual healer, though his peasant origins and unorthodox theology (which supposedly encouraged extravagant sexual activities) earned him many enemies.

Rasputin is perhaps most famous as a psychic for divining that the hemophiliac Tsarevich Alexei, who was believed to be dying at the time, would recover if his doctors were sent away and medical treatment stopped —an improbable prediction that proved correct.

At the time it was not understood that the aspirin that the Tsarevich was being given to treat his pain was an anti-coagulant that was actually making his hemorrhaging worse. A number of other similarly striking predictions and healings are also attributed to Rasputin, many involving members of the Russian aristocracy.

Rasputin also strongly opposed Russian involvement in WWI, believing it would lead to disaster —though one didn't have to be psychic to see that. Rasputin was assassinated on 29 December, 1916, by a cabal or aristocrats who supposedly resented a peasant having so much influence over the imperial government —though recent theories suggest that Rasputin's anti-war stance may have actually been the motivating factor, and that the assassination may have been backed by or even assisted by the British government in order to keep Russia in the war.

Rasputin famously predicted that if he died peacefully the Romanov dynasty would survive for a thousand years, but if he died by violence the dynasty would fall and the Tsar's immediate family would be dead within twelve months –which is exactly what happened.

ALEX SANDERS

Alex Sanders was born Alexander Carter, on June 6, 1926. Alex Sanders was son of entertainer Harold Carter who subsequently changed his family's name to Sanders.

Sanders' grandmother Mary Bibby was a Witch, who supposedly initiated the boy into Witchcraft at the age of seven when he caught her at ritual. Though many have questioned the veracity of this claim, Maxine Sanders affirms that Mary Bibby did in fact practice a form of Witchcraft and that psychic and magical practices were common occurrences at her home.

Sanders was a gifted psychic and spiritual healer. From his grandmother Sanders learned how to scry using ink-in-water and crystal gazing techniques. Sanders also practiced spiritual healing by laying on of hands and other methods. For a time Sanders practiced spiritual healing through the Spiritualist Church, using the name Paul Dallas.

Whatever Sanders may have learned from his grandmother, he augmented his knowledge of Witchcraft with Gardnerian ideas after studying with and being initiated into a Gardnerian coven in 1963, and these strongly influenced the Alexandrian Tradition that he founded. By 1965 Sanders claimed to lead 100 Alexandrian covens, who gave him the title "King of the Witches" as head of their Tradition.

In 1965 Sanders was handfasted to Maxine Morris Sanders, whom he legally married in 1968. Maxine was Sanders' second wife. Alex and Maxine had two children, Maya born in 1968, and Victor born in 1972. Although they formally separated in 1973, Alex and Maxine's relationship would continue until his death in 1988.

Among Sanders most famous initiates were Stewart and Janet Farrar, both initiated in 1970, who would do a great deal to popularize Alexandrian Witchcraft.

Like Gardner, Sanders avidly courted publicity and was anything but secretive about his Witchcraft. Sanders was featured in dozens of newspaper articles, and in the film "Legend of the Witches" (1969). Sanders wrote no books of his own, but was featured in *King of the Witches* (1969) by June Johns and *What Witches Do* (1971) by Stewart Farrar.

Alex Sanders died on May Eve of 1988.

SILVER RAVENWOLF

One of the most popular of all Pagan authors, as well as one of the most controversial, Silver RavenWolf has authored seventeen books on Witchcraft and magic.

Born September 11, 1956, as Jenine Trayer, Lady Silver was first known in the Pagan community as SilverRaven the artist and Lady RavenWolf the High Priestess, later merging these two names to become Silver RavenWolf.

It was as an artist that Lady Silver first became famous, later founding the Wiccan/Pagan Press Alliance as a forum for Pagan publishers and editors to share resources and experiences, and finally rising to prominence as an author. Lady Silver has also been an activist in Wiccan anti-discrimination issues.

The unprecedented popularity of Lady Silver's books was due to their accessibility and straightforward manner. Unfortunately the very popularity Lady Silver achieved, led to a backlash against her works in some quarters.

Lady Silver trained as a Priestess of the Serpent Stone Family, achieving her Third Degree initiation through them. Later Lady Silver founded the Black Forest Tradition, with covens throughout the US and Canada. Lady Silver is also a practitioner of Pow Wow, a form of German folk Witchcraft.

Lady Silver currently resides in Dillsburg, Pennsylvania. She is married and has four children.

Lady Silver has also written several novels.

Some of Silver RavenWolf's many books include: *To Ride a Silver Broomstick* (2002): *TeenWitch!* (2003): *HedgeWitch* (2008)

CROSSROADS MAGICK

by **A.C. Fisher Aldag**

Acts of magick performed during times and at locations where two or more energies meet can be especially successful. Ever wonder why so many old-time spells take place at midnight, or on Midsummer Eve, or at a crossroads? The reason is because places and occasions of duality or convergence seem to be more powerful than other locations or times. Any time or place where one condition begins and another ends, or where there is a meeting between two or more directions or circumstances, contains a special magickal force.

In the old days, witches or magick users were sometimes called "hedge-riders" or "style-jumpers". A style is a wall or fence separating two rural fields, and thus symbolizes dual or variant states of being. The hedge or style represents the boundary between the visible and the unseen world. It is the borderland between the known and unknown, the tangible and intangible. The Witch straddles the physical world and the realm of the psychic. He or she may jump or transcend the familiar world of form, thus entering the world of force; making the change from an untenable condition to a more actualizing state of being. Another metaphor is the veil, or sheer fabric. Wiccans often say that on Samhain / Halloween, the "veils between the worlds are thinnest". Symbolic veils are found in locations and at times where two conditions meet or overlap. One side of the veil is concrete and available, the other side is obfuscated or mysterious. The image of the style, hedge, fence or veil between day and night, indoors and outdoors, above ground and underground, between the worlds, or a time when seasons begin and end, is a powerful ritual tool.

If you wish to add extra power to your spells, workings and rituals, try performing magick during times and in places where the veils are thinnest or where energetic boundaries occur. You may want to consult an almanac, and seek the exact moment when these situations occur – when summer ends and autumn begins, planets align, the sun rises, the moon turns full, or the sun moves from one Zodiac sign to another. Likewise, you may intentionally locate your ritual in a place where two conditions meet, such as the doorway between your home and yard, or at the shoreline of a lake. Even envisioning the image of a door, or picturing a crossroads in your mind, can increase your energy. Ideally, the symbolic time or location should reflect the intent of your rite. For example, you may wish to perform a banishing at the exact time the moon turns from full to waning, while standing on the basement stairs, both of which represent a "drawing away" or diminishing. These occasions of duality or convergence are also beneficial for transformation magick – creating intentional change from a certain life condition to a new situation or to greater awareness.

Locations that are on the edge between the visible world and the land of magick can include the abovementioned crossroads, doorway, fence, wall, or hedgerow. Other representations of this magickal boundary are a window, a fireplace hearth or chimney, bridges, thresholds, alleys and gateways. Many older rituals and spells include hiding a poppet in a chimney, placing a Witch's bottle beneath a threshold, or putting old shoes inside a wall for a protective talisman. Inside a wall, up the chimney, beneath, under or above are locations of duality. Basements and attics are also optimal, especially those where people do not dwell on a regular basis, rooms used only for storage. These locations have the dual aspect of being within the home but not an actual living space, empty yet full. Basements have the manmade features of a building, and the natural aspect of the earth, while attics have the elemental feeling of air with the manmade quality of structure. In popular literature, there is the story about the wardrobe in the nursery with Narnia beyond... the closet or wardrobe being a place that is between the land of concrete reality and fantasy. Gay people and Witches are said to "come out of the closet" when they tell their loved ones about their lifestyle, thus emerging from a situation of hiding and anonymity into a spotlight of truth and hopefully, acceptance. Any manmade place of duality or convergence is useable for crossroads magick.

Mirrors are especially powerful for journeying rites, as they represent a transparent boundary between the visual world and the spiritual realm. Many of us have heard legends of magickal beings who dwell within a mirror. Alice went through the Looking Glass to enter Wonderland. A spooky Halloween story tells of lighting candles before a mirror to envision the ghost of a bloody queen. Jewish folk cover mirrors when someone passes away. All of these legends speak to the belief that a mirror is a borderland between this world and the next, a reflection of this reality yet a container for the mysteries. The image seen in a mirror is also a vision of duality: there when we seek it, non-existent when we do not look, a semblance in reverse. Mirrors can be used to "capture" an image and magically retain it, such as focusing the glass on a representation of success. They can also be useful in a binding ceremony. A box lined with mirrors can reflect infinitely back on itself, and create a situation where a harmful influence is nullified. Care must be taken to not entrap one's own image in the mirror's borderland.

Natural locations can be used for crossroads magick, including the mouth of a cave, the entrance of the forest, the tideline of the ocean or large lake, the edge of a cliff, a swampy place that is neither fully land nor water, and under certain bushes or trees. In literature, magickal beings often inhabit thorn bushes, Rowan trees, elderberry groves, marshes, or hide beneath toadstools or mushrooms. These places all are thought to have the distinction of being gateways between the magickal realm and the mundane world. Alice fell down a rabbit hole to enter Wonderland. Dorothy was swept away by a tornado to Oz. Of course, during high winds or lightning storms, you should find shelter, but you can still work magick by using the energy of wind meeting earth, or a bolt of electricity connecting the air and the ground, to power your ritual.

You can also stand in these physical locations that represent a boundary while mindfully journeying between the known world and the hidden world, seeking wisdom. Wade through a flowing stream from one bank to the other. Cross a bridge. Travel a woodland pathway. Stand at a crossroads at midnight – this became a magickal cliché because so many of our ancestors did it – because it works! The "force lines" or "ley lines" of earth can also be tapped, as the spots where these energetic fields converge are especially powerful. The folks who constructed the stone monuments in Europe and the pyramids of Egypt and Mexico were likely using the "crossroads" energy of these locales, further connecting the earth and air with their buildings.

You can also seek magickal tools that have the benefit of two or more conditions meeting, converging or diverging, ending and beginning. The first snow of winter can be used for purification, a lightning-struck branch can make an excellent wand, the water of a fast-moving river can be used for a cleansing rite, the dirt from a crossroads can facilitate a binding, and so forth. Manmade items can also be utilized – a brick from a building that is being demolished, for example. One symbology of the May Pole is the connection between land and sky. Objects that take on the aspect of two locations, such as a seashell, can be used for crossroads magick, where the elements of both water and earth are needed. If you wish to ask for cooling, healing, grounding, and quenching of thirst, the seashell is a perfect talisman. Autumn leaves can be used to start a ritual fire, symbolizing the past being used to fuel a new, brighter situation. Another image that we can use for our magickal rites is a butterfly emerging from a cocoon, symbolizing growth. Any duality, polarity, convergence or a dividing principle will suffice.

As mentioned previously, times when the veils are thinnest, or when two or more natural occasions conjoin, are also advantageous for energetic workings. Gerald Gardener's "Charge of the Goddess" tells us that the Lady is most responsive during the hour of the full moon, and thus we should make our requests to Her during the Esbat. The time of the full moon is actually very short, when one side of the moon is fully exposed to the sun, facing the earth. However, its influence can be felt for nearly three days, the most powerful being the actual day when the moon is fully reflecting the sunlight. Check your almanac for when the tides turn, and use the symbolism for your magick, as well as the feeling of the moon pulling on the water. Astrologers can predict optimal times for rituals, and will inform you of a "cusp" situation, when one planetary influence seems to overlap another. For instance, if you're arguing with a loved one, you may wish to perform a rite when Venus aligns with Mars, and then Mars moves slowly "away", taking with it your heated emotions. Eclipses can be the best time for creating positive change – our family did a ritual for gaining a new home during a total solar eclipse. We used the darkening of the sun behind the moon to symbolize the ending of the time in our current dwelling, and the emergence of the sun to represent acquiring our new homestead. Planning for your ceremonies, and using the most beneficial occasion possible, can do much to strengthen your magick.

The times of magickal crossroads include the Wiccan Sabbats, especially those of Beltain and Samhain. Shakespeare wrote about traditional belief in Fairy activity in his "Midsummer's Night Dream"; and yes, the magickal entities really do seem to be more lively at certain times of the year. Spirits of the departed seem more inclined to visit on Samhain, at night, when legend speaks of a gateway opening between our world and the realm of the dead. This may be because the Sabbats are held during midpoints or times the seasons end and begin. The solstices and equinoxes are particularly good for some workings, as the longest day or night, or a time of equal darkness and light, sunshine and night time. These dates have an astrological significance as well; for example, on the

Autumnal Equinox, the sun enters Libra. Many older spells state that the Witch should perform a working at midnight, but dawn, dusk, and noon are also perfect for certain rites. Just like the new, waxing, full and waning phases of the moon, the daily phases of the sun can create specific magickal situations.

Many legends of the Gods, Goddesses, and ancestors correspond with times and locations of duality. The crossroads are a symbol of Hecate, the Celtic Maeva / Mab / Macha and Brighid / Brid / Briget, and Boann are represented by rivers, Aurora is the Goddess of the dawn, Nix the Lady of sunset and night time. Charon carried dead travelers on a boat across the River Styx, Janus guarded a gate, and many magickal beings stood as a watcher or guardian of a doorway. When planning your ritual, you can look up any Deities or entities that symbolize particular times or places. Ask their permission to be there, and of course bring them a gift of a stone, food, drink, a poem or song. Good luck and blessings in your quest for the Crossroads!

YOU WERE THE FIRST ONE

Holy Mother! Holy Mother! Holy Mother of Life!
You were the First One – Mother of Existence! Holy Mother of Life!

We are Your children! We are Your children! Holy Mother of Life!
You were the First One – Mother of Existence! Holy Mother of Life!

Holy Mother! Holy Mother! Holy Mother of Life!
You were the First One – Mother of Existence! Holy Mother of Life!

We are Your children! We are Your children! Holy Mother of Life!
You were the First One – Mother of Existence! Holy Mother of Life!

Holy Mother! Holy Mother! Holy Mother of Life!
You were the First One – Mother of Existence! Holy Mother of Life!

We are Your children! We are Your children! Holy Mother of Life!
You were the First One – Mother of Existence! Holy Mother of Life!

SHADOW AS A SPIRITUAL FORCE

by **Raven Digitalis**

This article and meditation focuses on the idea of *shadow* being something metaphysical and sacred. Interpretations of what shadow means span numerous traditions crossculturally, is viewed in a myriad of forms, and is applicable to Neopagan practice and philosophy.

As a spiritual force, shadow manifests in countless forms — just as countless as its equal-opposite counterpart, *light*. At the same time, is there really any division between darkness and light ... black and white ... good and evil ... or does reality operate and fluctuate in varying shades of gray? Why do we have distinctions such as these in our reality? I've come to believe that easy-reference labels can be beneficial for purposes of identification and discernment. On the other hand, it's all too easy to latch onto labels of any sort, becoming dependent on them, which can change an occurrence of *discernment* into one of *judgment*.

Some spiritual systems teach that identifying something under *any* of these extremes (dark/light, black/white, good/evil, and so on) is spiritually counterproductive, and is both inaccurate and limited thinking. In this view, looking at reality with an eye of categorization only leads to hierarchical thinking, distorted views, and divisive mental cataloging. Many spiritualists, magicians, and esotericists tend to perceive reality, and all its facets, as a massive grayscale. All is One, and divisions of any sort are there for convenience. Qabalah (Kabbalah) sees Oneness dividing itself tenfold (or more, depending on the school of thought), as per the vision of the Tree of Life discussed in the *Sepher Yetzirah*. While monotheistic religions tend to draw strict lines of division between "this" and "that" (generally the *sacred* vs. the *profane*), polytheistic religions tend to recognize the duality in all things, but see *both* sides of the spectrum as sacred and holy in their own right.

In terms of the force we label "shadow," its existence is highly interpretive. What can be termed shadowy for one person may or may not be termed the same by another. Going back again to monotheistic viewpoints, *light* is often aligned with the *sacred*, while *shadow* is aligned with the *profane*. As Neopagans, we realize the folly in this type of extreme dualistic thinking: reality makes no distinction between extremes, and is indeed constantly fluctuating between them. There would be no day without night ... no life without death ... no joy without sorrow ... both polarities are equally sacred, and both must be examined to cultivate spiritual wholeness. Neither shadow nor light can be neglected if one is wishing to make their life a truly holistic spiritual experience. Witches, magicians, and spiritual seekers of all varieties must examine *all* sides of reality's divine spectrum.

The word *shaman* originates from the Tungus people of Siberia (Russia), but is now frequently used to refer to particular practices of indigenous people across the globe, often citing Native American shamanism, Amazonian shamanism, Aboriginal shamanism, and so on, even if the term was never originally applies to these cultures. Part of the shaman's role — which can be seen in a variety of forms across the globe, yet all with similar characteristics — is to voyage the depths of darkness to uncover the light of awareness, revelation, and insight. This can be done for a person, a community, and so on. Shamans are initiated through pain and trauma, or have inherent abilities borne from living on the edge of a society (as a necessity, such as having a disability). Shamans were and are venerated for their abilities, and are often simultaneously feared for their power. When shamans and shamanistic practitioners help clients, they often work to heal them from a platform of interpersonal darkness. Parallels can be drawn between this and Jungian psychology: it's from the repressed, deeper portions of the self that shadow accumulates (to degrees either healthy or unrestrained), and it's from this deeper psychospiritual that the Light of Awareness is born.

Contrary to popular misinterpretation (even within some Neopagan circles, sadly), the force of shadow is not purely destructive, evil, or manipulative. At the same time, "black magick," predatory sorcery, and manipulation *can* be aligned to the shadow-side ... but there's more to it than that. Can dreaming or astral projection be classified as benign aspects of shadow-work? Heck yes! Can illusions of perception, such as an *artificial mask* of compassion (false-kindness), be classified as a negative aspect of "light?" Most definitely.

I have personally come to see the shadow under a number of forms, and tend to catalog these along a certain spectrum. For the convenience of this article, allow me to review my own perceptive divisions of shadow, and propose what can be included in each. I examine a number of these points in my book *Shadow Magick Compendium* (Llewellyn, 2008). These lists can easily be expanded, and even rearranged and altered to some extent, by any reader who has their own personal interpretations of shadow and light:

> **The Internal Shadow**: The Internal Shadow is the darker side of human nature, and is purely psychospiritual. Herein exists portions of the emotional body that have been repressed by the mind. When denial occurs, thoughts are pushed to the back of the mind, and into the unrecognized Internal Shadow. This draws on the Jungian view of the psychological shadow. When darker emotions palpably arise, such as sadness, anger, and apathy, it may be considered a conscious surfacing of the Internal Shadow. Just the same, a person may be objectively aware (or at least somewhat aware) of their darker characteristics, which is the first step in magically and spiritually working with one's Inner Shadow.
>
> **The External Shadow**: One's External Shadow can be seen as a projection of the Internal Shadow. Gone unrecognized, the External Shadow can manifest through *projection*. For example, a person may believe that no one thinks they are smart, when the truth of the matter is that they do not accept their own intelligence themselves. External projection can happen in limitless ways, and can arise from any repressed beliefs. Also included in this definition of the External Shadow are the shadows of others. In other words, any shadow aspects that are not your own can be considered external. External Shad-

ow-work relies on external forces, yet connects with and affects one's internal reality, such as with fasting or godform assumption (invocation). Demonic evocation, Qlippothic pathworking, binding, and cursing magick may also be categorized here.

The Astral Shadow: The astral plane is an etheric reflection of the physical world, and carries energies that are generally invisible to the untrained eye. The astral is also a realm of guides, guardians, and ancestors. Thoughtforms, deities, dreams, and etheric beings are said to exist on the astral plane, and magickal workings concerned with these forces can be considered operations of the Astral Shadow. Naturally, the astral plane carries currents of darkness that are directly linked to the shadow of the human psyche and the natural world. The astral plane and physical plane are intricately connected by the Web of Life — the threads of Wyrd — and connects all portions of reality (both seen and unseen) to each other. Many of the deeper mysteries of esotericism are indeed greatly astral, etheric, or energy-based.

The Shadow of Nature: As a prime example, the food chain may be considered part of Nature's Shadow, as one life form must feed on (destroy) another to survive. The "death" side of "life and death" can be viewed as a Shadow of Nature. The destructive aspect of nature may be included here, such as natural disasters and even poisonous plants. Additionally, shadowed aspects of nature like eclipses, the infinite night sky, the dying season, the dark moon, and the dark half of the year may be considered the Shadow of Nature.

The Shadow of Society: The unseen, hidden, suppressed, or overlooked aspects of our culture and society can fall under this category. Insofar as my own definition, the Shadow of Society is predominantly *not* a positive one. Skewed cultural worldviews, underhanded corporate crime, religious fanaticism, prejudice of all varieties, and self-serving politics can be considered a part of the Social Shadow. The Social Shadow is greatly shaped by the Internal Shadow, which is to say that devastating sociopolitical crime is often no more than horrid projections of certain peoples' inner fears and psychoses. Personally, I feel that the most devastating aspects of the Shadow of Society are the two extremes of *fanaticism* and *apathy*.

A Meditation on the Shadow Self

The following is a meditation is designed to access fears associated with darkness. This is not in reference to physical darkness, but to darkness as a vibration. This contains repressed fears, forgotten memories, and subconscious habits — many of which influence our everyday lives. Of course, this does not make internal darkness inherently bad or malicious, but makes it something essential to navigate for personal development.

In reality, our Internal Shadows can take years, if not a lifetime, to accurately study and come to terms with. Mysticism and magick are ways to better *know thyself* (as the Greek axiom states), and the meditation that follows is a suggestion to help this process. Please read through the meditation a number of times before enacting so that you are able to perform it by memory.

> 1 — Situate yourself in sacred space and have some comfy pillows to lie down on. Be sure to perform this meditation in darkness; the Witching hour (midnight) is preferable. If you can perform this on a new moon, all the better. Light a single black candle to partially illuminate the space, and cast the circle in your usual way. Summon the elements and dedicate the circle to your patron and matron gods (if you have any) and the spirits of the nighttime. Do what is comfortable.

> 2 — When you feel connected, fully lie down on the pillows and declare your intent. Say something like, "Behold! Great spirits of obscurity and darkness, I now wish to enter the shadow of my mind. I do not fear the darkness, but rather embrace it as a force of creation and mystery. Sacred spirits of the inner planes, I humbly ask that you guard me and guide me *into* myself, that I may grow and learn with patience and accuracy. So mote it be."

3 — With your eyes closed and your body comfortable, visualize the room around you. Allow your mind's eye to focus on the room from your perspective, and feel the placement of your body in the room. Become aware of your environment, and visualize your body for what it is: a temporary vessel for your spirit.

4 — While performing visualization, practice deep breathing. Take deep breaths in through your nose and out through your mouth. Continue to alter your consciousness and become psychically aware of your body and the environment. Take a decent amount of time to expand your perception.

5 — Now sufficiently aware, envision your astral body descending through the floor and into the earth. Descend only a few feet beneath the soil. You are comforted by the sensations of peace and stillness in this place. Open your psychic senses and feel the burrowing creatures and worms. Feel the roots of trees and plants brushing your body. Feel the damp soil, recognizing it as a center of nourishment and (re)birth.

6 — At this point, knowing that you are safe and protected by the bounty of the living earth, bring to mind two or three occurrences in your life that caused you great amounts of pain and emotional suffering. Take some time to remember these; some things may pop in your mind immediately, while others may be shrouded and even willingly repressed. If you happen to remember a large amount of painful experiences, you may wish to write these down after the meditation so that you can perform this again with different focuses in mind. Focus on the most traumatic, painful, and emotionally-breaking experiences you have endured in your life. If tears surface during the meditation, allow yourself to cry. Process each experience individually, remembering them even if you have already worked through them in the past. Claim your power.

(Please note: If the weight of any memories are too strong to process on your own, please arrange appointments with a counselor or therapist – everyone deserves to talk to someone, so why not a compassionate professional? I highly encourage the therapeutic method of working with one's shadow.)

7 — Sort through each issue individually. For each one, take plenty of time to recall the specifics of each situation: how, exactly, did you feel at the time? What was your role in the situation? Were you a victim? How has the situation effected your personal development? How has it influenced your life, both positively and negatively? Are any of your current patterns of behavior or modes of reaction connected to the event? Spiritually, what could possible reasons be for having to endure the experience? What can you do to resolve your pain attached to these occurrences?

8 — When you run through each individual event in your mind, one by one, you should feel a return of emotional weight. Now, envision your astral body — still submerged in earth — as covered with a dense, black tar-like substance. This represents the extent to which your mind still holds onto the event; the extent to which it may plague you now, even unconsciously. When ready, visualize a healing soft green-blue colored light emerging from your heart chakra, radiating through your body and eventually to the dense astral matter surrounding your body. Envision this light as a conquering force against the astral junk, permeating through it and dissolving it. With a strong exhalation, envision the black substance breaking away from your aura, plummeting down into the earth. Envision the healing light surrounding your astral body, ensuring against its return. Feel free to take as long as you need.

9 — Once you have performed this with one memory, occurrence, or negative incident in mind, continue with others that may have arisen. When you feel finished, complet-

ed, and relieved, visualize your astral body rising up from the earth, through the floor, and back into your physical body. Wiggle your fingers and toes, breathe in deeply, and come to center.

10 — To close, state your intention, saying something like, "Sacred spirits here this night, I thank you for protecting and comforting me as I journeyed layers of my mind. I ask that I be able to understand and release these issues by continuing to face them bravely and accurately. Thank you for attending this rite. Blessed be."

11 — Take some time to come back to your body, and close the circle as you normally would. It's a good idea to write down your experiences afterward, and spend additional time meditating on the intricacies of each experience of the past. Do whatever it takes to peacefully come to terms with the experiences of your past — most of us have endured trauma to one degree or another, and every one of us deserves to heal and claim our power. Nothing is every fully released; our experiences are simply come to terms with and accepted. Everything in life, no matter how dark and painful, can hold profound lessons beneath the surface.

MINI BIO:

Raven Digitalis (Missoula, MT) is the author of *Shadow Magick Compendium, Planetary Spells & Rituals* and *Goth Craft*, all on Llewellyn. He is a Neopagan Priest and cofounder of an "Eastern Hellenistic" Coven and Order called Opus Aima Obscuræ (OAO), and is a DJ of Gothic and industrial music. Also trained in Georgian Witchcraft and Eastern philosophies, Raven has been a Witch since 1999, a Priest since 2003, a Freemason since 2012, and an Empath all of his life. Raven holds a degree in anthropology from the University of Montana and is also a professional Tarot reader, small-scale farmer and animal rights advocate.

www.ravendigitalis.com

www.facebook.com/ravendigitalisauthor

SUFFERING

by **Don Lewis**

This discussion of Suffering is based on a series of videos that aired between May 28 and June 8, 2010, as part of "Rev. Don's Vlog", a daily video blog that I do. The discussion began with a question from viewer Elvenbough, who asked "Why is there so much suffering in the world?"

Why is there so much suffering the world, you ask? Many different religions have wrestled with this idea, and perhaps I will contribute a couple of comments to it. We do talk about it a little bit in the various books that I've written. But I think that the most common cause of suffering is perspective. I personally don't know anyone who has as many problems as people have never ha real problems. Very often they will go through the agonies of ... horrible, horrible spasms of agony over situations other people would take in stride. Why? Because they've never experienced it before. Others who've experienced it look at it very differently. I think this is true for many aspects of human suffering – that its entirely a perspective of how it strikes the person and the level that they look at it from. Many years ago, when I was much younger, I watched talk shows – why? Because I had nothing better to do. But I used to watch Donahue quite a lot. And Donahue was a very good talk show, very thought provoking. And I believe that this was Donahue, it could have been the early days of Oprah. But they had a show on weight loss. And they had the mandatory weight loss guru. And it was a woman who had lost a huge amount of weight, and who was very much a cheerleader for weight loss – but she was also rather bitter. And she made the comment that no person who was overweight could possibly ever be happy. And I remember thinking, even at the time, "You know ... there were people who lived through the concentration camps in Germany, went on to rebuild

315

their lives and find happiness. There are people who are quadriplegic or otherwise severely disabled, who lead happy lives. What do you mean you can't be overweight and be happy?" Well, obviously, she could not. And that was fine. Others can. Perspective. Level. I have done a lot of work over the years with the disability movement, partly because I spent some time myself being bedridden and unable to walk. One of the things I learned both through my own situation and through later interactions with the disability movement, is that you can be profoundly disabled and have a wonderful life and tremendous amounts of happiness. Similarly, you meet able bodied people who have no problems by comparison – who are miserable. Well, in many cases I would say that suffering is a matter of attitude – and to some extent you just have to make up your mind that you're not going to, and that you're going to resolve your situations as they come up. Now I say that like I practice it all the time – and of course, everyone has certain moments of suffering, sorrow, and depression. And you don't always handle your problems as they come up – you don't always handle them correctly – that's part of being human. But I would still say that in many, many cases its how you look at it that determines whether it is or is not "suffering".

Now, I want to move on to another subject, and that is the idea that it is through the challenges of life that we learn and grow, and that one of the primary purposes of life is to learn and grow. Therefore we must have challenges to motivate us to improve, to grow, to become better. And often when we face challenges we perceive them as suffering –especially if we struggle against the challenges. And that struggling against the learning experiences that are put in our path is a major cause of what people perceive as suffering. Sometimes arguably it really is [suffering], sometimes arguably its perception – but again it's the difference between what they think their life should be and what their life really is.

And perhaps about understanding that challenges are our benefactors – they bring us knowledge, they bring us experience, and indeed it's the times that we are challenged that make us stronger, better, and more able to succeed. Even when we fail, if we learn from our experience, we are more able to succeed the next time. However many people, because they believe that they should always succeed, and they do not realize that challenges are learning experiences, will perceive that this is suffering, and terrible – and occasionally it is. But this I would say is the second reason for what we perceive as suffering in the world. In many cases, if instead of struggling against our challenges we would embrace them and grow willingly, we would have much less perception that we are suffering. Now out of my own life, I mentioned the other night that at one time I had injured my back very seriously, and was bedridden for a long time, and had a great deal of difficulty in recovery. And certainly this was not a pleasant experience, and there was much physical suffering involved. Looking back upon it however, it was also one of the greatest learning experiences of my life, and I have been a much stronger person ever since. And so I perceive that as not only something necessary in my life, but beneficial.

So, having talked about the role of perception and perspective in how people perceive suffering, and also having talked about the role of challenge in life and growth, let's now talk about Karma. For many people, and I was initially taught this way myself, Karma is a matter of action and reaction. As I have grown and matured, my understanding of karma has changed, and during my lifetime the understanding of Karma endorsed by the Correllian Tradition has changed – largely due to Past Life work on the part of myself and the Lady Krystel, and other leading Correllian Priesthood. My current understanding of Karma – our current understanding of Karma, if you would – is less a matter of action and reaction than a matter of "attachment." What that means is that when a soul encounters an experience which is particularly important to it -in any way – but usually especially in the sense of being traumatic or difficult, but also in the sense of being very pleasurable, it will "attach" to an aspect of that situation, and will afterwards be drawn back to it. As long as that attachment remains the Soul will be drawn back, until eventually they understand the nature of the attachment, learn the lesson involved in the attachment, and release it. And I have no doubt that this is the cause of a great deal of suffering our Karma, our Attachments. I believe that these things draw the soul back into situations, and variations upon situations many times throughout many lifetimes. And very often these situations will be traumatic, and will involve suffering. How do we deal with Karma? Well ultimately we must release it, we must resolve and heal it. One of the best ways to do this in my opinion is Soul Retrieval, which I talk about in various writings I have written and videos I have made. But I find it a very effective tool for working with Karmic Attachment. Karma, which is to say Attachment, is what brings us the situations of our lives, in an unconscious manner. Now of course we also create situations unconsciously, both before coming into life and all through our lives, and it is the act of taking conscious control of this process which we call "Magic." But Karma – Attachment – is also part of that process of creating our world. We draw those things to us to which we are attached, we draw them into our lives. For many people the traumatic, the "suffering" things, are the things they are most attached to. Releasing them can be very hard. Many people I have known actually define themselves more in terms of their suffering than any other thing – in fact, I think it was Carolyn Myss, the New Age author, who described this as "Woundology." People who live in their woundology, who are totally focused on how they have been hurt, how they've been damaged over the years, and never quite come to the point of letting this go. To me, the path of Magic, the path of Religion, the path of Metaphysics, is all about healing and releasing these attachments, releasing our woundology – not holding on to it.

Finally, I wanted to comment on the difference between objective and subjective reality. A number of people have made the comment that suffering is very often directly related to the actions of others, and this is certainly true. And when it is true those actions can be seen from one level as the cause of the suffering. This has to do with the level from which you are looking at reality. Reality, like all things, has a number of different levels that you can look at it from. From one level reality is very objective, its very external, it's something that is very solid and must be interacted with as it is. From another level, a more spiritual level, reality is very fluid, it's very subjective, and very much manifested from within, rather than experienced without. In metaphysics we try to more consciously create our reality from that inner level. Therefore when we speak of things like suffering, we do tend to look at the inner causes, because ultimately that is where we would see the root. Even when the apparent cause of things is external, we believe that it is attracted to us or created by us – or co-created by us, or any of a number of different ways of looking at it- because of inner issues which could arise in this life or be held over from previous ones. This does not mean by any means that that objective aspect of reality should be disregarded, rather it means that when we go trying to work with our spiritual self, work with our Higher Self, work with magic and trying to consciously create the world around us, that we must look for internal origins. Now in terms of the world around us, whatever the internal origins or our circumstances may be, there certainly are right and wrong ways to behave. And when people go around intentionally inflicting suffering on others, this is a wrong way to behave, regardless of whether there are also internal origins on the part of those receiving this treatment. That really has nothing to do with whether it's the right or wrong way to behave. And the whole issue of right and wrong ways to behave also is one that is a very deep subject, because of course it's very subjective. Living here in Salem I am very aware of the Salem Witch Hunts, because it is of course the big tourist industry. And you know, the people who were conducting these Witch Hunts certainly thought they were behaving in a right manner – although nobody today, for the most part, would think that. Looking either at what they did or how they did it we are rather amazed. Even more amazing is where they drew the line between what they considered to be Witchcraft and what they did not, because apparently a number of them were practicing kind of magic that today would come under that heading, and they seem to have had what we would consider rather eccentric definitions. Of course it was several hundred years ago, and definitions do change, ideas about what is right and wrong change. They also considered themselves very right when they persecuted the Quakers, who they persecuted mercilessly – in way that we would never approve of today or consider to be right. So ideas of right and wrong behavior are also very subjective and they do change with our social understandings. These things are part of what I consider to be, to use the general term, part of a social contract that we make with each other so that we can live together in peace, in terms of what we will and will not accept. And I think that having such a social contract is completely appropriate for society, as is constantly revising it. In terms of moral behavior and right and wrong action, I think that we need to be very conscious of such things. And of course within the Wiccan religion the Wiccan Rede, "An It harm None, Do As You Will," is considered one of the primary statements by which we judge what we consider right and wrong action – that, and the general social contract of the society in which we live. So to recap our basic subject – yes, certainly, people's wrong actions can inflict suffering upon others. That being so, we would say that there are still internal reasons which have brought these things into the other persons lives, and if they wish to deal with this it is not necessarily enough to deal with the external, objective cause of your suffering, but you must also deal with the patterns underlying – the metaphysical patterns underlying. Many of us have known – I certainly have known – of people who deal with one situation after another which when you look at them are nearly identical, going from one situation of suffering to the next. And every time they deal with the objective cause of it – and yet find themselves confronting exactly the same thing, because they have not dealt with the internal causes that are underlying it.

MOMENT OF CHANGE

The world is re-created
In the beauty of the moment
The beauty of the moment
Of change
-
The world is re-created
In the beauty of the moment
The beauty of the moment
Of change
-
The world is re-created
In the beauty of the moment
The beauty of the moment
Of change

KINDNESS

by **Abby Willowroot**

*Kindness flows like water
smoothing roughness
softening sharpness
nourishing all it touches*

*Kindness replenishes
the spirit & the heart
with strength and hope
building bridges of humanity*

*Kindness is keeping alive the hopes of our better selves;
nurturing the inner wisdom of connection among us all.
With Kindness all things become possible, even the impossible.
Compassion always triumphs over indifference*

It is easy to become hardened in our hearts. The pace of the world forces many to put up walls of indifference. Our inner nature cries out to connect with those around us in a meaningful way. Kindness expressed daily in a 1000 small ways is the key that liberates us from personal isolation. The simple kindnesses you express to others benefit you abundantly. They lighten your spirit and bless your path. Kindness offered without question or motive enriches the giver.

Pausing a moment to let a car enter into your lane, holding a door open for someone, sincerely thanking a person who waits on you, are all small, but important ways of expressing kindness. Everyday there are an unlimited number of opportunities to act with kindness to strangers as well as those close to us. With each act of kindness your heart opens a bit more and your sense of isolation diminishes. Developing the habit of being kind changes a person and draws to them many unimagined gifts and blessings.

Blessed are the Kind
for in their hands humanity is nurtured
in their spirits wholeness grows strong
in their presence all things flourish
in a kind heart abundance grows

We all are capable of changing the world through our beliefs and our actions. This is not any great revelation, but we sometimes forget how much power we really have. The way we live our daily lives has an enormous impact on those around us. Remembering to act with kindness and move past our own insecurities is a challenge for us all.

Quan Yin...Goddess of Peace
Mother of Compassion & Kindness

Help me to show unlimited kindness
restore the sacred balance of Yin & Yang ... my natural state
keep me grateful for the abundance that has been given me ...
may I remember to always use it well, sharing it with others.

It is easy to get caught up and forget that we are a living, breathing, manifestation of the sacred universe. Remembering who we are makes us strong, kind and unstoppable.

http://www.spiralgoddess.com/Kindness.html

SPELL WORK: THE POWER OF NOT

by **A.C. Fisher Aldag**

Spells, incantations, chants, prayers. Many Pagan, Wiccan and Ceremonial Magick spells end with the words "So Be It" or "So Mote It Be", to cause the words to become Law. Asatru has the practice of Galdr, using the voice and the power of the Runes to bring word into manifestation. The Khemetic paths have the concept of Mhaat, represented by a feather, meaning that words can be measured against the weight of a feather to determine truthfulness. If every word that is spoken is literally true, then all words spoken by an individual will become truth. Many cultures use prayer or chanting, and almost every civilization taps into the power of sacred song. Breath and voice give rise to spiritual power, which enacts result. Words bring force into form. Optimal situations are brought about by the energy of the spoken word.

When performing acts of verbal magick, we must be very cautious about using precise words to invoke the desired condition. The Power of NOT must be considered. How many times have we heard a parent say, "Don't do that, you will fall"? Or heard someone announce "I am trying not to gain more weight"? This semantic problem sometimes occurs even in the midst of a magickal ritual. "Let there not be any more war in the Middle East." Unfortunately, the Gods, or the Universe, or the Powers That Be may only hear the end of the statement. The parent has declared "You will fall". The individual has spoken the words "Gain more weight". And all of the participants of the rite have summoned "More war". Of course, our intent is exactly the opposite. We wish for our children to be safe, our physical body to be healthy, and for our world to be peaceful. Thus, we must NOT state what we do NOT want to happen. We must avoid invoking the negative. We must resist the power of NOT.

When we are speaking our will into manifestation, we must ensure that we say exactly what we mean. It is best to make positive statements about what we desire to happen. The parent might say, "Please keep your feet on the ground." The leaders of a magickal rite must carefully consider the message that they wish to announce to Deity or the Universal Mind. Use positive declarative statements. "We invoke peace in the world. We request that all nations cooperate. We ask that people get along with each other." If you ask for it NOT to rain during your picnic, the Rainbirds may hear / sense / feel the word "Rain", and the idea of rain will be entered into the cosmic register. The reality of a rain shower might be the result. Instead, we should request "Good weather during our picnic, sunshine until five o'clock." This statement deliberately avoids mentioning the R word. Often, we receive exactly what we ask for – even if we do NOT know what we're requesting!

Our will may be spoken into reality during a spell, prayer or a religious ceremony. Yet sometimes, Deity and the natural world may have other ideas. If you request nice sunny weather for your picnic, you may get your wish. However, if the local area has experienced a drought for the past month, the farmers are praying for rain, the frogs are singing in the rain, and Nature truly needs it to rain, your little working for sunshine may go ignored at this time. The spirit beings may choose NOT to respond to your spoken word. We must respect that the universal consciousness often has worldwide best interest at heart.

To help ensure that we get what we actually want from our verbal request, it's beneficial to consider exactly what we desire. Give thought ot time, place, situation, person, and any other issues. Write down your prayer in advance. "Ceres, dear Goddess of Agriculture, please bless my garden. Help my plants to be healthy, and to produce enough vegetables for me to feed my family this summer. Grant us enough vegetables to preserve by canning for the cold months. So be it. Thank you." This spoken prayer contains specific time parameters. We want the garden to grow enough vegetables for an exact period. We made sure to say "plants to be healthy" rather than "plants to not be diseased" or "not have insect pests". We left part of the working open-ended; it is up to Deity to fulfill our desire for "enough".

Sometimes we must make a declarative statement about a particular condition in order to vanquish that situation. Let's return to our prayer for peace: "My grandson is serving in the Army, fighting in the war in the Middle East. I pray for his safety. I ask that the war be ended." The declarative statement is truthful. However, NOT is gone from the prayer. Instead, the magick user has asked for a desired condition. The Powers That Be will hear "War be ended".

An exception to the power of NOT is during banishing spells or rituals. Many magicians perform this type of working during a waning moon, using energetic tools such as black candles and sea salt to remove certain unwelcome influences. The objective is to stop undesirable conditions from occurring. Intentionally saying the word NOT can be beneficial in these particular circumstances. Speak about a true situation and your desire to discontinue that state of being. "I am unemployed. I do NOT wish to be unemployed. Instead, I wish to have a good job that uses my skills and pays well. Please remove any mental impediments which cause my unemployment. Change conditions which result in my lack of employment. Banish that which impairs my goal of gainful employment. So Be It."

Of course, after performing a banishing rite, it is best to invoke or summon the desirable condition that is opposite of the situation that you have banished. Once you have removed any influences that cause unemployment, then you may request that you be hired by the perfect employer, in the most wonderful job that is exemplary for you. Leave other options open, as well. The Universal Mind could respond to your request with self-employment or a money grant for study. Be certain to add a caveat about free will and to ensure that no harm is caused to others. You wish to be employed at a fascinating, high-paying job because an employee has retired or a new account has opened, creating a need to hire more personnel – rather than gaining a new career because someone in the company died in a car wreck. "Change conditions that result in my unemployment" could actually mean "Get rid of my new baby so I can work full time without having to pay for day care". We do NOT want harmful, negative energies to cause pain or trouble for other individuals. We wish for everyone to enjoy the bounty that is available in the world. "Please change conditions that result in my unemployment. Let my will be spoken into reality while causing harm to no other person. So be it."

One more caveat to the power of NOT: Some magicians who operate within the realm of chaos energy, such as Contrarians or Discordians, may use the spoken word to gain the opposite of their request. They might say, "I want it to rain today" in order to have sunny weather for the picnic. They might use the word NOT to bring force into form in reverse... but this is a large topic that should be explored in another article.

For the rest of us: The power of NOT works in the context of a ceremony, yet we must also attempt to mindfully remove the word from our vocabulary in regular conversation. We wish to experience optimal health, rather than to NOT get sick. Instead of hoping that the car does NOT break down, we want the engine to run smoothly, the tires to stay inflated, and all parts to operate well. You get the idea. Each time we speak, our words hold a power that interacts with the energy present in all things. We purposefully invoke our will, invite our desired condition, into reality. The consciousness present in the universe hears and responds... and we each hear our own words of power and may unconsciously bring about our spoken statement.

When we hear a loved one inadvertently use the power of NOT, we might wish to help them to manifest their true will. When a teenage daughter moans, "I won't ever get a date!" we may wish to state, "You will find a perfect loving relationship." Ensure that the individual is simply using an enculturated verbal phrase, so that you aren't interfering in their own free will. If your son declares, "I do NOT want to attend the prom," he may be expressing a true desire to avoid the dance. Another way our society uses the word NOT is in a sarcastic manner. "Oh no, it's NOT going to rain, is it?" "Please tell me that my car is NOT breaking down!" Again, these statements can bring about that particular undesirable condition. The Gods may hear "going to rain" and the Universal Consciousness might act on the words "car breaking down." We might wish to say, "The car is NOT breaking down. The car will run until we can get it serviced. The car will function perfectly well after the mechanic repairs it." Thus we bring our true will into manifestation.

Negative words: NOT, never, don't, won't, ain't, wouldn't, shouldn't, couldn't, is not, will not, did not.

MAGIC'S EVERYTHING

Magic in the fire
Magic in the flame
Magic in our heart
Magic in our name

Magic is the word
Magic is the goal
Magic's what we do
Magic is our soul

Magic's what we want
Magic's what we need
Magic's what we make
Magic is the seed

Magic makes the world
Magic's what we bring
Magic is the power
Magic's everything

WELCOME TO THE DARK, STILL WATERS OF SEA PRIESTESS TRAINING

by **Stephanie Leon Neal**

Chapter One
Spiritual Shadow Work

"Since once I sat upon a promontory, and heard a Mermaid on a dolphin's back. Uttering such dulcet and harmonious breath, that the rude sea grew civil at her song. And certain stars shot madly from their spheres, to hear the sea mist's music."
~ William Shakespeare

Water people are now showing their selves, for now is the time to once again, open the next great transformative gates. Therefore compassion, selflessness, and grace will be assets once again while selfishness and greed will be blown away. The water mysteries reveal that up is down and down is up; when philosophies are turned inside out. Most of humanity will not be frightened, and conversely, will be given a grand opportunity to grow into their new expanded consciousness. Some individuals will not be able to receive such a grand notion because they have enjoyed the concept of high and low, saying, "We are higher than them," that only a select few are the "special ones," and that there are only a very few that are truly divine. That concept will be torn asunder because it is a complete untruth and has always been an untruth.

Thus bad news for the arrogant and good news for all humanity.

If you think becoming a Sea Priestess is focusing on things of the Sea; you would be incorrect. It is essential, even paramount we start with you and who you are. .You will be untaught and complete much shadow work to earn the title Sea Priestess. You will be surprised how much shadow work is done and in the end you will return from where you began, in the deep waters of the cosmic sea.

Becoming a Sea Priestess/Priest is threefold:

First, Sea Priestess' students are "untrained." They are turned right side up again, enabling them to uncover all their treasures and tools within. In doing this, we come to the second precept; discovering and identifying all shadowy waters which have clouded our perceptions in the past. When clearing is done, we dig to discover our tools, and our heritage.

Thirdly, we pick up our tools and enter our divine purpose as a Sea Priestess or Sea Priest; fully prepared to work as pioneers, doing our part within the Great Evolution, the Great Work. Some of us will be drawn to set up training groups to help women and men to remember their sea heritage, while others will travel throughout the land and sea to find the others.

When studying the Sea Priestess path, each lesson will include exercises to insure a meaningful journey to our full creature-hood. The exercises also reveal many more lessons. Lessons are not learned through just the written or oral communications.

So called "power" will be laid out for all to see and for all to pick up and utilize for themselves. Ego centered individuals will soundly reject the notion that the Universe has given every one all they need to be whatever they desire, with no middle man. The Universe trusts us to carry out this most sacred task. Some will not want to be untaught, which is their free choice.

Becoming a Sea Priestess is easily reachable, if you have a pure selfless heart and pure motives. That is all which is needed to take this journey across the seas of consciousness.

Becoming a Sea Priestess means you have done extensive spiritual shadow work; while focusing on the positive side of issues, in balance. Balanced to the point that there is no balance because the two will become One. It is important to focus on what you desire, not what you do not desire or hope to obtain someday; someday never comes. Sea Priestess' are pioneers and un-philosophers; meaning we are brave enough to look at old precepts and turn them upside down, thus becoming a Sea Priestess philosopher.

We will focus on shadow work from the positive view. If we only focus on the so called negative aspect of a problem or try and find the "root" of a shadow, then we gain nothing, except spending more time in shadow. If you like to always focus on the negative side, then these lessons are not for you. If you want to spiritually heal, at soul level, and live a bombastic life, then you will. It is all up to you. Everything is up to you. In other words your life is your responsibility.

Here is the tough part - all outside gifts must be put down. The Tarot, stones, herbs, charts, reference books, everything that has a perceived power over you must be stripped away so that you may discover your own power, your own voice, your own core This freedom enables you to dig for your treasures and cultivate a direct line to all that is. Only after you have experienced and applied your treasures may you pick up all those powers outside yourself and discover that they are more attuned to you, more powerful than before you laid them down.

Stones, charts, herbs and the Tarot have incredible power, a higher self, and an ever expanding consciousness. As you install each helper back into your life, both you and your tools will be more developed and strengthened to hold the mantel and energies of a Sea Priestess, a living spring directly connected to Source, for there was always nothing between us and Source or It.

Yes, you will need to meditate, astral travel, and lucid dream like you have never done before. You are able! Everything is reachable to you!

Rise up, so that you may claim your rightful heritage and help usher in this great work. We will need all hands on deck to turn everything back to right side up again. Sometimes you will think, "What does this have to do with water?" Then other times, while reading about Water, you will think, "What does this have to do with me?"

As you travel across the seas with me, you will see how shadows and water work together unraveling your philosophy, unraveling you back to your very core. Our main focus is you, because everything unfolds from here.

"Gifts from the Sea, I give. Thus says the Sea."

Dive

As you dive into these teachings, know you are entering into another world, a world that has been waiting for you for eons. Each chapter has many levels of communication, deliberately installed. There are also three threads that run throughout all chapters. What you see within these lessons will depend on your perception, your astrological sign, your world view, your mind training, your shadows, and your philosophy. To some extent, this is a fact for everything and any event that comes in contact with you. There are lessons between the lines, under the surface, waiting for you, in every lesson.

As meditation becomes deeper, and you experience your power points, your personal core, you will be ushered into another frequency so that you may see all that has been lovingly placed on these pages, i.e. symbols, pictures, harmonic sounds, and colors that you have never seen within this life. If this sounds impossible, I challenge you to do the exercises and see who you are by the end of these lessons. These lessons will either push you away or draw you near to the water's edge. I challenge you to do the work and see the changes within you, changes that will reach the farthest four corners of the earth, at the very least.
Yet, know that nothing has ever been hidden from you, ever.

You will receive the exact measure of what you put into this journey, no more and no less. These un-lessons ensure that your shadow and your promise will be revealed together, one diminishing while the other flows, if you do the work.

Some statements within these lessons will push many away from this Sea Priestess path because they are not Sea Priestess', which is excellent. It is good to find out what you are not. I bid a fond farewell and blessing as you find your true journey, your true purpose. Your true purpose may not be here, for only the Sea Priestess will remain in these quiet waters.

Buckle your seats; it is going to be a bumpy ride!

Reading is Not Enough

Reading mere words does not mean you know the precept; there are many hidden lessons that can only be realized when a Sea Priestess enters a pearl precept, and experiences it, for only then will she be able to apply that knowledge. Only then, is the precept genuinely her own. Are you willing to change, to evolve to pure love? Are you willing to experience, not just read the words on these pages and say to yourself, "I know because I have or want to experience what I just read."

To know something is to experience "it" first hand, not receiving information second or third hand, resulting in watered down information. If you are just going to read the words and do not allow the spirit behind the words to enter your heart and life, then you are not willing to do the shadow work and are not willing to experience and apply the pearl precepts. Pearl precepts are transformative believe systems, if applied to one's life. I hope you enjoy the mere words, as they will become seeds for the future. It is wonderful to "know," however knowing without experiencing is not enough because one misses all the lessons that are within the experience and concept application. There are so many more lessons that can only be revealed through action and application. Reading is not enough.

Unless you have entered into the experience, felt the experience first-hand and applied the water to your life, then you are not an active participant within this circle of water. When you have done this, then you are no longer a spectator, but actively using your life as a transformative force of nature.

As you move through each sentence, feel your very core energy. Receive every ounce of pure love imbued within every pearl precept. This is your time to develop and activate all your senses, all your gifts. You are reading about this subject because you have a deep abiding sense of your purpose, you may or may not know your purposes and found yourself attracted to this subject. By the end of these lessons, you will, without a shadow of a doubt, know what you are capable of, or at the least see everything with new eyes, through the lens of water, through the lens of the sea, through Goddess.

Consider each word a soothing, fragrant sea balm; a love letter written just for you. These words were written just for you. It takes courage to allow yourself to be touched and comforted, maybe for the first time in your life. It may have been a very long time since you were uplifted, or validated in any fashion. Your soul will begin to speak this very moment, saying, "Now is the time to reclaim my purposes and joy!"

Every lesson is a water love letter to you because indeed, you are loved beyond measure. My desire is that you will stand in your full glory by the end of these lessons, because the world is waiting for you, the world is waiting for your gifts. The seas are waiting for you. That is a fact! You are not here by accident. You are here by your design.

If you are reading these words and have judgments, bitterness or un-forgiveness in your heart, regain back your authority and power so that you may receive what you need to become sovereign. Though not impossible, it will make self-discovery more difficult to uncover what is rightfully yours, the hidden treasures that lie just below the blue surface.

Warning! If you are reading these lessons for just the purpose of accumulating knowledge, be careful, because you may fall into the water and become more than you could have ever imagined.

Let us end all the outside stimuli, everything robbing us of our time and our power, as we work through this study. Let us put down everything that hinders us from clearly seeing the big picture. End the outside influences, so that we may hear our own inner voice, not someone else's voice our voice. Stop trying to make ourselves into what a book says; we are not in any book, none. Books are good outside tools, but we cannot find out how we work, from where we came, and who we are within any page. This un-training will push away all outside powers and push us into our power, our gifts that were given directly to us. After you have discovered your own voice, then pick up books and see how much more will be gleaned from them.

Decide right now that no "middle man" shall come between you and your journey.

Once we have found, experienced, and applied our gifts, then as Sea Priestesses we may pick up all our external tools, at which point they will be even stronger and will sing for us louder than they did previously.

Mutterings

"You are safe; you are needed to usher in this great evolution. Nothing will be hidden from you. Enough of humanity is ready to directly hear my voice because you are enough, my pioneers. You are more than enough."

> *"He who takes his teachings and applies them increases his knowledge."*
> ~ Hawaiian Proverb
>
> *"Only through knowing, does one attain liberation, only through knowing does one come to know oneself, only through knowing is truth revealed."*
> ~ Taoist saying

WELCOME TO THE DARK, STILL WATERS OF SEA PRIESTESS TRAINING

by **Stephanie Leon Neal**

Chapter Two
One Pagan

Under the Sea, most sponges, shells, and seaweed are used as a protective covering for their underworld inhabitants. As a hiding place to birth young and a home and filter to see their watery world, all good reasons to stay among the sponges and seaweed. But alas, the young fish grow up and know, instinctively, it is time to come out of their covering and explore a wider world and to embrace a wider vista that is theirs to claim. Just as the dragonfly, instinctively, knows to come out of her veil, emerge out of the protective water, and develop her wings, so that she may fly into the horizon. A dragonfly does not need to be taught to fly, nor a fish to swim, this is true for the Sea Priestess. Sea Priestesses only need to lay down all perceived outside powers, all external influences, for a time and remove all shells that are now a burden. All were good to be among, for a time, but have now outgrown their purpose. Come out of all seaweed tangled paths that lead you to everywhere, but you.

The main purpose for this lesson is to gently untangle you from all over complication.

Over complication is a time and joy thief, designed to rob you of your free-will, your divine thoughts, giving you permission or excuses to remain in the struggle. People have been trained that life and their "path" is one long awful struggle. That is only true if you live under that shell. It was a choice you made, long ago. It is not a good or bad choice, just a choice that needs to be re-examined, if you want to learn something new. Decide now if over complication is out dated or useful for your growth; only you can answer these questions. Consider quietly settling into your own presence, your own journey, your own heart, and your own thoughts, your own life. Some individuals do not know their own thoughts! They need to wait and find out what others are saying before speaking. Do not enter other people's drama, another's journeying, another's stories, another's purpose or another's thoughts for they only rob you of your own life.

As a Sea Priestess, you will see many personality types but know they are all just trying to find their way back home. As a Sea Priestess, you are a spiritual healer, a spiritual counselor, a Hevic healer to the Soul, a voyager, traveling all seas. Seeing problems from a new perspective, we now begin our un-training.

Un-training

We have been taught so-called truths will serve us well within our lives yet actually, they have been colossal blocks, veils, and strong sedatives to cause us not to live in our full potential. So-called truths designed to keep the waters muddy, so that we remain unmovable and unclear of our purpose; always trying to be one of them, over there. We are not over there and we are not them. A huge eye opener!

Some Personality Types

There are folks that desire to experience lessons through the veil of need and/or some form of pain. If this is how they believe then this is how they learn most of their lessons. Remembering it is us that design our life. There are other individuals that enjoy the veil of drama, if this is you, and have no desire to change, then enjoy that choice; know you will experience life and learn many valuable lessons through those veils, but know it is you whom selected your learning method. All methods are equally valuable. You will deal with people that think they see reality very clearly and will be glad to tell you all that they know, and tell you how they see your reality. Be patient with these sweet souls; after a while they run out of steam and look up to see the sublime of what is, and begin to experience what is. They want to impress people with all they know and all they do, in hopes people will look up to them. In reality, they are doing it backwards and by approaching people backwards, they are creating the very opposite results they are trying to achieve for themselves. Someday they will rest, not within their head knowledge, but within their own Being. They will see they are already fathomless love, as all of the above personalities highlighted so far. They will begin to ask wonderful questions; not about things outside themselves, but inside the soul.

Let us consider the person that desires everyone to admire them, through continual bragging these folks have selected the big ego veil from which to learn their lessons. The big ego is trying to be validated every waking moment. The truth is, they already are validated, and they just don't see it yet.

Be aware, that some folks may enjoy wearing their veil. As an "Un-teacher," you do not need to convince anyone to do anything. Remember you are a facilitator to un-teach people; it is they that do the work, not you. Many other personality types will be highlighted as examples, yet our main focus is you and what you need to remove from your life, so that your life sparkles under the noon day sun. I believe everyone, inherently, desires to be a true asset and genuinely wants to be the best person they can be. Some personalities are just trying to figure out how to show up in life.

Example: A person desires to become a leader. They think they need to put the spot light on themselves, essentially saying, "Look at me." Un-teaching says put the spotlight on the students and say, "Look at you!" More individuals will listen to you if you first listen to them and acknowledge their gifts they bring to the table.

Words are not enough; all your actions convey that you are focused on others' gifts.

Everyone desires to be magnificent, so let's begin to ask the tough questions.

Are you carrying an out-grown shell on your back? Are you lying immobile on a sea sponge, doing nothing? Are you tangled among the high seaweed, causing you to not see the Universes' vast vistas? Today, before you read one more word, identify what is holding you back from what you want. If you want to do nothing and think nothing is holding you back from action, then excellent.

If you do want to see life differently, then ask yourself, "What are my shadows?"

You instinctively know what they are.

I told you this was going to be a bumpy ride.

Lay down everything you perceive as an over complication. Let us pretend that we only are given one life...ask yourself, "Am I living my life to the fullest!?" Am I helping others?" "Am I relying on others to tell me what my shadows are?" "Am I relying on outside things to tell me about me?!"

If the answers are difficult to answer, do not worry. That is why you are here to clear the waters, to make a path, and maybe end up a Sea Priestess; receiving instruction from the best life coach on earth, for you, you.

What's That on Your Head?

We think we see clearly when actually we see through a veil, or many veils. We think we know what reality is for ourselves and even for others; we do not. Some veils have been lovingly placed on us by our parents, some by our teachers, some by our friends, some by our culture, but most by our own hand. We think we have keen insight on other people's lives, interpreted not as they really are, but seen through veils on our own head. Some of us think our training and experience is superior to any other training or culture. We value or devalue others by our own shadow standards, which only causes people to move apart from each other, instead of moving closer to each other. We only need to focus on our shadows, while other people focus on their own shadows, bringing everyone back into the world ocean; all supporting and affecting each other as they cultivate their own water energy field. If we focus healing our shadows it will affect the entire world energy field.

We are rewarded when we work on our shadows. As we explore our shadows, our gifts automatically rise up to replace every shadow. Situations change around us, because we change. We find it easier to lay down physicality and replace it with Spirit, yet never losing focus on practicality. For it is important, as Sea Priestesses, to have one foot in both worlds.

Exploration beyond physicality brings all of us to a place where our focused thoughts become our reality, while realizing all realities are mutable. All physical realities, history, and concepts are all veils. To enter the portal of cosmic omnipresence is to look beyond our physicality, beyond our mentality; to run towards the limits of reality is to find none! Thus boundaries are eliminated. It is the ego centered mind that runs amuck, reminding us, ultimately, there is death there is an end, which is the biggest cosmic lie of all. The ego says we will "die." The Universe says, "How can consciousness die?" It cannot, thus we cannot die; it is an impossibility. As Westerners, we are too focused on the body and the ego conscious mind, thus our perceptions are tied to those very small aspects, instead of the larger, none linear systems.

We are all here learning and experiencing different lessons that we have pre-chosen before we popped into this reality plane. We choose to be here and to experience life to its fullest. For some, they go out of their way to do the opposite and not fully live. Due to our choices, and our own veils we all perceive our world as reality. Truthfully, it is not reality in its fullness; it is only a small part of the entire picture. Our limited minds cannot perceive all that is right here, right now, within the practical mundane plane. However, our Divine Mind can and is connected to all realities all multi-dimensional realities.

Open minded folks, not attached to the physical excel in this concept. Or should I say people that are willing to step out of their mundane minds and enter their Divine Mind through meditation, deep lucid dreaming, astral journeying, and/ or living life in complete fullness. Understanding individuals work on different life lessons, using different methods; no two people have the same reality, or the same consciousness. However, we all are able to clearly see and explore our Divine connection and see no one is apart from us. When we see we no one is lesser than anyone else, we see.

Some Realities that people Live By

The following list are just a few realities I have heard through the decades:

One Pagan

One Pagan said, "90% of Pagans are rebellious against other groups."
One Pagan said, "90% of Pagans are poly."
One Pagan said, "90% of Pagans are Playgans."
One Pagan said, "90% of Pagans are single."
One Pagan said, "90% of Pagans are negative."
One Pagan said, "90% of Pagans are spiritual."
One Pagan said "90% of Pagans are not spiritual."
One Pagan said, "90% of Pagans are talented, wonderful explorers!"
One Pagan said, "90% of Pagan groups do not last, by reason of blah, blah, blah"
One Pagan said, "Most Pagans are positive."
One Pagan said, "Life is difficult, and then you die."
One Pagan said, "We learn mostly through pain and failure."
One Pagan said "We learn through many methods, not just pain."
One Pagan said, "We grow through balance."
One Pagan said, "We grow through imbalance."
One Pagan said, "Life is joy."
One Pagan said, "Life is quiet peace."
One Pagan said, "Life is a fight."
One Pagan said, "Life is Drama."
One Pagan said, "Drama is foreign to me."
One Pagan said, "Most people are against us, so we must build the bunkers thicker."

One Pagan said, "There are many good non-Pagan people that respect our choices.
One Pagan said, "All Pagan groups are political."
One Pagan said, "Many Pagan groups are doing well and have lasted for decades."
One Pagan said, "When Priestesses get together they are catty."
One Pagan said, "When Priestesses get together they are supportive loving humans."
One Pagan said, "When Priests get together they gossip."
One Pagan said, "When Priests get together they are non-judgmental."
One Pagan said, "… there are always Witch wars."
One Pagan said, "I chose not to be involved with a Witch war."
One Pagan said, "All Pagans around here do not want to join a group."
One Pagan said, "Many Pagans want a group with which to fellowship."
One Pagan said, "Success comes easy."
One Pagan said, "Success is difficult to achieve."
One Pagan said, "You need to know your limitations."
One Pagan said, "You have no limitations, except the ones you place on yourself."
One Pagan said, "I have no control of what happens to me."
One Pagan said, "I have created my life, by my own hands."
One Pagan said, "It's necessary to struggle through life to experience one's own conscious unfolding."
One Pagan said, "A person does not need to go through pain to become enlightened."
One Pagan said, "A person needs to go through pain to become enlightened."
One Pagan said, "People must focus on the Shadows to see their light."
One Pagan said, "People can focus on the light to see their Shadows."
One Pagan said, "What if I keep going through the same thing over and over, learning the same lesson, time and again." My answer: "The second you learn the lesson this situation will stop, so stop doing what you are doing so the negativity that results from the situation will stop."
One Pagan said, "I am a Pagan out of rebellion."
One Pagan said, "Living as a Pagan is fulfilling."

Every one of those quotes are "true," only to that individual and those that selected to live that way. Many believe that everyone lives and experiences life somewhat like them. The truth is there are many ways to live. Depending on how you designed your story, will bring into your life the individuals and experiences that will affirm your believes. No statement made regarding "One Pagan said" is incorrect in the cosmic sense, because it is a truth to some individuals, none "bad or good;" only experiences and lessons to be learned by all those different types of personalities. No-one wrong, since each person was seeing their reality, through their own shadows, their own veils, through their own eyes. While pulling that reality into their lives, thinking everyone lives their way and they do not.

Everyone is unfolding their awareness in their own way. Everyone attracting the people working on the same shadow work, which only confirms for them that everyone is essentially thinking and experiencing what they are! Everyone is not approaching life the same way, which is a good thing. Life would be incredibly boring if we were all learning the same lessons, in the same manner.

There are times we need to take a closer look at what we are learning and ask, is it time to move on to our next lesson? Instead of learning the same lesson over and over. Moving on is identifying and removing distortions and filters we think are there protecting us when they are not. Thinking and behaving in such a way, that show ourselves we truly learned the lesson, so it does not need to be repeated again and again, unless we enjoy the lesson.

Be gentle with yourself when you ask the following questions.

> Have you lived life to your fullest?
> It is sad to say that some folks say "no."
> Ask yourself the hard questions, i.e.,
> > "Why can't I attain what I desire?"

Examine all your excuses, but know there are no real excuses to hold you back for a life time. A person may have one or two excuses and they, indeed, can be valid. However, if a person shoots excuses out like a machine gun, then they are not ready to move forward into clear waters. This person needs to ask their self the dreaded question, "Why?" Your mind, with a small "m," has a zillion whys, ultimately, all the person's excuses will find it difficult to remove their own veils, before they remove their excuses.

What restrictions are you placing on yourself? Who are you blaming? Blame is just an excuse dressed in a blame costume. Are you allowing your past to make your decisions for you? Are you allowing your fears to make decisions for you? There is not one excuse we can use that can stop us, not one. Even if the excuse is, "I have nothing." That is still not a valid reason to move forward, to achieve what you desire. You have everything you need; you just don't know it yet. Out of nothing, you can create something; this is magic.

It scares some people to think they are directly connected to everything now and everything is not what most people think everything is, thus it scares them to take on accountability and find answers for themselves. Once again, because we are so physically oriented, to time and space bound, all these become our veils; making us forget what we have learned in past lives, causing apathy for our very own lives! Thus fear and apathy become security blankets that we hold onto for dear life.

> *Since everything is but an apparition,*
> *Perfect in being what it is,*
> *Having nothing to do with good or bad,*
> *Acceptance or rejection,*
> *One may well burst out in laughter.*
> ~ Tibetan Buddhist teacher, Long Chen Pa

Everyone knows deep within our soul that we are working on a much larger plan than any human behavior modality has ever fathomed. We are getting glimpses of how big we are. All our varied aspects of our development are, in fact, Deity developing through us. Divinity cannot be complete without us. Divinity cannot grow apart from us. We are Her hands, we are Her eyes, we are Her voice, and we are Her movement. She explores Herself through us. She unfolds Herself through us. She expands through us. As we expand through Her.

REJOICE AND GIVE THANKS!

Rejoice! Rejoice! And in rejoicing sing!

As the pattern of Eternity unfolds in everything!

Give thanks! Give thanks! And in thankfulness dance round!

As the blessings of Divinity within our lives abound!

DISPELLING

by A.C. Fisher Aldag

Unfortunately, there comes a time when users of magickal energy must learn to do rituals for dispelling, which means removing harmful or baneful spells, or for banishing negative energies. Someone may have deliberately used words of power or magickal actions to cause us problems. This is sometimes called a curse or hex. They might have knowingly raised energy with the intent of doing harm. Or it might have been an inadvertent, unconscious action. A co-worker or neighbor might feel jealous of our position or our material wealth. Someone who is undergoing relationship troubles may be angry that their love life is encountering difficulties, while our life seems easy by comparison. A person with an axe to grind might even want to purposefully harm us. This is a sorrowful state, but occasionally, it happens.

Other people's negative energy can affect our job, our transportation, our position of authority within our community, or even our home and family. Yet before we conclude that someone is deliberately performing magick to cause us harm, we must first look at other problem areas. Are we doing our best? Is our job performance satisfactory? Are our once docile children going into puberty and becoming independent? Is our relationship suffering from neglect? Is our home or our vehicle undergoing normal wear and tear, and can it be repaired on a mundane level? If the same awful thing keeps happening repeatedly, you should analyze what might really be occurring. If you keep getting fired for tardiness, that isn't the result of baleful magick ... that is on you. However, if an event happens repeatedly that is beyond your control ... several car wrecks, constant illness with no discernable cause, a long string of sorrowful events ... there just might have been some deliberate spell workings with the intent to cause you misery. Or it may simply be the result of the unintentional anger or jealousy of a person you interact with in everyday life.

Do divination to attempt to determine the source of baleful energy. Is it something that you caused by your own actions? Is it a "stuff happens" situation? Or did some person deliberately inflict a curse on you? Use your intuition. Listen to your inner voice. Consult your guides, the spirits, or your deities. You might want to go to a neutral party for divination, readings and advice. Talk with trusted friends or family members. Even if they do not believe in magick, they might have some insight about who is upset with you, and who might be throwing harmful energy your way.

Some magick users insist that the source of negative magick must be known. Think about who in your life may be causing you problems. Has a relative changed their attitude toward you? Was a co-worker passed over for promotion? Are you arguing with anyone? In most cases, it isn't always necessary to know who the culprit is; you can banish negative energies, dispell, and shield yourself to prevent further mishaps, without knowing who caused the trouble.

Even if you realize who has cast a harmful spell, it is imperative that you do not retaliate. Sending negative energy back to the source can sometimes "bounce", gaining force, so that it comes back to you stronger and more harmful than before. The "threefold law" is not a law like "do not jaywalk", the threefold law is a law like gravity. It is a magickal occurrence. Sending destructive power anywhere runs the risk that you will be the recipient of three times (or nine times, or a hundred times) the "bad" energy... even if you weren't the original sender. It can also harm the culprit's family, friends, loved ones, including innocent children, who had nothing to do with casting negative magick. No matter how angry you get, please do not curse anyone else. Be careful that in a ritual, you do not say anything like "I wish so-and-so would drop dead". Your words have power, and in a sacred space, your words can become magickally charged.

If you know who has cast a harmful spell, you may first try speaking to them privately, or writing to them online. Ask them what is wrong, if you have done anything that has caused them pain. Determine if you have inadvertently hurt their feelings or given them trouble. Discuss matters with them candidly. This may be enough to end the conflict, and thus end the bad feelings that may have inadvertently caused negative magick. Some issues can be resolved by negotiation. And some cannot. If you are absolutely certain that someone has performed a baneful spell on purpose – you have a witness, or the person has bragged to their friends – and you confront them with no result, then you might have to take more drastic measures.

Again, do not retaliate. Do not send bad energy or hurtful magick back to the source. Do not curse, and do not maim. Negative energy can be removed in any number of ways, and the magickian who has bespelled you can be blocked from doing further damage. Curses can be broken. All of this can be done without causing further harm.

Dispellings can be performed at any time, but during the late night or early morning of the waning moon is best. Thursday or Saturday, days associated with justice, reaping and protection, are the most auspicious. Colors can include very bright hues which are high on the spectrum, such as white and yellow, which deflect light. Conversely, dark blues, dark green and brown are associated with Earth, as in, "earthing the power". Dark blue robes may help to invoke the image of justice. Dispelling is best performed alone or in a group of trusted friends, covenors or family, but ensure that the person who instigated the curse is not present! The rite should be done in a safe, protected sacred space, with rituals performed to sanctify, purify, and seal in power, which will be released and allowed to dissipate. If indoors, open a window to allow baleful energies to escape. Tools include salt, blessed or consecrated water, a feather fan, broom or wand, an athame, sword or other edged weapon, sage or other incense known for clearing a space, and purification and cleansing of a person. You may also wish to have music or percussion instruments, such as bells or drums, and paper and pen for writing.

Perform your usual rite to create and purify sacred space. Invite your ancestors, elementals, guides, deities or other holy beings. After invocations, be sure to thoroughly seal your temple or sacred place ... cast circle, summon wards or guardians, close off the area to intrusion. You may wish to do double the magick to encase your ritual area. Sprinkle salt and consecrated water around the perimeter. Envision a fortress or castle, or an impenetrable bubble made of unbreakable material, or crackling electricity surrounding your sacred space. Draw a circle in chalk. Or sweep the perimeter of the room with your broom, whisk the air with a fan. Light candles. Use oils or incense with a strong, purifying scent. Perform whatever rites normally used for your own protection. Use sound barriers or visual cues that represent safety.

Now for the working itself ... ritually cleanse and purify yourself as your tradition decrees. Smudge with smoke, perform sacred drumming or chants, aspurge yourself with water, sprinkle your head with salt, hold ritual objects, absorb baneful energy in an egg, let the negative power flow into a crystal or other holy item, envision baleful energies draining out through your feet to be absorbed harmlessly by the earth. Keep the candles, lanterns or incense burning. As you do this, simultaneously draw, write down your intent, or speak words of power. Do not use a journal, book of shadows, or other permanent record. You will want to destroy what you've written or drawn in the course of the ceremony. Speak words such as, "I intentionally banish any curses, hexes, baleful energies or harmful magick. Let it be gone. Remove it from me. Cast it forth hence-from." Or write some of the conditions that have become difficult for you, with the words "Remove" or "End", such as "End trouble at work, remove problems with my transportation." You may wish to safely burn papers in the fire during the rite, or wait until afterward to dispose of them. Visualize the harmful energy as a dark bird flying away, up to the roof, fluttering around, trapped. Or a slimy sea creature, swimming to the perimeter. You might concentrate on an image that signifies cleansing and healing to you ... a waterfall, a soothing balm, a clear pool of water, being immersed in pure sound waves or laser lights that sandblast any curses away. Feel the harmful situation draining away into the power objects, or to the edge of your ritual space.

Perform some action to raise power. Drumming, dancing, spinning in place, tying knots, burning a candle, singing, chanting, marching around the edge of your sacred space, playing loud music. This is to fuel the ritual, to remove the curse or to actually perform the dispelling. Continue to speak or write your intent. Then suddenly, release the wards or open an escape route, or make a hole in your protective circle, as would be done for releasing a cone of power. Erase a portion of the chalk. Sweep away the salt. Envision a door opening, a blank space, a drain, a lid lifted off a pot, or an empty place where negative energy can escape. If you have created a bubble, let it burst, and the negative energy is drawn away, as if into a vacuum. Let wards fall. Or chase hexes into the jaws of your guardians. Raise your arms and drop them, or abruptly halt your drumming, dancing, chanting or singing. Cut off the music. Chop away at envisioned difficulties with your edged weapon. Wad up the paper with your drawing or writing, or set fire to it. State intent through one or two easy words, such as "Curses leave!" or "Hexes begone!" or "Troubles END!" Don't be afraid to shout.

In the ensuing silence, visualize the problems leaving through the hole, or being absorbed by the power object, or being washed away in water, earthed, or cleansed by fire. Chase it away, out the open window, with a wand, feather fan or broom. If you have done the working by burning words on paper, wave away the smoke. If you have caught negative energies in a crystal, egg or power object, it must be discarded or thoroughly cleansed at a later time. Deliberately make the statement that the negative forces will cause no further harm. Say "Earth the power" or "Wash away this curse, let it be cleansed, let it be changed", or say "Remove (problem) from this plane, cast it forth hence-from." Ensure that the energy won't return, or go forth to harm some other person. Deliberately state that the vanishing curse will cause no further harm. Smudge, aspurge, sprinkle salt, and cleanse your sacred space again. You may wish to take a ritual bath or shower. Light more incense. Put on a fan.

After you've released and completely purified your ritual area, it is time to thank unseen entities and / or deities, and allow them to return to their homes. You might wish to make an appropriate offering. Devoke and dismiss according to your tradition. Discard any scraps of burned paper, pour water out where it will not cause problems – not into a plant or down the drains of your home. Sweep salt and dust outdoors. Extinguish candles. De-sanctify your sacred space appropriately. Take down a ritual circle, speak words of power that clearly indicate that the rite has ended. Afterward, cleanse power objects thoroughly, including any items used to trap negative energies, and ritual tools used for the dispelling. Scour cauldrons used for burning papers, wash chalices or aspurgers with mild soap. Immerse crystals in water, or place the object in running water such as under a downspout or in a stream, keep it outdoors in sunlight or under the moon for several nights.

At some later time, you may wish to perform a blessing and healing ritual, to invoke good, positive, beneficial conditions to replace the energy you've just removed. Nature abhors a vacuum. You want to ensure that blessings and optimal situations fill the void that has been left ... not more curses! Ask your guardians and deities for assistance. Draw positive energy to you. If you can emotionally and mentally do so, without prejudice, you might also wish to ask for blessings and healing for whoever has cursed you. If you believe that the person is actually good at heart, but acting under duress, you may wish to ensure that they know they caused harm to you. The individual might become mentally aware that their actions were hurtful to you, which may cause them to review their conduct and change their behavior. Approaching the situation with love and good intentions may be a very positive solution. (Blessing rites will be covered in a subsequent article, or look some up online.)

MOONLIGHT AND FIRELIGHT

Moonlight and Firelight
Silver and Gold
Magic is afoot tonight
Wondrous to behold!

-

Moonlight and Firelight
Silver and Gold
Magic is afoot tonight
Wondrous to behold!

-

Moonlight and Firelight
Silver and Gold
Magic is afoot tonight
Wondrous to behold!

TIME MAGIC
by Don Lewis

> This discussion of Time Magic is based on a series of videos that aired between July 17 and July 27, 2010, as part of Rev. Don's Vlog, a daily video blog that I do. It is one of the more interesting subjects that we have tackled on the Vlog, so I thought that it might make a good subject for an essay.

Time Magic basically is Magic dealing with time: dealing with the passage of time: dealing with movement forward or backward in time. And one of the principles that Time Magic is founded on is that Time is essentially illusory in nature, or at least is more illusory than we give it credit for. It's a standard principle in metaphysics that Time in the Spirit World either does not exist or is very different than Time in the Physical World –but it's also a principle of metaphysics that the Physical World Is only an aspect of the Spiritual World. Therefore although Time seems very concrete to us, it is not in reality. Those of you who have taken our Degree Courses will know that the first thing we talk about in our Chapter on Magic is that the Physical World, though it seems very concrete, is actually very fluid. And this is one of the reasons that Magic can work – because things that seem very solid are actually very malleable. Time is the same way. It seems very solid, it seems very inescapable – and it also can be very malleable. Time Magic is not as well developed an art as certain other forms of Magic, and so there is a lot of room for growth in Time Magic.

Time Magic is the art of manipulating Time in a Magical manner. It can be either speeding Time up, slowing Time down, or moving

357

through Time. It can go either forward or backward, and in theory it can go sideways as well –although normally when we talk about going sideways in Time we use the term "Probabilities." Those of you who have studied our Third Degree materials will know what I mean by this. Most people who practice Time Magic tend to focus on one or another area of it, and it's a relatively new art form, I believe. I don't really know anyone who's written much about it historically, but there are certainly people doing it today. And they are doing it often in what I would consider a fairly experimental manner. Time Magic I would consider to be certainly a metaphysical art form which is in its dawning phase. Time Magic can include things like slowing down Time when you need to get more rest, or you need more time to work on something: speeding up Time if you're on a trip and you need to make it go faster. My old friend Rosemary Fletcher, who is one of the better psychics I've ever known often talked about "Folding Time" when she was on a trip, and needed to get there faster – she would "fold" the time so that she would arrive sooner. Time Magic can also be going forwards or backwards in Time, which is more what you'd expect to see in science fiction, but it can be done and it is done to a certain extent. It isn't how you see it in science fiction however. And in fact none of this, or any aspect of Magic at all, is really all that close to what you see in film, or in many cases what you read about in fiction books. People who practice Magic, which I assume is probably the larger portion of the people watching this, know that as a general rule when Magic comes to pass in your life, it will come about in ways that are very natural, in ways that are very subtle, so that if you didn't know you had done the Magic you would perceive the outcome as a perfectly normal event – and this is the same with Time Magic. As a general rule if you do Time Magic you will probably be the only one who is aware that it has happened. And for that matter, as with ordinary Magic, you will read in our materials that everybody does Magic constantly – unconsciously. What we talk about by "learning Magic" is only actually learning how to do consciously what is really a natural process. And it's the same with Time Magic. We all do it unconsciously. The example that was given to me when I was learning this was, for example, where you might wake up on a Thursday morning thinking that it's Friday. And you go through most of the day thinking its Friday. And you meet other people who think it should be Friday. But it's really Thursday. And I was told that this usually means that people are repeating their Thursday, and this is why they think it should be Friday – because in the normal course of events it would have been. And this is a kind of unconscious Time Magic. It happens from the level of the Soul, the level of the Higher Self. When we learn to do this consciously, then it happens from our conscious level. I have had occasions of changing things in past time, we write about several of these in the Third Degree materials. And when you do Time Magic that's intended to affect something in the past it can be done in several different ways, it can manifest in several different ways. If you're doing for example a kind of healing of events that are intended to address the spiritual or emotional outcome of those events, you could address them on that level – and an argument could be made that if anything actually happens in the past it's within a different Probability but it still affects you here. And then there's where you actually try to change an event. This can in fact be done, however it something that you need to do very cautiously. Because in this sense it is a little bit like what you see in movies because you do kind of have to ask yourself "Well, gee, if I change this, what else changes?" And it can change things that you don't expect. As a general rule I don't think that there are a lot of people who do a lot of Time Magic for this reason.

Time Magic, like any kind of Magic, works because the world that we think is so very solid really is not – it's very fluid, it's very malleable, it reacts to thought, to emotion, and to physical action. Time, like space, is illusory in many ways. We do not have a perfect understanding of this – I do not think anyone CLAIMS to have a perfect understanding of this, at least in the metaphysical world. However, we do know that it [time] reacts, and that t is not the static thing that it sometimes appears to be. The reason that this is an issue and why it makes it [Time Magic] more difficult, is that we base our lives on the idea that the Universe is a solid, fixed entity: that 'A' will always lead to 'B', 'B' will always lead to 'C'. In the Magical world that is not necessarily true. When you start working with Magic, and even more with something like Time Magic, 'A' can sometimes lead straight to 'C' – or it can lead to 'M', or 'F', or 'G'. And if you are not exceptionally well grounded, this can be very bad for you – because the illusion of Time, the illusion of Reality, is how we order our experiences in such a way that we can make sense of them and understand them and in such a way that we can use this world to lead useful physical lives. When we cut those threads we sometimes lose that ability. I've known a number of people, some of whom were aware of it, some of whom were not, who had really lost their connection to reality by working with certain sorts of Magic – because it revealed to them the illusory nature of reality, and 'A' stopped leading to 'B' for them. This is what makes Time Magic in particular so very dangerous. It's not because you may "disturb the Space/Time Continuum", or the

"Timeline", or other things that you might see in science fiction. It's because you can disturb your own understanding of reality considerably. If you are going to do this sort of thing you need to be extremely well grounded – or it can really cut you lose. Traditional Qabalah at one time was restricted to people over the age of forty who had children. The reason for this was that people who had loved ones and responsibilities and dependents found it much harder to become ungrounded than people who did not. And although I don't particularly feel that that prohibition is a necessary one, I do understand the reason for it, and I would recommend to people practicing Magic in general that they really make an effort to stay grounded. If you read our materials and our exercises you will see that we really emphasize grounding. If you lose your groundedness you lose your place in reality – and in the Magical community we see a lot of people who've done that. It is very important if you are going to do this level of Magic – and this series is not going to be talking about 'how to' particularly, although we'll talk a little bit about that. But f you do try to do things like Time Magic, it's imperative that you also work really hard to stay grounded, and that even as you try to look through the illusion of Time that you also remember that that illusion has a very important purpose and you don't just cut it out. So – that's my caveat on Time Magic. And to continue our conversation – it [Time Magic] really can be a very effective tool. I myself primarily use it in order to try to get more rest than my actual physical life allows by manipulating particularly those periods of time when I am able to rest. Now, I once had a Priestess of our Tradition – the Correllian Tradition – remark to me when I had made the comment that there were not enough hours in the day to get done the things I needed to do that [since] I wrote about Time Magic I ought to know how to change that. And you know – it doesn't really work that way. There are things you can do, but it [Time Magic] does not give you a perfect mastery of time any more than the practice of Magic gives you a perfect mastery of space. It [Time Magic] does give you additional tools. To this day I do not have enough hours in the day to get done the things I need to get done – even though I do definitely feel that I Magically extend to some extent the hours that I am working with. I have also known people who do the opposite, who shorten their hours, particularly if they are traveling or doing other unpleasant business. When I was taught these things I was taught specifically that it was not a good idea to shorten time – because we only have so much of it no matter what we do, and therefore we should not take away from it but only add to it. And generally speaking that's what I have done. I am particularly fond of a technique called "Psychological Time", and we discuss this in our Third Degree materials. Psychological Time basically involves extending the duration of a certain activity such as rest, or sleep – but it could theoretically be any activity. I particularly tend to use it for rest, because there have been many times in my life where I have not had the opportunity to get enough of that, and so I alter it metaphysically. We could argue whether that is actually affecting time or affecting our perception of time – but to be perfectly honest I don't really know that that matters, because both would be forms of Time Magic. I will leave the details of Psychological Time to those who are studying Third Degree, where we talk about how to do it. But what I will say – and I say this in Third Degree – is that many of the details of this are things that people are still learning, still studying. And you know, we often in the metaphysical world act as if we are trying to rediscover things that people knew long ago – and many people actually think that that's what's going on.

The truth is we are blazing new trails all the time. Time Magic for the most part is a very new metaphysical trail. Not that nobody has ever done it, but in terms of knowledge of it there's not really that much. And a great deal of it is in effect a metaphysical frontier. So there's only so much to say about it because there's only so much that people have done so far. It's one of those things that I expect to see continue to expand during my lifetime, and I'm actually very curious to see what people do with it.

Now let us talk a little bit about how Time Magic is done. I mentioned in an earlier installment my good friend Rosemary Fletcher, who is now in Spirit. But Rosemary is one of the best psychics I have ever known, she also is one of the widest ranging psychics I have ever known – a very kind, very nice person and also immensely talented. One of the things she did was Time Magic. And her Time Magic was very different from my Time Magic. When she did Time Magic she used a technique that she described as "folding" time. Now it does involve some of the same idea, but she perceived Time as being not unlike a fabric. And when she wanted to move through it more quickly than ordinary physical existence would allow, she "folded" it. You might say she created a pocket in Time and moved through it. She did this particularly for long driving trips. Now, interestingly, Rosemary also felt that that time that was folded must eventually unfold, and she experienced this in the following way: she would often "fold" a long trip, which would then become shorter, and she would do this two or three times, and the fourth or maybe the fifth trip would suddenly become much longer than she expected. And she attributed this to the "folded" time unfolding. And it would often happen unexpectedly. Now, I'm not sure that that is... I have not found it to be the case in my Time Magic. However because she believed it, of course it became true. And plus she was extremely talented – perhaps she knew better than I, I don't really know. But I don't normally find that the Time Magic I do undoes itself in any way. When I do Time Magic I perceive it as passing through a barrier. I'm not going to go into a lot of details about how the barrier is dealt with or how it's conceived, although we do talk about this in much greater detail in our Third Degree book. But by the time you get to Third Degree you should have a good basis for it, whereas people watching this video do not necessarily and I do not want to give you a technique that might be dangerous to you. But I perceive it as a barrier and pass through it, and in passing through it I charge what I want to happen. And I have found – as I say, I don't find that it "unfolds". But then I'm not folding it either – I'm passing through it. I have however sometimes felt – and this also is a difference in my Time Magic versus Rosemary's, Rosemary was frequently trying to shorten Time, I almost always am trying o lengthen it. And that has to do with the way I live my life – I find myself almost always with too much to do and too little time, and so I create more time. And I sometimes think that just because in the physical world that time doesn't always chronologically show doesn't mean that it's not accruing. And so sometimes I feel that I am significantly older than I am [chronologically] because I have lived parts of my life at double speed. And that is a possible side-effect of Time Magic – but as I say, Time Magic is in its infancy, and it seems to affect different people different ways. My cousin Krystel, who some of you know, is almost always taken for being years younger than she is – and she had done just as much Time Magic as I have, yet it affects her differently. Understanding the affects is something that we are still working with. And as I say, I don't know anyone that I would call really an expert in Time Magic, in the sense of being able to answer all these questions, because it is an art that's in its infancy. And, as I say, for me, it is basically a matter of moving through barriers – or maybe it's better to say, of objectifying Time in the form of a barrier and moving through it. I also have a wide range of techniques that I use that involve creating a "Room in Time". Creating a Room in Time basically is programming what you want to happen in a certain period in time. Again I'm not going to give the step by step instructions for it because I think it's something one needs to work up to. But I've found it very effective. And it also is something that you have to have built the "muscles" for. One of the things we talk about in our Degree materials is the fact that psychic and Magical work is very much like a muscle. It's like a physical muscle – the more you do with it, the stronger it gets. The more you do, the more you can do. And it really does react very much like building a muscle. The same is true for Time Magic – if you haven't built the muscle you won't be able to do it, or it will really hurt. If you have built the muscle it becomes much easier. I think this probably pretty much concludes what I want to say in Vlog format about Time Magic. Now we have written about it much more extensively in our Third Degree materials, and those who are members of the Order of World Walkers work with it a great deal more. But I think for the purpose of explaining what it is I think we have pretty much exhausted the topic. But I do want to say that I think it's extremely important, with arts such as Time Magic but also many others that are really kind of still in their infancy, that we really understand that we are not recapturing ancient knowledge but are building new knowledge. And that we in fact need to build it. And we do this experientially. Magic is not a science, Magic is an art. Although we sometimes describe it as a science it really is an art – it's very subjective, it's very individual. And only through individual experience and sharing that experience among ourselves are we really going to learn more about it [Magic]. And we really need to be doing that. We need not only to be learning the Traditional arts, we need to be expanding them. We are not playing dress-up in other people's clothes; we are building our own world. One of the things that I find most exciting about being the Head of a Tradition is the fact that some of our Priesthood are in fact on the frontiers of the metaphysical arts and are in fact expanding them – and I really would like to see more of that. Time Magic is certainly an area that needs expansion. But as I say, it's extremely important to pursue it in a very grounded manner because it can extremely ungrounding to a person. And so, I think that concludes our discussion of Time Magic.

SURVIVING THE SEASON

by **A.C. Fisher Aldag**

Part Two – the "C" word!

Last time, we discussed surviving winter holidays in general, and Thanksgiving Day in particular. This time we'll tackle the big-C … Christmas!

This time of year can be very stressful for those of us who do not celebrate the Christian holiday. Despite the "war on Christmas" discussed in the media, it seems to take over society, invade every aspect of life. It's on television, it's in your neighborhood; you can't escape! However, there are ways to minimize the Christmas aspect and focus on activities, symbols and culture more in keeping with Winter Solstice traditions.

You may feel pressured to decorate your workplace, or take part in a "Secret Santa" exchange or office party. Take the pulse of your job … will you face the label "not a team player" if you opt out? You might want to participate on a level you can stand, such as putting up real holly boughs or glass "witches' balls"; only you will know the true meaning of the decorations. Greenery, reindeer, Santa Claus, candy canes, candles and elves all have Pagan origins and symbolism. If it's anathema to your belief system to participate, explain that while you value others' religious rites, you are unable to take part because of your own religion's prohibitions. That's the only explanation you owe. You can probably stand to dress up and eat a catered dinner with co-workers – or you might suggest an office charity, instead. Take up a collection for Toys for Tots or other children's non-profit, rather than exchanging presents. Or see if co-workers would rather go to a hockey game, or a concert with Yuletide songs, rather than hosting a Christmas party. If you really can't avoid it, make the best of it. Share something from your culture, such as a recipe or craft. Bring your personal touch to other folks' holy day.

Children's school activities are another matter. You might have to tell your youngsters that they're not to sing songs about Jesus, although you don't mind them standing silently and respectfully as other kids exercise their right to freedom of religion. This may require some parental intervention on your part – you might have to call a teacher or principal and remind them that religion is not compulsory in a public school. If your kids have to take part in some aspect of Christmas – decorating the classroom, portraying a reindeer in a pageant, or other activity – find something that fits in with Pagan themes. Winter scenes, snow, presents, drawings of candles, deer, stars and sun symbols, and bells are all appropriate for the season, and won't offend Christian students. Make colored paper chains, cutout snowflakes, decorate with cotton snow, and do various other crafts that are acceptable to Christians, Pagans, and other religious groups. Have your child play the bells or drum while others sing Silent Night. And what a nice time to share your own customs: "On Yule we light candles to celebrate the return of the Sun."

Many parents face the dilemma about what to tell your kids about Santa Claus. Some families discuss the legend as a cultural aspect

– there are many "origins of Santa" stories online. Read them for yourself first; some denounce Santa as demonic, others becry his Pagan beginnings. Once you've found some good origin stories, share them with your kids. Other families emphasize that Santa is a spirit, similar to the guides we magickally depend on, or that Mom and Dad avatar Santa as they give presents to others. "You know when Daddy becomes Cernunnos in a ritual? That's what we do with Santa, when we put presents under the tree!" You may wish to tell children that the legends are fun stories that people enjoy sharing. Others don't mind telling children that St. Nick is imaginary, or that Santa is a real being. Think about it, discuss it with loved ones, meditate on it and ask your guides, then have the talk with your children. Most can understand the concept of "real or pretend" around age four. They'll comprehend the idea of the avatar or spirit around age six or seven. Caution them to not ruin others' belief by blurting "Santa isn't real" on the school bus.

There are a few television programs that may be right for your children, including musical or variety shows, tales about kids from various cultures celebrating their holidays, and the more innocuous cartoon specials. However, you may have to explain that the kids on TV are observing a holiday that your family doesn't celebrate. "Sally's family believes that Jesus was born in a stable on Christmas." That might be enough for young people to understand. Look for shows that have values similar to yours – sharing, togetherness – and talk about them with your child. And beware the commercials, which are designed to set off a torrent of "I Wants!" Suggest that your children ask for ONE special toy, and check to see if it meets your standards. Does it have extreme gender bias? Is it made by slave labor? What your child likely desires isn't the toy itself; it's more the idea of happily playing with something fun with other kids. You may be able to substitute a toy more in keeping with your values. Or you may be able to suggest an alternative to material things – a trip to an ice rink, a delightful movie, a day at a children's museum. You could purchase some appropriate books and spend an afternoon reading them aloud with your kids. Likewise, encourage your children to pick out inexpensive yet special gifts for loved ones and friends.

Next we'll discuss the issue of presents ... even Pagans who DO enjoy celebrating Christmas with family and friends ... might not be able to afford costly gifts this year. We all are feeling a pinch when it comes to the economy. We may have to explain, in advance, that this year, everyone is receiving a handmade present. Or draw names from a hat, set a spending limit, and make the time to find that special present that is perfect for your loved one. Look in import stores, at local craftsmen's shops, "holiday markets", the art or historical museum gift shop. Record a mix of music. Crafty Pagans can create a scarf, placemats, or other home-made gift. Other ideas include printing a special t-shirt or cloth grocery bag with an image or message that is just right for your family member, or draw up a certificate for a service. If you can wash Grandpa's car every week during the summer, this may be more valuable than just another necktie. Or cook something fabulous, and serve it in a pretty container that your family member can re-use.

Okay, the presents are under the tree, and now you have to face the actual Christmas Day celebration. You can try to be tolerant of customs you disagree with – eating meat, buying ugly trinkets, prayers that run for half an hour. Aunt Betty is entitled to believe that the Savior was born on Dec. 25th, and Uncle Ralph might insist on watching hours of football or CNN during dinner. That is their right, and has nothing to do with you. You can choose to remain silent when someone states "Jesus is the reason for the season," or you can politely say, "Well, actually it's the Winter Solstice" and change the subject. However, some relatives may express disappointment in your choices, lifestyle, religion or orientation. Keep in mind what is right for YOU. If someone states that "God wants…" you might have to reply, "Yes, that is great for you. I have made a different decision". You may have to explain that you're pleased with your life, or that you're working toward a goal. Share your religion in tiny increments; when your cousin asks sarcastically if you sacrifice babies on the Winter Solstice, smile and say, "We Pagans shared our symbols with Christians, including the tree and mistletoe". If a loved one is truly interested, give them the "Cliff Notes" version of the Yule sabbat. Should your description encounter genuine hostility, you might want to switch topics – fun Christmas traditions around the world – or simply keep silent. Don't allow yourself to be drawn in to an argument. "I'm sorry you feel that way, Uncle Jack. How'bout those Red Wings?" Ask if they want to argue, or have fun on the holiday? At the end of this article, there are some resources that include Christmas coping strategies.

If it all becomes too overwhelming, and people seem to be spoiling for a fight, you might wish to take a walk outdoors, and enjoy the neighbors' light displays. Look for twenty signs of winter. Play with the dog. Or bring along a book to read, something that won't incite a riot, like poetry, the latest novel, or a history tome. Or find some task that needs doing – a closet to clean, a faucet to fix, a stovetop to scrub. If someone gets completely out of line, such as insisting that your children say a prayer to Jesus or sing a song with lyrics that you disapprove of, or insulting your Gay spouse, or calling you a devil worshipper, you may have to take the high road. Or leave. That's right, leave.

You do not have to endure a situation that is completely intolerable. If you feel it is necessary, you might want to offer some explanation. "This subject is making you uncomfortable, so it's best if we cut the afternoon short". Or if they've genuinely hurt you, "We do not get along, and this is difficult for all of us. I am leaving. Have a good holiday." You might want to follow up with a phone call to relatives who may be sympathetic, and make them aware that it's not them causing the problem. Suggest that next time, you meet a day or two before their holiday, share a meal or exchange gifts, and visit each other in a less stressful environment.

In the first article, we talked about opting out of holiday celebrations with family, when you truly do not get along, or in an abusive situation. If your relatives insist on telling you that you're going to hell for being Pagan, Gay, or otherwise somehow different from them, you do NOT have to subject yourself to enduring an entire day of verbal abuse. There are lots of other things that you could be doing:

Participate in a Yule party or not-Christmas dinner with a group of friends. Cook an elaborate dish, hold a potluck. Exchange funny or whimsical gifts. Or participate in some activity you'd all enjoy – watch a DVD of the Ice Capades, go for a horse-drawn carriage ride, rent sleds and find a really big hill, play board games, or listen to a music concert on the radio. Wear whatever you want, from evening clothes to pajamas. Have fun with "family by choice".

If you have small children, you might want to make an hour appearance at Grandma's, then do something with another family or on your own. Go to a children's movie, go ice skating, drive around and look at decorations or a light display, sing songs together, make cookies, play outside together. Do a craft or art project together. Make bird feeders. Read stories, make a tent out of a blanket over a table, bring in flashlights and popcorn.

Find a UU Church or Pagan organization. You may have to travel to a nearby city. Resources such as the Magickal Media calendar page, or the Witches' Voice events pages at www.witchvox.com can give you information about Winter Solstice events. Make Yule your primary holiday of the season. On the actual Winter Solstice, go outdoors and look at stars, light candles, exchange presents with loved ones, eat a feast. Or choose the weekend prior or after the Longest Night.

Volunteer to serve Christmas dinner at a VA hospital, soup kitchen, women's shelter, children's home or hospital, or other charitable organization. Wear a Santa had and red and white clothes or a jingle-bell necklace or bracelet. Advantages are: you won't have to cook, you'll meet nice people (both the clients and other volunteers) and you'll be doing something worthwhile. Or volunteer at an animal shelter.

If all of your family is Christian but you – spouse, children, parents – why not take a day off? Explain that you do not celebrate Christmas, but you will happily spend a different vacation day with them. Then spend Dec. 25th by yourself. There's no harm or shame in taking a calendar holiday alone, by choice. Take a long hot bath, give yourself a facial or pedicure, watch DVDs of movies that YOU like, read a book in bed, do a project you've been meaning to get to, wear whatever you want, perform a ritual that lasts for hours, listen to music, eat food that everyone else in your household dislikes. Or go somewhere by yourself. While many places are closed on Christmas, often truck stops, movie theatres, convenience stores and similar places are open for a few hours (or all day). Many hotels and restaurants owned by East Indian people remain open.

If you are in an essential job, work so that Christian people can spend the day with their families. An advantage is that many businesses will pay overtime or holiday pay. Hopefully the boss will reciprocate and offer you a Pagan holiday off from work.

Have a blessed Winter Solstice / braw Alban Arthan / blod Jul / merry Yule!

Resources:

Some survival tips from the "About.com" site's "Pagan / Wiccan" page ... http://goo.gl/m1AlpF

From "Wiki-How", ways to celebrate the holy days in a Pagan manner around non-Pagans ... http://goo.gl/AFakM2

From a family therapy site; advice and suggestions apply to Pagans, too ... http://goo.gl/ljy01n

BIOGRAPHIES: PART FIVE

by **Don Lewis**

OLIVIA ROBERTSON

The Most Reverend, the Honourable Olivia Robertson, Co-founder and Head of the Fellowship of Isis, was born on Friday April 13, 1917. She was the daughter of Nora and Manning Durdin-Robertson.

In 1925 her family was able to return to their ancestral home, Huntington Castle in Ireland. Today Huntington Castle is more commonly known as Clonegal Castle.

Before becoming a religious leader Lady Olivia was a well-known author. Lady Olivia published her first book, *St. Malachi's Court* in 1946. Several more books followed including *Field of the Stranger* (1948) and *The Golden Eye* (1949). Lady Olivia's last work of popular fiction, *The Dublin Phoenix* (1956) sold out on its first day.

Lady Olivia had her spiritual awakening from Isis in 1946. In 1963 she would join with her brother, Lawrence Durdin-Robertson, 21st Baron Robertson of Strathloch, and his wife Lady Pamela, in founding the Huntington Castle Center for Meditation and Study.

In 1975 Lady Olivia wrote her spiritual autobiography, *The Call of Isis*, detailing her psychic and spiritual experiences as a follower of Isis. The following year she joined with Lord and Lady Robertson to found the Fellowship of Isis at the Spring Equinox of 1976.

The Fellowship of Isis is open to people of any faith who reverence a feminine aspect of God. Today the Fellowship of Isis is the largest Goddess Spirituality organization in the world, with over 24,000 members nearly 100 countries.

Over the years Lady Olivia has created an expansive liturgy for the Fellowship of Isis, much of it using the distinctive Mystery Play format. The practice of bringing through Oracles is also extremely important in Isian practice, and Lady Olivia is the foremost living master of this art.

Lady Olivia's proudest moment came in 1993 when she was represented the Fellowship of Isis at the Centennial Session of the Parliament of the World's Religions in Chicago, Illinois. This was the first time that Goddess religion was publicly recognized as a worldwide faith at this level.

Lady Olivia was one of only two women and sixteen men to offer a blessing during the Opening Plenary of the Parliament, and hers was the only one of these prayers to be networked via radio around the world.

Even in her nineties as the last of the three Founders, Lady Olivia continued to lead the Fellowship of Isis and travel around the world each year making appearances at Isian events with amazing energy and dedication. Lady Olivia died on 14 November, 2013 at the age of ninety-six.

MOTHER SHIPTON

Mother Shipton is England's most famous prophetess, and is generally considered the English answer to the French Nostradamus.

Ursula Southeil was born in 1488, in Knaresborough, England. She was the daughter of fifteen year old Agatha Southeil, who gave birth to her in a cave beside the river Nidd, in North Yorkshire, England. Legend holds that Ursula was deformed in some way, possibly with scoliosis, and that her mother either died giving birth to her. Ursula nonetheless received a good education being literate and writing her famous prophecies in verse form.

Ursula was noted for her psychic and magical abilities from an early age, and though most famous for her prophecies and predictions, she was also a spiritual healer.

At age 24 Ursula married Toby Shipton, a carpenter. As she grew older she came to be known as "Mother Shipton".

Many different collections of Mother Shipton's prophecies have been published over the years, the first appearing in 1641 – eighty years after her death. Some of the predications attributed to her are definitely forgeries, others may be original to her – many are very famous.

Mother Shipton is said to have predicted the defeat of the Spanish Armanda in 1588, the Great Fire of London in 1666, and the development of many modern technologies. Notably, she also predicted the end of the world – to happen in 1881.

The famed diarist Samuel Pepys records that at the time of the Great Fire of London he heard members of the British royal family discussing Mother Shipton's prophecy of the fire.

Among Mother Shipton's most famous prophecies is the fall of Cardinal Wolsey. Mother Shipton had made a prophecy that Cardinal Wolsey would never come to York, despite being its Archbishop. Because the Cardinal was in a politically sensitive position owing to King Henry VIII's desire to divorce his Queen, the prophecy was politically damaging to him.

The Cardinal sent emissaries to question Mother Shipton about this prophecy, and afterwards swore that he would come personally to York and when he did would have her arrested as a Witch.

Cardinal Wolsey duly set of from London to York but ten miles short of the city he was ordered to return to London to stand trial for High Treason, dying during the journey.

Mother Shipton died in 1561.

The cave where Mother Shipton was born is known as Mother Shipton's Cave and together with its associated "Petrifying Well" has been a popular tourist attraction since 1630.

SOCRATES

Socrates, born in 469 BC., was a great Athenian philosopher.

Socrates was the teacher of Plato, and thus had a great influence on Platonic thought, one of the leading spiritual systems of the ancient world whose ideas are still very important in modern metaphysics today.

Socrates' own teaching was primarily concerned with issues of virtue and right behavior. Socrates taught that the highest virtue was to "Know Yourself", and that no one knowingly does wrong but rather always does the best thing they know to do.

Socrates taught with a method termed Socratic Dialogue or Dialectic: teaching through question and discussion. Socrates is said to have created the teleological argument for the existence of Deity, which states that anything which exists to fill a useful purpose must be the work of an intelligence which designed it to fulfill that purpose.

Socrates was an opponent of the powerful Sophist movement, and his activities against them led to his being accused of impiety and corrupting the morals of the young. Socrates denied having done anything wrong, but refused to offer arguments to support his point of view and was convicted and sentenced to commit suicide by drinking hemlock, an herbal poison.

Socrates trial and death occurred in 399 BC. Since Socrates left no writings of his own, our knowledge of his teachings is derived from the works of his student Plato and the memoirs of the historian Xenophon: plus a few comments in the works of Plato's student Aristotle.

THERESE DeVOE (THERESE PENDRAGON)

Born and raised in Salem, MA, Therese Pendragon is truly a Salem Witch. Born into a large family of French, Sioux and Algonquin heritage, Lady Therese was raised to speak French as well as English, and has also studied Latin and High German.

Lady Therese has practiced Witchcraft and the spiritual arts for four decades, has studied under several famous teachers, notably Laurie Cabot – the Official Witch of Salem. Lady Therese holds several initiations and is a High Priestess in both the Cabot-Kent Tradition and the Alexandrian Tradition.

In 1979 Lady Therese was part of the historic photograph of Laurie Cabot and the Black Doves of Isis in National Geographic magazine. The photo is famous in part because it captures psychic energy on film, and is considered to have "put North American Witches on the map, internationally."

Lady Therese and her youngest daughter Michelle also marched with the Salem Witches in their historic first-ever appearance in the "Heritage Day Parade" in August, 1978.

Lady Therese is a professional performer and musician. She has recorded several albums along with Michael Pendragon including *13 Moons*, *Eight Solar Holidays*, *Dragon Tales*, *Angels and Aliens*, *Sun Child*, and *Peace Moon*. Lady Therese and Michael Pendragon also performed with the rock band Original Sin in the early 1980s.

Lady Therese has danced for 35 years, specializing in Sacred Dance, and various styles of Belly Dance. She designs and creates her own costumes and jewelry. Lady Therese also creates original art work, ritual tools, and pan pipes.

Lady Therese has appeared on the CBS Evening News with Dan Rather in 1985, Lifetime Channel's "Nature of Witches" in 1995, and National Enquirer TV in 1999. Lady Therese has also made several appearances on Magick TV.

For many years Lady Therese and Michael Pendragon operated Salem's famous Oracle Chamber. The Oracle Chamber featured Lady Therese's art and ritual tools, as well as a wide range of metaphysical tools and supplies with an emphasis on the unusual and hard to find. The Oracle Chamber also offered Spiritual Counseling, Tarot, Palmistry, Past Lives, Astrology, and workshops on a wide variety of subjects, as well as classes Belly Dance.

ABBY WILLOWROOT

Abby Willowroot is a world famous artist and jeweler. Nine pieces of her jewelry are in the permanent collection of the Smithsonian Institution in Washington, DC. A fourth generation artist, she is the daughter of painter Charles M. Kerins.

A Wiccan High Priestess holding High Priestly status in several Traditions, Lady Abby is the founder of Spiral Goddess Grove. Lady Abby has been a practicing Pagan since 1960s and a full time metaphysical and Goddess artist since 1965.

Lady Abby is also the proprietor of Willowroot's Real Magic Wand Company, where she manufactures magic wands using the same high quality techniques she uses to create her famous jewelry.

Lady Abby is most famous for the Goddess 2000 Project. The Goddess 2000 Project was an international art project dedicated to creating Goddess art. The slogan of the Goddess 2000 Project was "A Goddess on Every Block".

Anyone was welcome to take part in the Goddess 2000 Project regardless of their religious or philosophical background as long as they recognized a Feminine aspect of God and wanted to portray it in art. Consequently Witches and Pagans of many different Traditions were able to come together to make Goddess artwork despite the philosophical differences which might otherwise have separated them, as well as people from many other religions which recognize a feminine aspect of God.

The Goddess 2000 Project was an epochal moment in the Magical Community because it was one of the first international movements within the community to cut across Tradition lines and create common ground that everyone could sharer regardless of their background. This broke down many walls to create one of the most unifying moments in the modern Magical community.

OBERON ZELL-RAVENHEART

Among the most prominent leaders of the modern Pagan movement, Oberon Zell Ravenheart was born Timothy Zell on 30 November, 1942.

In 1974 Oberon married his lifepartner Morning Glory Zell. Together Oberon and Morning Glory founded Mythic Images, a company dedicated to Goddess themed statuary and fine Pagan jewelry. Mythic Images is particularly famous for their meticulous reproductions of Neolithic Goddess figures, as well as innovative modern works such as the Millennial Gaia.

A man of many accomplishments, Oberon is perhaps most famous for taking inspiration from science fiction, fantasy, and legend to create real-world structures and events.

On April 7, 1962, Oberon co-founded the Church of All Worlds with R. Lance Christie – a Pagan church based in part on ideas from Robert Heinlein's Stranger in a Strange Land. Oberon served as Primate of the Church of All Worlds until 1998, and then again from 2005 to the present.

Oberon is the creator of Green Egg Magazine, one of the most famous of all Pagan magazines. Oberon published Green Egg magazine from 1968-1975 and again from 1988-1996. In 1970 Oberon had a profound vision of the Living Earth. He published an account of this vision in Green Egg magazine as an early version of the Gaia Thesis.

Oberon is also famous for breeding unicorns. Together with his wife Morning Glory Zell Ravenheart, Oberon learned the secret of breeding unicorns in the 1970s. Using a simple technique of animal husbandry that causes the horns of any two-horned animal to grow together as a single horn, Oberon and Morning Glory created their famous herd of unicorns. In the 1980s Oberon, Morning Glory, and their unicorns toured with the Ringling Bros. Barnum and Bailey Circus.

In 2004 Oberon founded the Grey School of Wizardry, an online school with students world-wide that celebrates magic as an art form and a science, independent from its religious aspects. Oberon runs the school together with the Grey Council, a group of prominent Wizards, Witches, and Pagans.

Oberon and Morning Glory also did a great deal to popularize the idea of polyamory, or group marriage. Morning Glory coined the term "polyamory" in her 1990 article "A Bouquet of Lovers", published in Green Egg.

Morning Glory Zell-Ravenheart passed from this life on May 13, 2014 at the age of 65, after a long battle with cancer. Oberon and Morning Glory had been married for forty years. Morning Glory was buried at Annwfn, the sacred land of the Church of All Worlds.

The story of Oberon and Morning Glory's life is told in the book "The Wizard and the Witch: Seven Decades of Counterculture, Magick, and Paganism".

AN ELEMENTAL DEGREE SYSTEM SUGGESTION

by **Alan Salmi**
Hermetic Fellowship of Chicago

While many Wiccan traditions use a three degree system for advancement in knowledge of the craft, that is by no means the only way to organize a person's advancement in their experiences and spiritual pursuits. A Five Degree elemental system was used in the tradition known as The Pagan Way, originating on the east coast of the United States and an outline is given here for those groups that may want to organize in this fashion.

An important distinction is to be made between those who are an "outer court", those who are merely seekers and/or who do not want initiation but wish to practice the faith of Wicca in a group, and those who wish initiation and eventual ordination in the craft.

In many groups that distinction of membership but not yet initiation uses a "pre-degree" status known as "Dedication". A Dedicant could be considered an entry point into the group, and may be a further steppingstone into the path of Wicca, or they simply want to have a declaration of their intentions to practice a spiritual life.

The elemental degrees however imply a deeper commitment to the path, and to going through a tradition of knowledge and experience that could take months to, as often as not, years, in each of the degrees. Since much of craft symbolism is contained in the elements, the elemental system of advancement is a natural extension, and easily understood way of advancing for most members of a coven. Suggestions will be made here for the knowledge and experiences to be contained in both the Dedicant and Elemental degrees. Of course, each group will have to round this out for themselves, and are free to add or subtract from the suggestions given here.

The Dedicant "proto-degree"

We will not go into the issues here of how open or closed a particular coven should be. Rituals may be advertised or announced online or in local newsletters or a flyer at an occult shop. A group could likewise be only known by word-of-mouth or by invitation. The dedicant ritual is best done, in any case, once the person gets to know members of the group and the group likewise is willing to spend time putting forth energy in a short ritual to allow the person to make a public declaration of their willingness to take on the spiritual path in life.

The ritual itself should be carefully explained to the person about to undergo it. The ritual does not obligate them to the group itself, but should they wish to move forward their public declaration of taking on a spiritual path, in whatever form it takes, is a prerequisite to further entry into the group. The dedicant ritual is set up in such a way that the person could simply do that ritual, and then walk away and find their path in a totally different tradition. In a sense, as well as being a public declaration, the coven itself gives a form of blessing to the person in their declaration of wanting to move forward into a "path of light".

Typical elements seen in this ritual are the following:

- The person would purchase or borrow a white robe, and have available a white cord that could be placed around the waist, symbolical of a clean, unadorned state to start things with.

- A ritual purification of the four elements, emphasizing that the person is being cleansed and prepared for another stage in their life is then done. This could easily be done by either those who are officiating or with the help of people who are assigned to elemental places in the ritual.
- Having been purified, the person is then gently challenged with an oath. The oath should be as general as possible, neither binding the person to the group, nor to a particular manifestation of a spiritual path. The oath however can be seen as a public declaration of their willingness to add spirituality into their life in a meaningful way. They declare they are to move forward in a manner dedicated to their own advancement and spiritual knowledge and the spreading of light to others.

Once this is done there could be one or both of the following to be given to the dedicant:

- A ritual blessing of the senses, with an opening to the eyes for being able to see more clearly, the ears to be able to hear truth, the mouth to be careful in their speech, and the heart to be filled with light of the divine to help them in the pursuit of their path.
- Also there can be a blessing to be performed with either a lower level of divine force such as a blessing of angels or elemental powers or a blessing from higher divine sources such as the Lord and Lady.

The completion of the ritual would be to have members of the group tie the cord around the person's waist to symbolize their connection to all of those who are also on the path of light in whatever spiritual tradition that they follow. This white cord would then be a reminder of following the light and keeping their eyes and ears open for truth.

The entire ritual act would take no more than 15 or 20 minutes, and may be done with two or three people at the same time if needs arise. Often times this is a very lovely little rite, and makes people feel more included into the outer court of the group. If the group wishes to set things up this way, it would be a prerequisite to gaining some knowledge before the first initiation into an elemental degree. The amount of that knowledge, in the course of study, would be left up to the group. It may also be possible to leave all deeper instruction for those who are initiated.

Typically a course of study for a dedicant would however be one of the general Wicca 101 classes with an introduction to philosophy, history and practices as well as knowledge of the altar, ritual objects and the basic form of ritual that is seen in their open participation. This class is an opportunity to get to know the dedicant better, and give a standard basic knowledge to them before they are initiated. In the older days however, such knowledge was given only to initiates, so that form is not completely unusual or without precedent. Considering however, nowadays most of such information is available publicly in books and on the Internet, it would probably be most prudent to give your particular form that your group wants to work with to the dedicants to prepare them for further work. An obvious format would be to take the relevant parts from this book as a group study effort.

The Elemental Degrees

The Earth Degree:

The earth degree is meant to be the basis for most of the other work of the other degrees. This degree starts to move the person into the actual use of magic and basic understandings of the magical path. It is suggested that a number of different topics be covered under this degree with the following the major areas that are investigated:

- A basic reading list comprising of both the Common Book of Wicca and whatever supplemental materials the group or coven decides upon.

- The body and exercise: accomplished with martial arts, dance, exercise systems such as Pilates, movement awareness systems such as Alexander work or Feldenkrais or Rudolph Steiner's Eurhythmy. Gurdjieff's movement work could be included here, as well as yoga practices such as traditional schools of hatha yoga or even modern acroyoga.

- Basic understandings of the subtle bodies (chakra systems, acupuncture meridians, Qabalistic power centers)

- The basic structure of ritual, the uses of rituals for the seasons, the lunar tides, special occasions such as weddings and/or handfastings, memorial services etc. While the level of understanding for these rituals is not as exact as someone who is about to be ordained, knowing the basic patterns and being able to help with or conduct new or full moon and seasonal rituals would be a goal for this degree.

- A basic understanding of elemental magic and especially of the elements would be required in this degree. This would eventually build to a major project that could be used as a "final earth degree magickal discipline" which would be a working that would culminate in a seasonal body of exercises and meditations done for each season and its element.

The year-long seasonal/elemental working could be designed by the group to include such things as ritual word done at the proper time of day, with numerous other correspondences. The correspondences with food, incense, sacred names of elementals, etc. can be devised as part of this working by the elders of the group Once the group puts together this format, it can be refined over the years and/or used as a rite of passage in itself.

Once the earth degree has been gone through, the person should have the basic idea of magic and ritual as well as an understanding of the seasons and the elements. This becomes a strong foundation for the rest of the elemental degrees. The discipline gained in the areas of diet and exercise will have obvious positive effects that will form a basis for further discipline in other degrees.

Of course the particulars of this degree would need to be worked out carefully with all the members of the group. Typically it would take some design of checklists and books to be read with an understanding that at least a year would be spent in this degree work, and probably several years.

The Water Degree

Water degree consists of a deeper understanding of the unconscious, along with a mastery of divination and the beginnings of an effort at psychological and spiritual self-knowledge. To this end, the following areas would be examined and mastered:

- Dream interpretation and the reading of symbols

- Personal psychological work via psychotherapy, support groups, psychological systems such as NLP, experiential focusing, parts work (Internal Family Systems or Allione's "Feeding Your Demons" work), family constellation work, all depending on local resources. Shamanistic journey work would do well here, since it deals with both inner realms and has elements of divination in the practice itself.

- Divination: mastery of two major systems is recommended, such as tarot, astrological geomancy, numerology, runes, astrology (especially horary astrology) or even Eastern systems such as the I Ching. A minor method, such as oracle reading, dice divination or working with a pendulum or other divining tool is also suggested.

The main goal of the water degree then is to gain a certain sense of self-mastery and self-understanding, with being able to understand symbols and the wider range of coincidences and correspondences in the world for divination work. While this is a degree that can be considered to never end, by the time that water degree has been engaged in for at least a year or two, this person should be able to grasp the possible motivations or unconscious processes of other members of the group and have some skill in negotiating and working through difficulties. This will greatly help to alleviate problems with drama within the group as well as gaining the obvious benefits of self-discipline and self-knowledge for further work down the road.

The Fire Degree

All the previous degrees could be considered challenging, the fire degree will be one of testing the discipline of the person as well as their ability to grasp and understand the changes that can occur in others as ritual work is done. This degree is the one in which one learns mastery of both group processes and the ways to read where a person is at and how best to design a ritual to cause change in their life.

The areas of study in this degree are:

- Ritual Design and construction, particularly the ability to formulate initiations that are personalized to the needs of a candidate.
- Strengthening the Will
- Manifesting from inspiration to the actualization of a major change in one's life in the material or spiritual realm.

Fire, being the element of change, is mastered when you are able to bring all of your previous knowledge and experience together to produce change for both yourself and others. In the ritual sense, understanding the person's life stage, personal values, their life myth and the needs for the change that will be induced in the ritual is a necessary integration.

In many groups, the fire degree is also the place for ordination or elder status, since the amount of knowledge and the level of ritual ability needed flows into the usual duties for elder or full priesthood status. There should be a mastery of all the "womb to tomb" rituals, as well as all those rituals needed for initiation into the lower degrees. Areas of leadership, of course, should be mastered by this time, with an understanding of group patterns and dynamics and the structure and functioning of groups. In particular, the mastery of the self, to be able to step outside of a group process and observe what is happening and what is needed next, is a high level of attainment to be sought at this stage.

A personal project of one's own would also be most appropriate at this stage. A long-term goal that would directly work on one's own weaknesses or areas to enhance should be well formulated, stages set and then commenced. This project could be almost anything: improvement of health, a discipline of some sort that may be emotional or mental (in anticipation of the further air degree) or a community project would fit with this need to show mastery of manifestation through the power of will/fire.

The Air Degree

When a candidate moves into air degree, they either have to gain mastery of a particular system or path of magic and bring it to a new level, or they would synthesize a number of different systems bringing about the new formulation.

Obviously this work will be a major study for some time, the previous attainments in some system of magic, such as natural magic, Qabala, or even astrological magic, will be brought to an entirely new level. This may take several years to work through, and the ability to travel to other realms astrally to gain information will be essential here.

point in their own evolution where they have completely cleared themselves of their issues or personal challenges, they are operating on a level and with subsequent challenges that few are able to reach.

This is truly the attainment of the long path of magickal work. Ultimately, they should be continuing to contribute their wisdom to others, if even to just a select few. At this point also, it would be appropriate to designate someone as their special successor for their lineage, to help them in their own level of attainment to continue the teachings to future generations.

Conclusion

Obviously, this is only an outline. Any group that attempts to implement this would do well to consult with elders of the Wiccan tradition, especially those using this system. If none are available, a well-run group could have a focused committee to work on the specifics of what they would like to see in these degrees in the ways of specific work. It would be up to the group/coven itself to determine if they would want a connection via formal initiation to a lineage or to work in a manner in which the group would support each other in their ongoing levels of attainment.

Notice that, aside from a few suggestions for the Dedicant degree, no mention is made of the form of the initiation rituals to be used. This would either be communicated from such Elders as the group can contact or find to advise them in a particular tradition or devised by the group itself from the knowledge of the patterns of ritual and the needs for initiations. In this latter instance, the old saying "of course it's true, we made it up" is perfectly appropriate!

Possible example projects here might be:

- A new synthesis of natural magic, done by in-depth study of the natural world, evolution, or astral or shamanic travel into fairy realms.
- Another project might the examination of a particular school of mysticism and how it may apply to Wicca.
- Further, in-depth study of some subject such as astrology, including it's ancient history and its place in Western esoteric thought would be an appropriate study for this point, especially if it could be applied and adapted into a Wiccan worldview.

At this point, the intellectual attainment and discipline would be the equivalent of graduate study in the humanities. It would be natural for someone at this level to have a considerable library of their own as a resource or, in this digital age, to have e-books and online reliable materials (being able to identify unverified personal gnosis in writings of others would be an obvious skill to have at this level).

Not all are called to the Air degree, just as many are not called to active leadership in a group, but for those who work in this area, there is a chance to contribute to the community and the magickal path in a whole new way that may well have an effect on future generations.

The Spirit Degree

Once the intellectual/air degree is mastered, the only thing then is to continue to travel the path. This level of attainment would probably not be reasonable to consider before at least two decades of work on the magickal path. The things that may happen here are really up to the individual and their own connection to the divine. There are few areas that would not be at least familiar to, or mastered by the person in Spirit degree. While this does NOT mean that the person is more than human, nor even at a

The Common Book of Witchcraft & Wicca

CHILD OF LIGHT

Mother of Darkness, Child of Light
Born in the darkest hour of the night
Moment of promise, promise of life
Now a new year begins, begins
Now a new year begins

Sun growing stronger, winter declines
Days growing longer, summer on our minds
Light warms the Earth, Earth warms to life
As the young year unfolds, unfolds
As the young year unfolds

God joined with Goddess, blade in the cup
Crops growing higher, babies growing up
Life brings forth bounty, bounty brings forth life
As the good year goes on, goes on
As the good year goes on

God falls in autumn, shadows grow long
Make bread from His body to keep us all strong
Death of the crops means survival of life
As the old year winds down, winds down
As the old year winds down

Darkness comes on again, rebirth draws near
Daylight dwindles down with the dying of the year
Goddess prepares to again bring forth new life
As a new year is born, is born
As a new year is born

TESTAMENT OF ED THE PAGAN

by **Ed Hubbard**

I love Life. In all the glory of the living, I love life. I cherish all the parts of living, the joy of being part of all creation. There is no separate part of me away from nature, as there is no part of us that is separate of nature in any way. Nature is all the living, and all the living on our planet is Gaia, the living mother of us all. It is by Her will, Her gift of life that we continue, as my body is part of all the living.

I am a witch. I am a Wiccan. I believe in the power of a natural world, a spiritual world, and a supernatural world. I believe in what my mind can understand, and that my mind seeks to answer the unknown. It is the glory of knowledge the unending part of my inner nature, the curiosity that is divine in its search, to seek the laws that God has written into the cosmic tapestry. For my mind reflects the unending curiosity of God seeking to understand my point of view. So it is, all I do is a reflection of God, and God is all that there is.

Thou Art God, Thou Are Goddess.

The say Witches have magic and I testify that is true. We have the way to move our will and the cosmic reality shifts along with us. All that seek the unknown is the witch, for it takes the power to face your fears reflected against the infinite darkness of our own ignorance. It is this fearsome curiosity and courage born of the soul, that makes a Witch that to be feared but much to be loved.

As a Wiccan, I ask what senses I have for what I cannot see hear, see, or feel. I feel the sense that want to be more, the ability to see more, listen intensely, speak truer, touch fully, taste distinctly, and smell deeply of all the world offers. My empathy allows me to feel more and to share the feeling with those around me. My inner vision allows me to sense a reality that is more connected then my eyes allow me to see, and enhances that which my physical self knows. The psychic sense is the power of humanity emerging, and the Wiccan in me rejoices in the practice.

I have seen ghosts. I have seen Fairies. I have seen demons and I have seen a devil. I have seen the shadow people. I have met people who were spirits hidden among us. I finger touched a Sasquatch child, who laughed at me. I have seen angels in the skies. I have bargained with a demigod upon a hill. I have played with dragons that dwell near us. I have met the dead and I have met the living. I have met an extraterrestrial and had a conversation with them. I have met those who reincarnate and remember their lives, and I will join them in my next life.

I have met wizards, witches, shamans, high priests, high priestesses, and all manner of folk. I have shaken the hands of presidents of the nations, of senators, and mayors. I have been blessed by the Dalai Lama, twice. I have been in the presence of the assembly of the world's religions and it profoundly moved me. I know entrepreneurs, business folk, and even the idle rich. I know poor people, people who live off the grid and people who live the happy minimalist life. I know those who struggle with money, with mind, and with life itself. I have met those who love, who kill, and people of every walk of life. In each is the reflection of the God and their bodies are of the Goddess. We are complex and beautiful. For the Goddess said all acts of love and pleasure are Hers, and I have indulged in all acts that I have found along my way. It is said that a Pagan worships in their lovemaking, and I have truly loved, having the lovers, the living goddesses and gods that Gaia has matched me with. I have had the softest loveliest lovemaking a man can have ever desired. I have had frantic sex, I have hard quickie thrills. I have had intercourse until we dripped with sweat and our backs and legs ached from undying exertion. I have tasted every part of the human body with my tongue, and I enjoy the feel of skin between my lips. There is no act that can shame me nor create guilt with me, for all acts of love in pleasure in consent of all the willing is the act of worship that Gaia creates in all the living. There is only freedom in the acceptance of love in all its forms.

My God is an infinite God, who knows no bounds, and is within me as without of me. My God is a God of all the universe, of all the cosmos, within all creation, and has given us all the universes as ours. My God cares not to judge us, as we would judge ourselves. God allows us all to reflect what we desire in the divine, and in that moment god can miraculously become finite enough for us to comprehend a portion of the whole. My God is so powerful that nothing I say or do can be truly forbidden, nor is what you say or do forbidden, nor does the divine force stop us from expressing ourselves in any way. There are only consequences. This is a sign of a God that understands all things, and allows all things, as we are able to understand that we are the choices God has made, and through us God continues to make choices.

As a Pagan it is said we worship many Gods, and that is true. For us the Gods above are real, tangible, and make themselves known to us. It is said that they are part of one god, and that is true. The breath of gods and humanity blend together without boundaries, so even the Gods are part of infinity, and are living expressions thereof. Yet, I tell you that the Gods and Goddesses are their own beings as well, serving in the complexity of the cosmos. In ways we yet do not fully understand, they manifest as spirits, as powers, as thoughts and as miracles among us. They too have a life with us, and while we may argue their nature, as a Pagan man, I accept they exist and they have a relationship with me. So it is that Gods and Goddesses exist among us, and dwell in equal measure with the infinity that is god as well.

My life has been about the search for God, the search for meaning, and I discovered one truth above all others, The Universe Endures. My understanding is limited in thought and senses, unable to see even 2% of all that surrounds me, unable to hear but the tiniest spectrum of noise, and to house within my brain only the smallest fraction of knowledge I have gained, I have learned that the universe endures, it continues, and it is a wonder to behold. It is at that moment I feel the tug of a soul, of a spirit, who has been born in this flesh, and yet has been born in other flesh, and will yet again be born into flesh again, and know that I too shall endure, that I am the universe in action. Nothing is as simple and as profound as to understand, "I live because I am."

So do I think thoughts I thought yesterday, or will I think thoughts I will think tomorrow. Where do we exist but in a place, in a time, and in a pattern, created by forces beyond all our understanding, and yet our bodies embody all that the universe has created, and we are the timely creation of billions of years of cosmic evolution. From the birth of stars, which devoured gases and energy, and in their cycle secreted elements needed for their next generation of stars, life itself played out. So it is the whole of the universe, that is to say God evolves, and we can see it as a living being which we are just a small mote of. Not to say we are insignificant because of our size but our significance is in the idea we can explore that which is around us. We are small but we are large; after all, Thou Art God, Thou Are Goddess.

In the time that I live, the moments I am aware of, is the time of the greatest lies ever being told, or the greatest truths being played out. The powers of humanity say the world is changing, and that I tell you is true. The world is always changing, and because we have come to dislike change, they say Nature is striking back, attacking humanity and seeking to destroy us. This is petty nonsense used for personal power, and all that say these things, want to in some way change the behavior of all those around them. It is a necessary interplay as Gaia seeks to grow, but She does not hate us, for She does not hate herself. We are as much Gaia, as we are ourselves. Our flesh, our Code of Life, our DNA, is the same as it has been since the beginning of life. Every one of us is Gaia, a cell and a component, and we are behaving according to Her will. So while we may not understand Her evolution, Her billions-of-years life, Her continual recreation, we are a manifestation of it, and our will and behavior has been developed by Gaia Herself. So this self-loathing of humanity towards nature is a contamination of spirit against the flesh, and those who promise to destroy Gaia, do so because they believe in Gods that want to separate humanity's spirit from our enduring flesh. Gaia does not hate us, for if She did, we would all die. Gaia is expressing Herself through us, and our instincts and drives are an answer to Her desires. We are Gaia, and we are never separate of nature. It is impossible for us to be separated in any way and live.

I have said God is in everything, and I believe this is true. The universe is sentient, and that our will is expressed within the will of the universe. Yet we are not alone. We are with each person, each plant, each animal, and every living thing in these choices. This is expression of choices being played out. So it is true of gods, whom humanity, has come to know. For the Gods may be born of flesh or they are born of the interactions of the cosmos we do not yet understand. Yet these Gods do exist, and they, as much as humanity, make claims, and seek power. Our stories of them say so and whether you believe they are a manifestation of the human mind or something more, understand they have will and ego, the same as us. If it were not true, the Gods could not war, would not war amongst themselves. So Gods are living entities which at the very least dwell within the minds of their worshippers, and can act through them. Many can have even greater manifestations. So in this way humanity and the Gods are the same, and they all seek to glorify and manifest themselves, according to their divine will. So it is they drive us towards their ends and society, just as nature creates a forest or a jungle. They manifest their will, and we choose to join them, for whatever promises or protections as they offer. So it is some Gods seek to divide humanity and control them, to form them in their own image, and to claim their spirits as their own. So it has been among humanity, this play of Gods and Gaia, whom provides the body for our spirits.

My life was lived in a miraculous time, a time of amazing wonder. I am a planetary cave dweller, looking out of the mouth of my gravity well, into the ocean of stars beyond. I stand in awe and wonder, as humanity begins Gaia's sacred task of evolving out of the womb and onto unliving matter. For humanity is the expressive force that is so tasked, and so driven, that we must follow this path, or destroy ourselves in trying. Gaia has made way before, creating infinite diversity, to meet the needs of all the living. So we are the next great species and we are the carriers of Her seeds, Her ever-living flesh to the heavens and to worlds beyond. If we as humanity cannot evolve to carry out this task, Gaia will simply evolve another way; for what is the main drive of life but to procreate and carry on? So it is not a wonder that such a desire and hunger to space has always been with us, and I am in the fortunate time to see the first true cosmic steps. This alone is enough to love Gaia and to seek life in God's Universe.

I am a Spirit, which has dwelled upon the earth, since the beginning. I was a witness to creation, and that which cloaks me, is simply God. To understand, God is infinite, omnipresent, and creative beyond all. We are simply God expressing infinite knowledge and everlasting diversity. All things we imagine of God is God, simply because we say it is so. In this God is a verb, since we already acknowledge that if we can imagine God as a verb, then "to god" is a true act in our universe. To god means you express yourself as God would, which means you live as you desire, for if you are God all things are possible. Once people understand God is not an entity but the force of all creation, then to god makes sense that the universe understands and fulfills God's will. I am the current spirit which expresses God, godding into my body and flesh from Gaia, and in union act as the force of will and action for Lord and Lady. If you believe this is true for me, then it is true for you. For we are part of the same manifestation, regardless of when you read or hear these words, and it will always be true, regardless of what flesh we wear or lives we live. As Gaia lives and grows into the cosmos, we too join her, as we choose. After all, to god the universe is so utterly human.

So this is the testimonial of Ed the Pagan, who is God, shares God, and gods the world around him. Within him is a spirit which has returned and will return again to join all those who seek to seed Gaia among the stars. For in the end, the flesh made spirit, and the spirit made flesh, is the sacred union of creation, and we are able to create god within ourselves, and manifest the lives of the truly living, those who endure and in evolve. It is the Now we live.

AFTERWORD

by **Brendan Tripp**
Editor, Eschaton Books

As Ed Hubbard noted in the Preface, the intent for *The Common Book of Witchcraft & Wicca* was that it would be shared, not only in .PDF form, but in other editions as well.

This means that if your group wants to produce your own printed version of this, with whatever additions, subtractions, and reordering you care to make, that's *great*... with a few caveats.

On page *iv* here, there is credit for the image used on the cover of this particular edition. Needless to say, were you to use a different image, you would want to change that to credit the source of *your* image.

Also on page *iv*, there is information dealing with the publication of *this* edition, and its accompanying hard cover and ebook editions. **DO *NOT* use the ISBNs listed there for *your* edition**. Please remove the Eschaton Books information there, as well as the copyright notice from Witch School (which is there to simply to establish publication precedence). However, you *do* want to keep the Creative Commons licensing info there for your version.

Frankly, if you are doing a variation of this and only distributing it as an e-book, it probably does not *need* an ISBN, but if you are going to be *printing* a new version, please get your own number (it really messes up the book business when ISBNs - which should be *unique* identifiers of books - get reused!). Information about how to do that can be found via a web search, with this being a good overview: http://goo.gl/um2hBr

In the U.S., http://www.isbn.org is the official source, but they are quite expensive for buying just *one* number, so you might want to check out other services which buy blocks of numbers and sell them individually, sometimes packaged with a barcode graphic. Needless to say, if you *are* going to be producing a print version, you will want to use your own ISBN and related barcode graphic rather than the one that's on Eschaton's editions.

http://EschatonBooks.com

info@EschatonBooks.com

The Common Book of Witchcraft & Wicca

www.ingramcontent.com/pod-product-compliance
Lightning Source LLC
Chambersburg PA
CBHW060104170426
43198CB00010B/762